Add Red Hat® Linux® 7 to Your Windows Desktop

Send Us Your Comments

To comment on this book or any other PRIMA TECH title, visit our reader response page on the Web at **www.prima-tech.com/comments**.

How to Order

For information on quantity discounts, contact the publisher: Prima Publishing, P.O. Box 1260BK, Rocklin, CA 95677-1260; (916) 787-7000. On your letterhead, include information concerning the intended use of the books and the number of books you want to purchase.

Add Red Hat® Linux® 7 to Your Windows Desktop

In a Weekend

Brian Proffitt

PRIMA TECH

A DIVISION OF PRIMA PUBLISHING

A Division of Prima Publishing

Prima Publishing and colophon are registered trademarks of Prima Communications, Inc. PRIMA TECH and Fast & Easy are trademarks of Prima Communications, Inc., Roseville, California 95661.

Publisher: Stacy L. Hiquet
Marketing Manager: Judi Taylor
Associate Marketing Manager: Heather Buzzingham
Managing Editor: Sandy Doell
Project Management: Echelon Editorial & Publishing Services
Project Editor: C. Michael Woodward
Development Editor: Joell Smith
Technical Reviewer: William A. Schilling III
Indexer: Grant Munroe
Cover Design: Prima Design Team
Interior Layout: Marian Hartsough

ISBN: 0-7615-2851-2
Library of Congress Catalog Card Number: 00-10733
Printed in the United States of America

00 01 02 03 04 II 10 9 8 7 6 5 4 3 2 1

"I do not fear computers.
I fear the lack of them."

— *Isaac Asimov*

ACKNOWLEDGMENTS

It goes without saying that you would not be holding this book in your hands had not some very talented and creative people lent their skills to help me get this done in what may be record time.

I can never express enough gratitude to my editors. For those of you that think this brilliant writing is the sole product of my fevered work (all two of you), you would be wrong. And I thank Kim Spilker, Michael Woodward, Lori Swan, Joell Smith, Marian Hartsough, and Bill Schilling profusely for their hard work.

They say no man is an island. I am fortunate enough to have three spectacular women in my life who know how to treat me right (or drive me insane, depending on the time of day). My wife and two wonderful daughters get the big thanks and smooches for putting up with me squirreled away in the office for days at a stretch.

ABOUT THE AUTHOR

BRIAN PROFFITT is the author of several Linux books, such as *Install Configure and Customize Red Hat 7* (Prima, 2000), *Sun StarOffice for Linux* (Prima, 2000), and *WordPerfect Office 2000 Fast & Easy* (Prima, 2000).

Brian loves being a dad and husband and in his very limited spare time, Brian does some swooping of his own as a soloing student pilot, trying to get his private pilot's license before it starts snowing. Which in Indiana means October.

CONTENTS AT A GLANCE

Introduction . . . . **xx**

FRIDAY EVENING
Getting the PC Ready **1**

SATURDAY MORNING
Installing Red Hat Linux 7 . . . . **45**

SATURDAY AFTERNOON
Initial Configuration Issues **81**

SATURDAY EVENING
Playing Well with Others **141**

SUNDAY MORNING
Adding to Your Linux System **187**

SUNDAY AFTERNOON
Using Some Popular Linux Applications. **215**

SUNDAY EVENING
Clean Up Any Messes **261**

Appendix A
The Linux Primer **279**

APPENDIX B
Online Resources **329**

APPENDIX C
Hardware Compatibility Journal **333**

Index **347**

CONTENTS

Introduction xx

FRIDAY EVENING
Getting the PC Ready 1

Assessing System Capability 4

Gathering Information about Your System 6

Checking Your Device Manager in Windows 6

Checking Your BIOS for Information 10

Checking for Network Information 14

Checking for Hardware Compatibility 16

Resources for Checking Compatibility 17

Red Hat Support 17

Linux Hardware Database 18

Hardware Supported by Red Hat 21

Video Card 22

Memory (RAM) 23

Monitor 23

Hard Drive. 24

Ethernet Card 24

Sound Card 25

CD-ROM and DVD-ROM 26

Zip/Jaz Drive 27

Tape Drive. 27

Modem 27

Printer 28

Mouse. 28

Keyboard 29

Notebook Computers 29

SCSI Adapters 30

Backing Up Your Old Data 30

Making Room for Multiple Operating Systems 36

Why Partition? 37

PartitionMagic 5.0. 39

When to Use fdisk. 40

What's Next? 44

SATURDAY MORNING

Installing Red Hat Linux 7 . . . . **45**

    Starting the Red Hat Installer **48**

        Creating a Boot Disk **49**

            Procedure **50**

        Navigating the Installer **50**

    Running Your Installation **52**

        Determining Language, Keyboard, and Mouse Settings **53**

        Choosing Installation Class **56**

        Selecting Your Partition Options **59**

        Networking Your Computer **64**

        Setting the Time Zone **66**

        Configuring Your Accounts **67**

        Selecting Package Groups **68**

        Configuring the X Window System **70**

        Finishing the Installation **72**

    Other Installation Concerns **77**

        Text Installation **77**

        Configuring LILO **78**

            Dual Booting Explained **78**

            How to Dual Boot with Windows 95/98 . . . . **78**

            How to Dual Boot with Windows NT **79**

    Conclusion **80**

SATURDAY AFTERNOON

Initial Configuration Issues **81**

    Seek Out and Explore Strange New Desktops **83**

        Exploring Gnome **84**

            Understanding Desktop Elements **84**

            Starting Programs from the Main Menu Button **86**

            Using Buttons, Menus, and Dialog Boxes **88**

Exploring KDE. 90

   Understanding Desktop Elements 91

   Starting Programs from the Application Starter 93

What Is X?. 93

Using Xconfigurator 97

Starting Up the xf86config Tool 106

   Configuring the Mouse. 107

   Configuring the Keyboard. 108

   Configuring the Monitor 109

   Configuring the Graphics Card. 112

Using the Control Panel. 114

   Configuring the Keyboard. 115

   Configuring the Mouse. 116

Properly Logging Out of X 116

Choosing a Desktop Environment 117

Login Options. 118

   Switching Desktop Environments. 119

   Failsafe 121

Configuring Your Desktop. 122

   Menu Customization 122

   Desktop Icons. 124

   Panel Icons. 125

   Desktop Themes 126

      Changing Themes 126

   Getting a New Theme. 130

Configuring Your File System 133

   Using the Linux File System 133

   Functions and Permissions 135

Working with Non-Linux Partitions 139

Conclusion. 140

SATURDAY EVENING
Playing Well with Others **141**

    Setting up Your Internet Account **144**

        Configure the PPP Dialer **146**

        Connect to the Internet **155**

    Networking and IP Addresses **158**

    Printers **167**

        Adding a Local Printer **168**

        Adding a Network Printer **173**

    Sound **176**

        Configuring Sound with the sndconfig Utility **177**

        Applying Sound to Events **182**

    Plug and Play Using the ISAPNPTOOLS Utility **183**

        Performing a PnP Dump **184**

        Editing the isapnp.conf File **185**

    Conclusion **186**

SUNDAY MORNING
Adding to Your Linux System **187**

    Installing Software Packages **190**

        Understanding Packaging **190**

        Installing a New Desktop Environment **192**

        Using the Update Agent **194**

    Installing Software with Setup **199**

    Adding New Hardware and Peripherals **204**

        Adding New Devices **206**

            Adding External Devices **207**

            Adding Internal Devices **208**

        The Kernel Boot Process **209**

            What Is Auto-Detection? **212**

Configuring Your Device 212

Conclusion. 213

SUNDAY AFTERNOON
Using Some Popular Linux Applications. 215

Using X WindowTools 217

Editors 218

Graphics. 220

Personal Information Managers 223

Internet Tools 224

Using Netscape Communicator 225

Configuring Netscape Navigator. 227

Home Page and Other Easy Stuff 228

Setting Cache Properties. 236

Defining Helper Applications 238

Configuring Netscape Messenger 238

Setting up E-Mail 239

Setting up Newsgroups 241

Using StarOffice 5.2 for Linux 243

StarDesktop: A Better Interface. 243

StarWriter: A New Way to Write 247

StarCalc: Figure It All Out. 249

StarChart: What Those Numbers Mean 252

StarMath: Equation for Success 253

StarBase: Track Your Data. 254

StarImpress: Show What You Know 255

StarDraw: Create Works of Art 256

StarMail: Communicate with the World. 257

StarDiscussion: Join Online Communities 258

StarSchedule: Keep Your Life in Order 258

Conclusion. 259

SUNDAY EVENING

Clean Up Any Messes **261**

Installation 263

Boot Issues 265

X, Your Monitor, and Your Video Card 267

Fixing LILO 268

Hardware 268

I Can't Hear You! 269

Making Printers Work 269

Those Touchy USB Devices 270

Software 272

Connecting to the Internet 272

Networking Fixes 274

Getting E-Mail Working 275

Security Alert 276

Conclusion 277

APPENDIX A

The Linux Primer **279**

Getting Started: The Login Prompt 280

Getting Familiar with Multi-User Operating Systems 281

Using Virtual Terminals 282

Using the whoami Command 282

Understanding and Using File Permissions 283

Finding Hidden Files 285

Working at the Shell 286

Understanding the Linux Philosophy 287

Piping Input and Output 287

Using Direction and Redirection 287

Common Commands 288

Copying Files: The cp Command 288

Example 1: Copying a File into Another directory 289

Example 2: Copying Multiple Files into
Another Directory 290

Moving Files: The mv Command. 290

Example 1: Moving a File to Another Directory. 291

Example 2: Moving Multiple Files into
Another Directory 292

Example 3: Renaming Files with mv 292

Creating Directories: The mkdir Command 293

Example 1: Creating a New Directory 293

Listing and Finding Files with ls 294

Example 1: Listing Files in Your Home Directory 295

Example 2: Listing Hidden Files in a Directory 296

Example 3: Listing All Files ad Their Attributes 296

Making Links 297

Example 1: Creating a symbolic Link to a Directory 298

Moving around the Command Line Interface: cd 298

Example 1: Changing to the Parent Directory
of the Current Working Directory 299

Example 2: Changing to a Specific Directory 299

Example 3: Going Home Quickly. 300

Example 4: Going Back to the Previous
Working Directory 300

Where the Heck Am I? Using pwd 300

Example 1: Using pwd to Find the Present
Working directory 301

Mounting Filesystems. 301

Example 1: Mounting a CD-ROM. 304

Example 2: Mounting a Floppy 304

Unmounting Filesystems 305

    Example 1: Unmounting the CD-ROM 306

    Example 2: Unmounting the Floppy 306

Deleting Files 306

    Example 1: Removing a File 307

    **Example 2: Removing a Directory and
All Files under It** 308

    Example 3: Deleting Multiple Files with Wildcards 309

    Example 4: Utter Insanity 309

Viewing and Manipulating Files with cat 310

    Example 1: Concatenating a File to the Display 310

    **Example 2: Redirecting the Output of a
Concatenation** 311

Viewing Files with less 312

    Example 1: Displaying a File with less 313

Viewing Running Processes with ps 313

    Example 1: Show User's Current Processes 314

    Example 2: Show All Processes 315

Stopping Processes with kill 316

    Example 1: Killing an Errant Process 316

Getting Help with the man Command 317

    Example 1: Displaying the man Page for cp 318

Directory Structure 319

The / Directory 319

The /bin Directory 320

The /boot Directory 321

The /dev Directory 321

The /etc Directory 323

The /home Directory 324

The /lib Directory 324

The /lost and found Directory 324

The /mnt Directory 325

The /opt Directory 325

The /proc Directory 325

The /root Directory 326

The /sbin Directory 326

The /tmp Directory 326

The /usr Directory 326

The /var Directory 327

Conclusion 327

Appendix B
Online Resources **329**

APPENDIX C
Hardware Compatibility Journal **333**

Index **347**

INTRODUCTION

Many people think of Linux as an operating system that is way over their heads, that only techies can use this strange, arcane OS. It would be nice to use an operating system that didn't crash all of the time for no apparent reason, but I don't have a degree in computer science.

For all of you who've had these thoughts, this book is here to tell you that this is simply not the case. Linux—and Red Hat Linux in particular—have become very easy for everyday users to install and use.

Now you can find out for yourself, in just one weekend, how easy it is to get started using Red Hat Linux 7 and discover that there is life outside the Windows.

Is This Book for You?

Add Red Hat Linux 7 to Your Windows Desktop In a Weekend is for anyone who wants to get started using Red Hat Linux, and only has one computer at their home or business on which to install this new operating system. Think of this book as a personal tutorial, a one-on-one class with a Linux expert. You get to stay in the comfort of your own home (or office, if need be) and learn how to:

- Use Linux as a sole operating system or have it happily co-exist with Windows

- Gather information about your system to assess your system's capability to use Red Hat Linux

- Make room for Red Hat Linux and Windows to work on your PC

- Install the Red Hat Linux operating system

- Deal with any unusual installation issues

- Configure your PC to boot to Linux and Windows

- Examine the Gnome and KDE interfaces

- Configure X Window to work with your system

- Create a customized desktop

- Explore the Linux filesystem

- Create an Internet account

- Add a printer to your PC

- Add additional hardware to your PC

- Install software using RPM packages

- Install software using archived setup files

- Explore some of the essential tools packaged with Red Hat Linux 7

- Examine and configure Netscape Communicator to browse the Internet, read your e-mail, and read newsgroup messages

- Use StarOffice 5.2 for Linux office suite
- Troubleshoot many installation and configuration issues that may pop up

How Much Time Will This Take?

This book is organized in sessions from Friday evening to Sunday evening. Each session lasts about three to four hours. The Sunday evening session is a troubleshooting session, which means that if all goes well with your installation, you should not need to use it. If you have the time, you really can cover this entire book in a weekend.

If you don't have the time, however, you don't need to limit yourself to a single weekend. The flexible design of this book permits you to spread the information presented over a week, a couple of weekends, or even a month. You can do each of the sessions on a separate night, or split the sessions over a few days. Tailor the book to your schedule and preferred learning pace, and you're sure to be successful.

Some sessions, such as "Using Some Popular Linux Applications," may not interest you at this time. Feel free to skip these for now, knowing that at any time in the future you can spend just a few hours learning them. However, I do recommend that you read the introduction to the sessions you decide not to complete right away.

What's Covered in This Book?

Though it may seem an insurmountable goal to finish a full-fledged Linux installation in a weekend, you will find that after breaking it up into more manageable tasks, the goal is indeed very attainable.

- **Friday Evening: Getting the PC Ready** helps you through the most critical step of installing Red Hat Linux 7—getting a solid inventory of your PC system. Once you obtain this knowledge,

you'll be able to determine exactly how to install Red Hat Linux, since you will be able to check for any potential hardware trouble spots before the actual installation. You'll also learn how to back up any data on your current system and how to make room on your hard drive for the Linux operating system.

○ **Saturday Morning: Installing Red Hat Linux 7** will walk you through the steps you will need to take to get Red Hat Linux onto your computer with a minimum of fuss. Should you run into any difficulties, you'll find out how to deal with those as well. This session will also explain how Linux should automatically configure your system to boot either Linux or Windows.

○ **Saturday Afternoon: Initial Configuration Issues** takes you through the tasks you will want to complete just after installation. This includes getting a look at the two desktop environments that come with Red Hat Linux, Gnome and KDE and performing some basic configuration changes in these interfaces. You will also discover how to get into the guts of the graphical interface and change everything from the screen display size to the color of the buttons on the screen.

○ **Saturday Evening: Playing Well with Others** will show you how to get your PC sharing information with other computers and devices, starting with the biggest computer network of them all, the Internet. After your Internet and network connectivity is established, you'll learn how to connect your PC to printers and properly configure the sound card on your PC if it did not work after installation.

○ **Sunday Morning: Adding On to Your Linux System** explains how to get more stuff onto your computer. Whether its new software or new hardware, you'll learn how easy it is to get all the cool toys working on your Red Hat Linux PC.

○ **Sunday Afternoon: Using Some Popular Linux Applications** will start teaching you how to use some of this cool stuff that came with Linux, including Netscape Communicator, a full-featured Web browser and communications application. You will also explore an application you installed in the Sunday Morning session: StarOffice 5.2 for Linux.

○ **Sunday Evening: Clean Up Any Messes** that may have occurred during the installation and configuration of Red Hat Linux 7. Though rare, mistakes do slip in once and a while, and this session will show you how to address some specific problems. It will also tell you where to go to find more help should the need arise.

To help you on your way with Red Hat Linux, this book provides some reference material in the appendixes for you to use.

○ **Appendix A: The Linux Primer** will guide new Linux users through some of the basics of the Linux OS.

○ **Appendix B: Online Resources** will point you towards the most up-to-date Red Hat and general Linux resources on the Internet.

○ **Appendix C: Hardware Compatibility Journal** provides a journal for you to track the hardware on your PC.

What Do You Need to Begin?

There's not a lot you need to start using Red Hat Linux: just the software and an Intel-based PC. It does not even have to be a new PC. Linux works well on older model PCs, and has much better performance on older PCs than Windows.

With each new version of Red Hat Linux, Red Hat sells a box containing CD-ROMs and printed manuals for around $45. The same files that appear on the CD-ROM are also made available on Red Hat's public FTP server (ftp://ftp.redhat.com) for free. Anyone with a fast Internet connection (like a cable modem or DSL line) and a "writeable" CD-ROM drive can download the whole package and create their own CD-ROM. The only cost is that of the blank CD.

For people who don't want to spend much money and don't have access to a big Internet link, there is a third option. A few companies download each new version as it is released, create hundreds of CD-ROMs containing the complete Red Hat distribution, and then sell them for about $5. This reselling is perfectly legal, and it will cost you less than the original packaged box from Red Hat Software. You should know, however, that two important items will be missing from that low-cost option. First, free limited support from Red Hat Software is missing. When you buy the distribution from Red Hat itself, a certain amount of free technical support is included. If you decide to purchase the low cost CD-ROM, you are on your own. Second, no printed manuals are included, although they are available in electronic form on the CD-ROM itself. You can, therefore, read them on your screen or print them out on your printer. Three known companies that sell low cost Linux CD-ROMs are LinuxMall, Cheap*Bytes, and Linux Central, all of which can be found on the Internet.

 TIP Even easier, just use the copy of Red Hat Linux 7 on the CD-ROMs that accompany this book!

Much of the preparation for installation is discussed in the Friday Evening session. You should definitely read this session first so you can get ready for the rest of the weekend's activities.

Conventions Used in This Book

Many Linux X Window commands can be selected with either a mouse or the keyboard, so menu commands in this book are written in a way that enables you to choose the method you prefer. For example, if the instruction says "Choose File, Open," click on the File menu to open the menu, and then click on the Open option. Alternatively, you can press the Alt key and the letter F to open the File menu, and then press the letter O to select Open.

When you need to hold down the first key while you press a second key, a plus sign (+) is used to show this combination (such as Alt+f or Ctrl+z). When two keys are pressed in sequence, they are separated with a comma. For example, the hot-key sequence for opening a file would be written as "Alt+f, o."

Bold text indicates text you should type, typically in the console.

You will also find several special elements that will make using this book easier as you read each chapter.

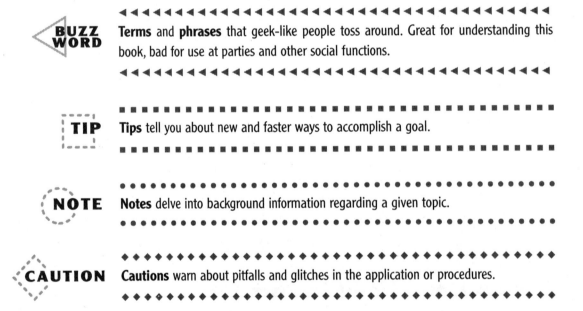

◀ ◀

BUZZ WORD **Terms** and **phrases** that geek-like people toss around. Great for understanding this book, bad for use at parties and other social functions.

◀ ◀

TIP **Tips** tell you about new and faster ways to accomplish a goal.

NOTE **Notes** delve into background information regarding a given topic.

CAUTION **Cautions** warn about pitfalls and glitches in the application or procedures.

Getting the PC Ready

- ✪ Assessing System Capability
- ✪ Checking for Hardware Compatibility
- ✪ Backing Up Your Old Data
- ✪ Making Room for Multiple Operating Systems

This is it—you're finally going to do it. For the last several months, all you've heard is Linux, Linux, Linux. The tech staff at the office talks about it constantly. The financial networks marvel at the rate of growth Linux companies are undergoing. Magazine articles speculate endlessly on whether Linux will be the David to Microsoft's Goliath.

These are all good reasons to be curious about Linux. Or maybe it comes down to just one simple reason: you're tired of watching your Windows system crash for no apparent reason.

On the other hand, there are all of those other stories out there: whispers of incompatibility issues with hardware, tales of PCs not booting properly, and more. Those stories represent the "dark side" of Linux. While it's certainly a bit exaggerated, there is some truth to these installation rumors. For these reasons, you should undertake every Linux application—including the new Red Hat Linux 7 itself—with a little forethought.

This evening, you'll do all the planning and fact-finding you will need to make tomorrow morning's installation of Red Hat Linux go as smooth as silk. By the end of the evening, you will have:

✪ Gathered information about your system to assess your system's capability to use Red Hat Linux

✪ Compared your system's properties with the Red Hat Hardware Compatibility List

✪ Learned how to fix or bypass problems with specific hardware

✪ Backed up your old data

✪ Made room for Red Hat Linux and another operating system

Before you start delving into the not-so-deep, dark, mysterious world of Red Hat Linux, let's examine why installing any version of Linux is so different from anything you've ever installed before.

Assessing System Capability

Since the inception of Microsoft Windows 95, most of us have become accustomed to relying on its ubiquitous SETUP.EXE file, designed to automatically identify your computer's components (often a compromise). SETUP then attempts to match the components with their appropriate files and then places those files in the proper locations on your computer (you hope).

Windows users can get away with this simply because Microsoft, with its very pervasiveness, has managed to keep hardware systems within a certain "compatibility window." For example, each PC manufacturer logically attempts to make small improvements over its competitors, changing and enhancing various component parts and then competitively marketing those enhancements.

However, if each manufacturer wants Windows users to buy their product, thus taking advantage of the huge Microsoft following, then despite fierce competition, each manufacturer will try to adhere to Microsoft's specs. This attempts to ensure that any enhancements can be reasonably identified by the Windows SETUP.EXE programs.

This phenomenon, for good or ill, has left us with a lot of very similar-looking PCs in today's market. The real differences between manufacturers are apparent only when you look at their service and repair programs or attempt to determine how easily their PC can be upgraded in the future.

Critics of Linux have said that Linux is too rigid and inflexible and thus too difficult to use. While Linux does indeed have its problems, inflexibility is not one of them. Windows only *appears* to be more flexible—but that's because its installation path onto a given PC has already been paved by hardware manufacturers whose components conform to Windows' suggested standards.

Linux, on the other hand, does not have cooperative agreements with PC and hardware manufacturers (although this is rapidly changing). So, like Scarlet O'Hara, Linux too must "depend on the kindness of strangers" to find its way onto different systems.

Okay, here's one of those disquieting facts about Linux: during installation, Linux may ignore some unrecognizable hardware devices, indifferently continuing through its installation process. As you can imagine, this glitch can be a real problem if the device in question is your PC's video card and you can't see anything on the screen.

Here's the good news: the number of devices that Linux cannot work with is decreasing rapidly, and this trend is expected to continue. Red Hat 7 certainly is more compatible with hardware than its predecessors. Linux programmers continue to add hardware drivers to the Linux kernel, including Plug and Play technology—Windows' method to install unrecognized hardware devices.

◀◀

Kernel: The core Linux software program, maintained by a small consortium of talented programmers led by Linux's creator, Linus Torvalds. Every distribution (or flavor) of Linux (Red Hat, SuSE, and Debian), all build upon the Linux kernel, which is freely distributed.

◀◀

Still, Linux is not quite there yet. Until the majority of common devices are automatically recognized by the Linux kernel, you'll need to first determine whether it will run on your computer. To do so, you will need to know where to locate the hardware information about your PC. Once you gather this information, you can spot any potential trouble spots before installing Linux on your machine.

Gathering Information about Your System

How well do you really know your PC? *Really* know it? Are you just passing acquaintances or do you know it down to its very soul (or at least the PIN settings on your sound card)? To find out just how well Linux will run on your PC, you need to know the workings of your machine fairly well.

If you're like most people, you may know the superficial information, like: "17-inch monitor, CD-ROM, floppy drive, printer, internal modem . . ." that sort of thing. To get a proper idea of compatibility with Red Hat Linux 7, you will need to dig a little deeper. For some, this can be the most intimidating part of the installation procedure. So it's a good thing we're getting this done this evening, right?

Actually, it's not so bad. For one thing, you will not have to open your CPU. In fact, I strongly recommend against this, since really bad things could happen. Even Windows has an application that enables you to see into the inner mechanics of your PC without cracking it open.

Checking Your Device Manager in Windows

As you begin examining your computer, first notice that a lot of the information you need to know is right there in front of you. Your monitor, for instance, is sitting on your table or desk with its brand name and model displayed on the front or back. Likely the same is true for your printer and any other external devices you might have. You'll want to take note of both the brand name and model as they appear on the device.

In addition to identifying external devices, you'll need to determine what's actually inside your computer. One place to start is by displaying a list of devices as identified by your existing operating system. Windows 95, 98, and 2000 use a built-in applet called the Device Manager to list known devices. In Windows NT, perhaps the best, most centralized place to view installed devices is the Windows NT Diagnostics applet, located in the Administrative Tools menu.

In Windows 95 and 98, open the Device Manager by clicking the Start button on the Windows taskbar, then choose Settings, Control Panel. When the Control Panel window appears, double-click the System icon to open the System Properties dialog box, shown in Figure 1.1.

Click the Device Manager tab to list the inner workings of your computer, as seen in Figure 1.2.

Now you need to do some old-fashioned detective footwork. Your computer may (or may not) actually use a device for each of the device types listed in the Device Manager. For example, to determine whether you have a CD-ROM drive installed in your computer and to list its brand, first expand the CD-ROM list by clicking its expansion control (the little plus sign in a box) shown in Figure 1.3.

As you can see in Figure 1.3, this computer has one CD-ROM drive, with a rather cryptic label. To find out more about a device, select it, then click the Properties button. (Alternatively, double-click the selected device.) For example, click the listed CD-ROM device, then click Properties. The Properties dialog box for the CD-ROM drive appears (see Figure 1.4).

Figure 1.1

The System Properties dialog box is the home of the Device Manager.

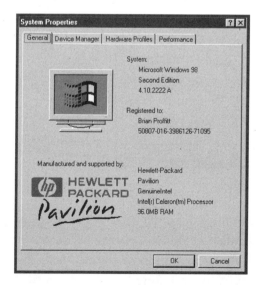

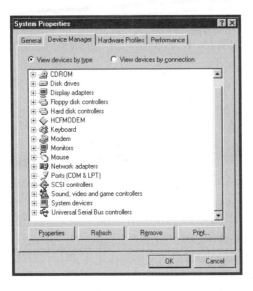

Figure 1.2

The Device Manager will show you nearly every hardware device used by your computer (at least as identified by your current operating system).

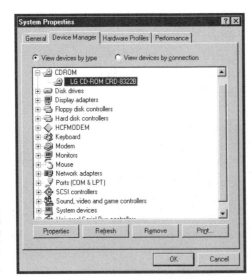

Figure 1.3

Open a list of devices by clicking the expansion box.

This is a classic example of a device that has been made to conform to Windows' standards—so much so that Windows does not care who manufactured it. As far as Windows is concerned, this is just a standard CD-ROM drive. It is still a good idea to record the non-generic

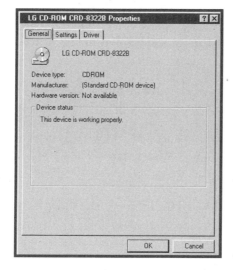

Figure 1.4

Not too much information here, but every little bit helps.

information so that it can be checked against the hardware compatibility list of Red Hat Linux.

You may find that other books urge readers to keep a Linux Journal used to track and record all of their PC's hardware along with any other issues that may arise while installing Linux. We agree with this approach, to the point we've included a working form in Appendix C, "Hardware Compatibility Journal," to use as you gather hardware data. Some sort of journal is a good idea. But jotting down all of this information with a pencil and paper can be an onerous job. Use these steps to simplify the task:

1. In the System Properties dialog box, click the Print button. The Print dialog box will appear, as shown in Figure 1.5.

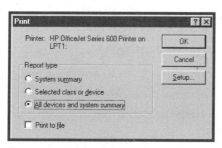

Figure 1.5

Getting your device information on paper.

2. Select All Devices and System Summary.

3. Click OK. All of the information available to the Device Manager will be printed.

You will find the printed document full of very technical information—most of which you will not need. Still, it saves time writing it all down.

How will you know what is needed and what is extraneous? Just by using only the information asked for during the Red Hat installation. Everything else is just gravy.

To successfully install Red Hat Linux 7, the most important information you need is for those devices that make your computer operable, as listed in Table 1.1.

In addition to the critical hardware, other not-so-critical hardware types that may be part of your computer system should also be recorded in your journal. These hardware types are listed in Table 1.2.

Most of the information you require is included in the Device Manager output you printed, but not all. For example, you can locate information on the amount of RAM installed on your computer by clicking the Performance tab in the System Properties dialog box. Another option might be to right-click on the hard drive icon displayed in My Computer or The Explorer, checking the Properties option to see how large your drive space is. A little detective work will go a long way toward making your Red Hat Linux 7 installation easier.

Checking Your BIOS for Information

The type of BIOS used by your PC presents another potential compatibility issue when installing Red Hat Linux 7.

The Basic Input Output System (BIOS) is firmware that exists on your PC regardless of what operating system you're using. It exists primarily to take care of the really basic housekeeping functions of your PC. For instance, the BIOS controls which drive boots up first and how power is managed on your PC.

TABLE 1.1 PRIMARY HARDWARE INFORMATION NEEDED FOR RED HAT LINUX 7 INSTALLATION

Hardware	Information Needed
CPU	Manufacturer, Model, Speed
Motherboard	Manufacturer, Model
Buses	Manufacturer, Model
Memory (RAM)	Size
Video Card	Manufacturer, Model, Video RAM size
Monitor	Manufacturer, Model, Horizontal and Vertical Synchronization Rates
Hard Drive	Manufacturer, Model, Size, Type (SCSI vs. IDE)
Network Card	Manufacturer, Model
CD-ROM Drive	Manufacturer, Model, Size
Floppy Drive	Manufacturer, Model, Size
Modem	Manufacturer, Model, Transmission Speed
Printer	Manufacturer, Model
Mouse	Manufacturer, Model, Type (PS/2 vs. Serial)
Keyboard	Manufacturer, Model, Number of Keys, Language
SCSI Card and Devices	Manufacturer, Model, Type of Device Controlled
IDE Adapters	Manufacturer, Model, Type of Device Controlled

TABLE 1.2 SECONDARY HARDWARE INFORMATION NEEDED FOR RED HAT LINUX INSTALLATION	
Hardware	**Information Needed**
ZIP/JAZ Drive	Manufacturer, Model, Size
Tape Drive	Manufacturer, Model, Size
Sound Card	Manufacturer, Model
Scanner	Manufacturer, Model
Infrared Device	Manufacturer, Model, Type of Device Controlled
Joystick	Manufacturer, Model
Serial Device	Manufacturer, Model, Type of Device Controlled
Parallel Device	Manufacturer, Model, Type of Device Controlled
PCMCIA	Manufacturer, Model, Card Type

◄◄◄

Firmware: Software specifically made to operate on a particular piece of hardware.

◄◄◄

The BIOS on your PC may have issues with Red Hat Linux's Linux Loader (LILO) application. LILO steps in after the BIOS is finished with its boot process and starts to load Linux (hence the name). When Linux is loaded, LILO first looks for the /boot directory. If you have put the /boot directory somewhere where the BIOS and LILO can't find it, then you'll have a problem.

Older BIOSes often can't handle more than two hard drives. They may not be able to locate data stored above cylinder 1,023 of any drive, either. New BIOSes have different, less stringent limitations, but these restrictions are still very prevalent. If you have an older computer, be sure you have the latest BIOS available for it. This will certainly ease your installation of Red Hat 7.

To examine the BIOS settings for your computer, simply restart your system. Then watch closely. Before your operating system begins to load, you will typically see a line that says "Press F2 for Setup," or something similar. Sometimes the message passes too quickly to read as your computer steps through its boot-up sequence. Before your operating system begins to load, try pressing the specific key to be taken into the BIOS setup program. Some likely candidate keys are Esc, F2, and Delete.

CAUTION

Unless you are very confident about what you are doing, you should follow a strict "look but don't touch" policy when changing BIOS settings. One wrong move and you could have major system problems.

Once inside the BIOS setup program, you should record information relating to your hard drives. Specifically, you are looking for how many and how large the hard drives are on your PC and whether they are IDE- or SCSI-type drives.

You may be wondering why getting this information here is necessary, since it may have shown up in the Disk Drive Info section of your device report. If it did, you're all set. However, many hard drives do not have their types listed for the Device Manager, so you'll have to fetch the information in the BIOS.

CAUTION

Be careful not to confuse the appearance of multiple drive letters on a directory list with the true physical presence of multiple drives. Partitioning software can divide one real (physical) hard drive into a number of virtual (logical) hard drives that operating systems treat as separate entities. The BIOS will only list information about your physical drives, while information regarding logical drives can be viewed through any directory utility such as the Windows Explorer.

Once you've noted your drive information in your Linux journal, exit the BIOS setup program as described by your PC's program, making sure **not** to save any inadvertent changes you may have made. The computer will then continue to load your primary operating system.

Checking for Network Information

Checking for network information now will save you time as you actually perform your Linux installation.

When you install Red Hat Linux, you will be quizzed on various settings, such as how your PC is connected to its network. Even if your PC is not on a physical network, perhaps you connect to the Internet or some other system using a dial-up connection. Therefore, if you'll want to access the Internet using that connection, it is a good idea to write down some important settings so that you can refer to them during Linux installation.

◆ ◆

If you typically use a dial-up connection to access the Internet via one of the national service providers such as America Online or CompuServe, be aware that Linux does not provide connection protocols to these services. AT&T Global Network Services is the only Internet service provider (ISP) with a *proprietary* connection format to which Linux will connect at this time. If you connect to the Internet via an ISP with the more common PPP connection format, then you will be all set.

◆ ◆

To check your dial-up settings, click the Start button on the Windows taskbar. Then choose Programs, Accessories, Communications, Dial-Up Networking. This will open the Dial-Up Networking window, shown in Figure 1.6.

If you have any existing dial-up connections, they will appear in this window. Right-click the connection's icon to open the shortcut menu. Select Properties from the menu to open the dialog box for your dial-up connection (see Figure 1.7).

Figure 1.6

Exploring your computer's connections.

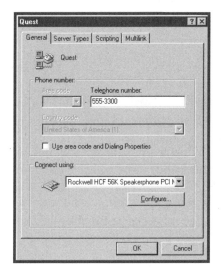

Figure 1.7

The properties of a Dial-Up Networking connection.

Click the Server Types tab. Note the Type of Dial-Up Server setting in your journal, as well as any other settings on this page of the dialog box. When you're ready, click the TCP/IP Settings button. The TCP/IP Settings dialog box will appear (see Figure 1.8).

The information contained in this dialog box is essential to any connection to the Internet. These settings dictate how your computer talks to

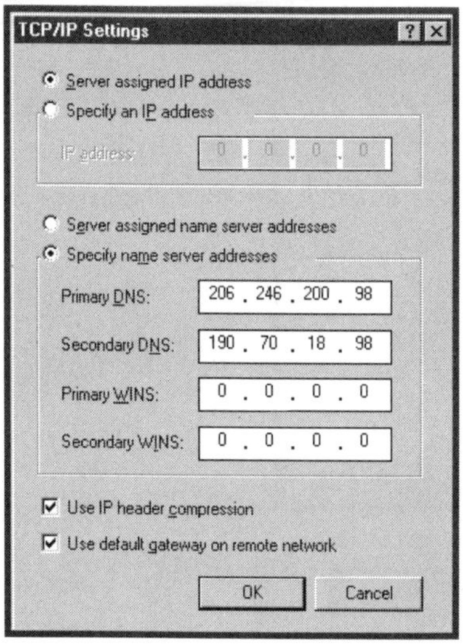

Figure 1.8

TCP/IP settings are the heart of most Internet connection settings.

the other computers once you have connected. Every connection may be is different, so you will want to record these settings exactly.

When finished, click the Cancel button to close the TCP/IP Settings dialog box. Then click Cancel once more to leave the connection dialog box.

TIP Don't forget to record your user name and password for the connection!

If you have any other connections in the Dial-Up Networking window that you'll want to retain in Linux, repeat the procedures in this section for each of them to determine their settings.

Checking for Hardware Compatibility

Now that you have record of the different pieces of hardware that make up your computer, it's time to start checking to see that hardware is compatible with Red Hat Linux 7.

Resources for Checking Compatibility

When purchasing software at the store, you can usually flip the box over to read the software's system requirements. For the most part, the listed requirements are usually complete. Alas, Red Hat Linux's requirements are woefully generalized on the box. Only broad parameters are detailed on the side of the box and with good reason: the hardware compatibility lists available for Red Hat Linux are pages and pages long.

Where do these famed lists exist? Fire up your Internet connection— you're going surfing on the Web.

Red Hat Support

It only makes sense that the best place to locate information about Red Hat Linux 7 is on the Red Hat Web site. Located at **http://www. redhat.com/support/hardware/**, the HCLs (Hardware Compatibility Lists) are gathered for all of the major releases of Red Hat.

Before you click the Intel Hardware link to begin examining the HCL, let me say a word about the different levels of compatibility that you will find in the list. Because of the huge variety of PC hardware available today, Red Hat supports a finite set of hardware. That does not mean that other hardware will not work with Red Hat—just that it is not directly supported.

Red Hat divides these differing levels of compatibility into tiers: Tier 1, 2, 3, and Incompatible. Each tier represents the level of compatibility or *comfort* Red Hat will have with a particular piece of hardware. Table 1.3 defines these levels.

The Red Hat HCL is very well organized. Each section focuses on a particular type of hardware and includes a definition of the compatibility levels. There is also an important warning about hardware names that bears repeating here.

In the hardware world, the *branding* of a given product occurs by keeping a popular name associated with what may be a completely different product. To provide you with a rather simplified example, a Pentium

TABLE 1.3 HARDWARE COMPATIBILITY TIERS	
Tier	**Definition**
Tier One	Fully supported hardware. Red Hat tested, used and approved. Go crazy.
Tier Two	Compatible and supported, but occasional problems have occurred. Red Hat support is limited. Proceed with caution.
Tier Three	Compatible and unsupported. Devices in this category may or may not work. Red Hat will provide very limited support, primarily pointing you to other potential sources for help. Danger, Will Robinson.
Incompatible	Very little chance of this working with Linux. Other daredevil users may have found workarounds, but don't count on it. Here there be dragons.

processor is very different from a Pentium II processor or a Pentium III. Even though the name Pentium is prevalent throughout, these are not the same products.

Other brand name differences are much more subtle and the product differences far more drastic. The point here is that if the exact model name or number is not listed in the HCL, the safest assumption should be that the hardware is incompatible.

The HCL is constantly evolving as more solutions to hardware compatibility issues are discovered. Later this evening, some of the highlights of this HCL will be discussed.

Linux Hardware Database

Unlike the Red Hat Web site, the Linux Hardware Database Web site does not offer a comprehensive look at all the hardware that can work with Red Hat Linux. It does, however, offer something the HCL does not: user-written ratings of how hardware really worked with Linux and tips on how to get around some of the sticky issues that can crop up.

The Linux Hardware Database can be found at **http://lhd.datapower.com**. As seen in Figure 1.9, it contains links to hardware organized by category types.

Clicking on a category link reveals a tabular listing of all of the tested hardware types for that category. The hardware is sorted by the rating the product has received (see Figure 1.10).

NOTE Hardware in this database is compared on different versions of Linux and different flavors as well. Be sure to read the testing specifications for each product. Hardware that tested well on earlier Linux kernels should work well with later versions.

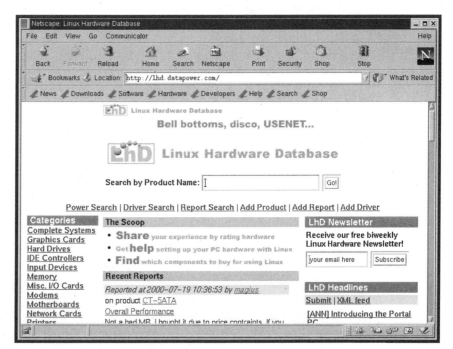

Figure 1.9

The Linux Hardware Database includes Linux compatibility reviews.

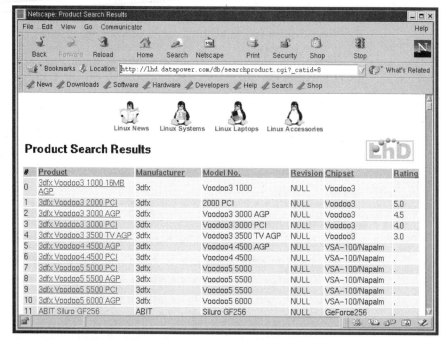

Figure 1.10

The best hardware to use in a category gets a rating of 5.0.

The rating system used in this site is based on the average of five categories:

○ Stability

○ Performance

○ Value

○ Ease of Setup

○ Overall

Each rating category is then based on six rather tongue-in-cheek values— from 0 to 5. The description for the top rating in the Performance category of 5, for example, is "Should be Illegal." (As you've no doubt determined by now, Linux users do not take themselves quite as seriously as do other computer folk.)

Click on the particular piece of hardware for which you want to view more information. You'll then see a detailed report on the item including any drivers that can be found for the hardware and user comments or warnings about the item (see Figure 1.11).

As you learn more about Red Hat Linux and become proficient at solving hardware issues, you can come back to this site and enter your own ratings about a product. All you have to do is register and that's free!

Hardware Supported by Red Hat

Gather your Linux journal and return to the Red Hat Linux Web site so that the HCL is on the screen in front of you. Now it's time to match up your PC's hardware to that on the list. Don't be discouraged if you find that any of your hardware falls into Tier 2 and Tier 3 categories. While it may take a bit more effort, it's not the end of the world. There may be a solution that won't involve going to the computer store. For more information on installing hardware, see the "Hardware" section on Sunday evening.

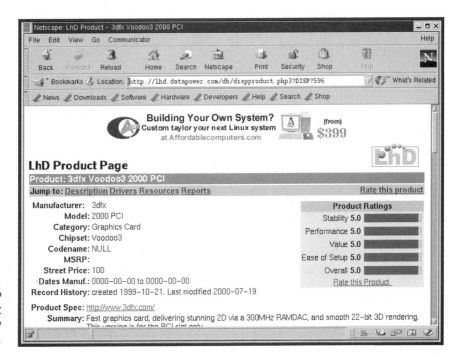

Figure 1.11

Real, honest opinions really help.

Video Card

Of all of the categories included in the HCL, the section for video cards is probably the most voluminous. That's because the video (or display adapter, as it's known in Windows) card could be considered the most important item in a PC, with the exception of the motherboard and CPU. Think about it. If nothing is displayed on the monitor, it's impossible to continue using the operating system. What's more, monitors don't control the video output of the PC—graphics cards do.

Because of this reason as well as the vast variations between cards, the HCL devotes a lot of space to listing different video cards. This devotion to detail is a bit ironic when you consider that compatibility with Linux is not the issue, the X Window System is.

Linux is a text-based, command-line operating system. It's a powerful system to be sure, but really just a collection of command lines much like DOS. To make Linux a more user-friendly system to use, Linux distributors often package a version of the X Window System (also known as X) with a release of Linux.

X is the source for all the cool windows and graphical user interfaces (GUIs) that come with today's Linux releases. XFree86 is the most common type of X server used for Intel-compatible PCs. Because XFree86 is required to display complex screens, XFree86, rather than Linux, is most concerned with video card compatibility.

Look carefully though the HCL for your video card. Once found, make a note in your journal of which X server will be used. The X server is the specific component of XFree86 used to display the graphics. Since different cards use different versions of X server, you may find it helpful to know this information should you later have problems with graphic display.

Table 1.4 displays the short list of video cards that are known to be incompatible with XFree86 4.0.1, the release shipped with Red Hat Linux 7.

Memory (RAM)

As with most operating systems and software, having at least the suggested minimum amount of RAM eliminates most problems. Table 1.5 lists the minimum requirements for RAM for various scenarios, as stated in the HCL.

Monitor

As mentioned earlier, the video card performs the lion's share of the work when producing the visual output from your PC. That does not mean that the monitor does not play a role in compatibility with Linux and XFree86. The place to make sure your monitor can relate well to XFree86 is not here in the pre-installation stage, however. Monitor compatibility is settled during the installation itself.

TABLE 1.4 KNOWN INCOMPATIBLE VIDEO CARDS	
Manufacturer	**Product**
SiS	530/5591/5596/5511 Pentium PCI/ISA Solution
SiS	600/620/5600 Pentium II multi-function integrated chipsets

TABLE 1.5 MINIMUM RAM REQUIREMENTS	
RAM	**Scenario**
16 MB	Bare minimum (will need at least 32 MB of swap disk space)
24 MB	Better performance for the Linux OS
48 MB	Recommended to run an X Window interface such as Gnome or KDE

To be sure that you are ready for installation, note in your journal the settings for your monitor's synchronization rates. These are usually found in the manual that came with your monitor. During installation, those settings will be matched to the X server component of XFree86.

 NOTE For more information on monitor compatibility, visit the FAQ section of the XFree86 Web site at **http://www.xfree.org/FAQ/#MONITORS**.

Hard Drive

Two types of hard drives are used in PCs: IDE and SCSI. If you haven't already, you can identify the type you have by examining your system BIOS (see the section titled "Checking Your BIOS for Information" you read earlier today). Most hard drives are compatible with Red Hat Linux 7.

Generally, if you have an internal IDE drive, you're okay by Red Hat Linux. Because Linux looks at the drive's SCSI controller, the same holds true for any SCSI drive, either internal or external. If the controller is supported, then all of the drives connected to it are supported by default.

 TIP External IDE drives, such as Syquest's removable drives, are the one incompatible type of drive mentioned in the HCL, but there is a workaround. Surf to the Linux Parallel Port Home Page (**http://www.torque.net/linux-pp.html**) to learn how to use this device.

Ethernet Card

During the installation of Red Hat Linux, the presence of a network card is typically detected. Linux will then ask you for your network settings. This section of the HCL reveals that many cards fall into Tier 1 and Tier 2 compatibility categories.

Given the history of Linux and its grandparent UNIX, this makes sense. After all, UNIX was initially designed to work on networks. Therefore, it's logical that network devices are largely compatible. Further, the communications protocols of the Internet are based on UNIX.

You should make sure your card is listed and find out where it falls in the compatibility tiers. Most of the big name cards fall into Tier 1, which is good. There are even Token Ring cards that have Tier 2 compatibility— very useful in today's mix-and-match corporate environments.

Table 1.6 lists the Ethernet cards that are known to be incompatible with Red Hat Linux 7.

 TIP While Xircom cards are listed as incompatible, there are workarounds to be found. Try the Xircom Ethernet Issues page at **http://pcmcia.sourceforge.org/cgi-bin/ HyperNews/get/pcmcia/xircom.html**.

Sound Card

Of all of the devices people will likely add to or upgrade on their computer, the sound card is likely to be near, or at, the top of the list. Sound cards, even in the Windows environment, can be difficult to install and configure. Maybe that's why the HCL lists no sound cards in the Tier 1 category.

TABLE 1.6 KNOWN INCOMPATIBLE ETHERNET CARDS	
Manufacturer	**Product**
Intel	EtherExpress Pro/10 PCI
Xircom	Ethernet adapters

Note that even if you have a compatible sound card, you will probably have to set it up through the sndconfig program before Red Hat Linux can use it. More information on sound cards can be found when you read "Configuring Printers, Sound, and Other Devices" on Saturday evening.

CD-ROM and DVD-ROM

Since hard drives were easy for Red Hat to utilize, you might think CD-ROMs would be equally as accessible. However, Red Hat is fussier about what CD-ROMs it will and will not use.

On the one hand, all 100 percent ATAPI-compliant CD-ROMs and SCSI CD-ROMs are Tier 1 compatible. Deviations from this can get a little tricky. This is one section you will want to review carefully.

Unfortunately, DVD players are not yet supported on Red Hat systems. While progress is being made, you're just going to have to watch your favorite video some other way.

NOTE Your DVD drive is not completely useless. Red Hat Linux will still be able to use it as an extra CD-ROM drive.

Table 1.7 lists the CD-ROMs that are known to be incompatible with Red Hat Linux 7.

TABLE 1.7 KNOWN INCOMPATIBLE CD-ROMs

Manufacturer	Product	Notes
Varied	Parallel-port CD-ROMs	Some BackPacks are Tier 3
LMS/Phillips	drive 206/cm260	Includes all clones
Liteon	All models	

Zip/Jaz Drive

It's not immediately obvious where to find Zip drives compatibility listings in the HCL. You'll need to look in Section 3.5, "SCSI Drives." Once you find the listing, however, you'll discover that external Zip and Jaz drives will work, including parallel port Zip drives.

Tape Drive

Most SCSI tape drives are likely to be Tier 2 supported. Remember that if the SCSI controller is supported, then any SCSI device attached to it will be supported as well. There is an exception to this rule in this very device class, which is listed in Table 1.8.

Modem

Your modem is the device this is likely to give you the most trouble. Simply put, if your computer has an internal modem, it probably won't work. This is because most internal modems use Windows-specific drivers and won't work in other operating systems.

TIP ■■

At this time, one internal modem that will work for sure under Red Hat: the LucentVenus PCI modem. If you are lucky enough to have this internal modem, return to the Modem section of the HCL after you have installed Red Hat to learn how to tweak your system to use the device. To find more internal modems compatible with Linux, surf to http://www.o2.net/~gromitkc/winmodem.html.

■■

TABLE 1.8 KNOWN INCOMPATIBLE TAPE DRIVES		
Manufacturer	**Product**	**Notes**
Varied	Non ATAPI parallel-port drives	
Onstream	30 GB drive	Includes *all* types (IDE, SCSI, and parallel)

The good news is that if you have an external modem, it will almost surely work. Modems that talk to the PC through a serial port rather than internally do not need Windows drivers to work.

Other types of external communications devices work under Red Hat Linux as well. ISDN routers, if they are external and can emulate a modem, will usually work, although Linux does classify them as Tier 3.

If you are lucky enough to live in an area of the nation that has cable Internet access, then you may have a cable modem. Cable modems that connect to a supported Ethernet interface are Tier 3 supported.

Printer

Setting up a printer in Red Hat Linux has a Windows-like feel to it. Basically, Red Hat Linux does not care what type of printer you have at installation. Setting up your printer is something you will do after installation (see the "Printers" section on Saturday evening).

The HCL has a good list of the printer filters contained within this version of Red Hat. These filters are directly analogous to the Windows printer drivers. Check the list to see if your printer is there, but don't worry if it isn't. There will be ways of getting the printer installed even if it is not on the compatibility list.

Mouse

The second thing Linux configures during its installation is the mouse. There are four types of mice: PS/2, serial, bus, and USB. The most common types are the PS/2 and serial mice, which are Tier 1 compatible. Bus mice fall into the Tier 2 category, and USB mice are classified as Tier 3.

Since your mouse will very likely fall into either a Tier 1 or Tier 2 category, this device doesn't require much concern. If you have a USB mouse, however, you should be aware that Linux is still in the experimental stages where USB is concerned. You might want to consider getting a new mouse type for your PC.

For more information on USB devices in Linux, visit **http://www.linux-usb.org/**.

Keyboard

No keyboard section exists in the HCL. Keyboards are universal to PCs (if any device can truly be called *universal*). Keyboards have long been held to the ANSI standard, which is an international set of standards to which all keyboards have to adhere. (Yes, someone actually sat down and thought this out.) This standard has used a specific code for every character the keyboard can create, no matter what operating system is being used.

This standard makes it very easy for Linux to access any keyboard, including the new natural keyboards and those keyboards with pointing devices contained within. USB keyboards, like their mice counterparts, should be utilized with caution.

Notebook Computers

A laptop or notebook computer is no more a single device any more than your desktop PC is. There is no one notebook PC that is compatible with Linux as a whole.

A section for notebook computers is included in the HCL, but it is a bit different, containing a great link to the Linux Laptop Web pages. You should follow this link if you are thinking about installing Linux on your laptop PC.

I also recommend you pick up a copy of *Linux for Your Laptop* (Prima, 2000) by my good friend Bill Ball. It contains a lot of valuable information on how to get Linux on your notebook computer, including a step-by-step guide to installing Red Hat Linux on a laptop.

SCSI Adapters

Finally, the section on SCSI cards bears a close look, if only because so many other devices could depend on the compatibility of the primary SCSI card.

This is a large section of the HCL and you should take the time to find your PC's SCSI adapter. While there are no incompatible SCSI cards, certainly you will need to use some caution if your card falls into the Tier 3 category.

Backing Up Your Old Data

After you have ascertained your hardware compatibility with Red Hat Linux 7, you will need to get your computer ready for the installation. One of the first things you should do is back up the data on your PC.

It is always a good idea to back up your valuable data, thus guarding against system catastrophe. At the very least, you'll want your data protected from power surges, virus attacks, computer theft, or anything else that can affect your ability to access the data on your machine.

Installing Linux certainly can't be classified as a catastrophic event. However, you are going to be changing your hard drive's partitions or perhaps even formatting your hard drive. These events can and will erase data completely.

The first thing you should decide is what data should be backed up. That really depends on what you want to do in your Linux installation. Especially if you plan to dual boot (running Windows and Linux on the same PC), then you will need to make sure you've safeguarded most of your Windows data. You'll find more information about dual booting in the section titled "Making Room for Multiple Operating Systems" later this evening.

Even if you plan to completely remove Windows, there is still merit to saving your data files. Some file types can be opened on a Linux PC, such as graphic files (GIFs and JPEGs, among others). In addition, Microsoft Office files can even be opened, compliments of a great office suite application called StarOffice that is fully Office compatible. You'll need to save, not back up, these files if you plan to use them on your Linux machine, though. Linux will not be able to read a Windows backup file.

Most computer applications these days use huge amounts of disk space, primarily because today's big hard drives enable them to do so. Backing up your data and your application files is a big job. If you have sufficient storage capacity (such as a tape or Jaz drive), then I recommend that you back up your entire hard drive.

For those of you that do not have a sufficient large-capacity device to hold an entire drive's worth of data, then just back up your data files. Your data files are the documents, spreadsheets, drawings, and other files that you have created over time on your computer. If you do run into trouble, you can restore your system by first re-installing your operating system, your applications using your original disks, and then restoring your archived personal data files.

If you have never used a backup program, you will find them easy to use. Many backup programs are available, including an excellent one found with Norton System Utilities. The principles for backup utilities are pretty much the same: locate and identify the files you wish to archive, specify the location of the new archive file, and then create the file. Restoration is simply the reverse of this action.

Microsoft Windows has its own utility for backup that can be used to archive your data. The next few paragraphs describe how to work with the Windows Backup utility.

From the Windows 95/98 taskbar, click the Start button, then choose Programs, Accessories, System Tools, Backup. The Microsoft Backup application will start with the Welcome to Microsoft Backup dialog box open (see Figure 1.12). You can now choose to create a new backup file, open an existing backup job, or restore archived data.

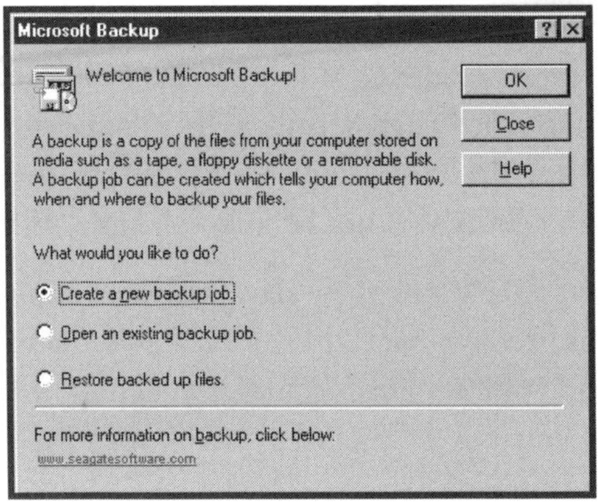

Figure 1.12

Microsoft's
Backup utility

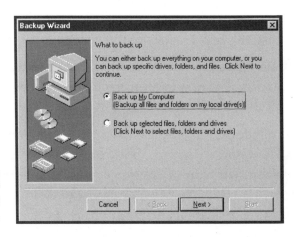

NOTE The Backup application in Windows 95 is similar to that in Windows 98, except for the lack of a wizard to step you through operations.

Select Create a New Backup Job, then click OK. The Backup Wizard will appear, as shown in Figure 1.13.

Here you can either choose to back up your entire set of computer files, or you can choose to only back up selected files. If you have the storage

Figure 1.13

The first step in the
Backup process.

space and the time, go ahead and archive your entire PC. If not, select the Backup Selected Files, Folders, and Drives option, then click Next. The second dialog box of the Backup Wizard will open.

On the left side of the dialog box, select the check boxes for the drives and folders you want to back up. As necessary, use the expansion icons in the directory listing to view subfolders. Note that selecting a folder automatically selects all of the files within the folder. Alternatively, select or clear the check boxes for the specific files you want to include or exclude from the file list on the right side of the dialog box. Figure 1.14 shows an example of selected files in the My Documents folder.

When you've selected all of the files you want to include in your backup job, click Next to continue to the next dialog box of the Backup Wizard. Now you are asked whether you want to back up all of the selected files or just the ones that have changed since a prior backup. Since this is likely your first backup, select the All Selected Files option and click Next to continue.

In the fourth dialog box (see Figure 1.15) you are asked where you want to store the backup file. Choose your preferred location and type a file name for your backup file. When complete, click Next to continue.

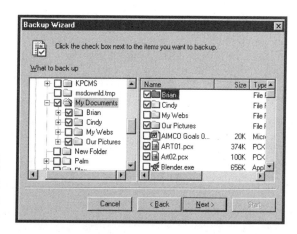

Figure 1.14

You can select all or part of a folder's contents.

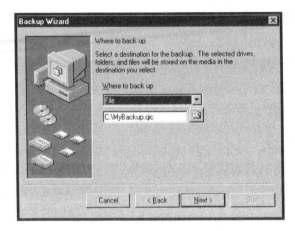

Figure 1.15

Where do you want to store your backup file?

TIP

Make sure you save this information on a drive other than your hard drive. Zip, Jaz, or tape drives are good places.

The fifth dialog box gives you two choices on how to back up your data. The first specifies that you want your data to be double-checked to make sure it was successfully archived. Double-checking your data as it's being archived will slow the process down, but I recommend that you do so. After all, what's the point of backing up erroneous data?

The second option asks if you want to compress the backup data. Unless you have virtually unlimited space to store your backup, you'll want this option checked. This will also slow down the backup process. Choose your preferences, then click Next to continue to the final dialog box of the Backup Wizard.

In the last dialog box (see Figure 1.16), you will provide a descriptive name for your backup file. This is different from the file name you previously selected. Use a name to help you remember the contents of the backup archive file.

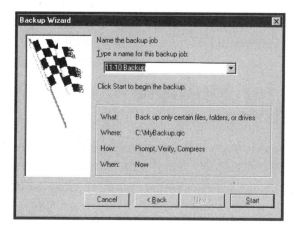

Figure 1.16

Confirm your backup choices in this dialog box.

After you confirm the choices you have made, simply click the Start button to begin the Backup process. The Backup Progress window will appear to display its progress (see Figure 1.17).

When completed, the Backup file will be verified (if you chose to do this) and you will be notified that the operation is complete. Click OK to acknowledge the notification, then click OK again to close the Backup Progress window.

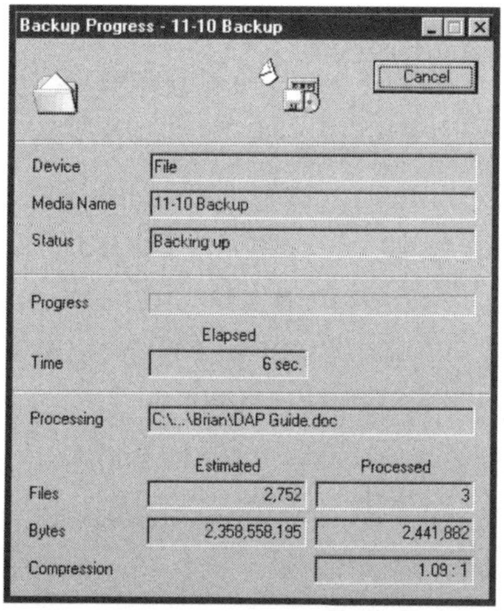

Figure 1.17

The Backup process in action.

Make sure the Backup file is stored away from your hard drive. As you will see in the next section, big changes may be coming to your drive.

Making Room for Multiple Operating Systems

Now comes the time where you have an important decision to make. Like all important decisions, you should weigh your options carefully. You must now decide whether you are going to run Red Hat Linux alone on your PC or whether you want to retain your existing operating system and add Linux.

There are several pros and cons for using multiple operating systems on one computer. The cons include the headaches of installing two or more operating systems on a machine, resulting in less memory available for each of the operating systems.

Nevertheless, the benefits of using multiple operating systems are huge. For instance, you will have the ability to run all of the programs available for each of the operating systems you'll have on your PC. You will also be able to use all of the hardware your PC has. Finally, you'll save money by not needing to buy another PC.

I recommend that dual booting is the way you should go—especially if you are just trying out Linux. This option gives you the benefits of using Linux without a lot of investment in time or money.

If you decide to include Linux on your PC in addition to Windows, you will need to make room for it on your hard drive. But making room on your hard drive for Red Hat Linux is a far different operation than making room for the latest computer game. You will need to create a brand new *partition* from which Linux will operate.

At this point in the evening, you get a crash course in disk partitions and why you can't write data to a disk without them, so hang on to your collective hats.

Why Partition?

Imagine the bee, buzzing around your garden. If you were to follow this bee back to its home, you would find a seemingly chaotic mass of buzzing insects, each looking as if they aimlessly wander about with nothing better to do than hang out and buzz.

As we all know, however, all bees have a specific mission in life: working together for the collective benefit of the hive. One group of bees has the job of taking care of all of the cute little baby bees after the queen lays her eggs. Now, think back to your science classes: where are the baby bees raised?

If you said the honeycomb, you're right. If you're wondering what the heck this has to do with partitions, hang on.

The honeycomb is an ingenious device composed of hexagonal cells made of beeswax, where honey and bee larvae are stored for safekeeping. Now, ponder this: how would the bees get by if they did not have honeycombs? The answer is they wouldn't.

Keeping the honeycombs in mind, you can apply this analogy to how data is stored on a disk drive. Data, you see, cannot be stored on a drive without some sort of structure already in place for the data to be organized.

When data is placed on a drive, it is written into this structure, called a file system in the Linux community. A file system is the format in which data is stored—a honeycomb of cells if you will, where each little piece of data is placed.

Computers being computers, it's a little more complicated than that. Data for a single file, for example, does not get stored in data blocks that sit right next to each other. The data may be stored in data blocks 456, 457, and 458 and then block 6,134, then block 7,111, and so on. (This is an oversimplification, but you get the idea.) It's the job of the file system to track where every file resides so that when you send a command to work with a file, the file system knows all of the separate blocks where the file is stored.

Because of all of this file tracking and retrieving, computer engineers came up with idea of keeping the file systems small, even on large hard drives. At that point, the idea of partitions came into play. Basically, the partition is a virtual barrier that tells the file system: "You used to be able to write to blocks 1-25000 all over the disk, but now you're only allowed to write to blocks 1-17500. A second file system will write to blocks 17501-25000, so hands off!"

Thus, you have partitions. Each partition can use a different file system. As an analogy, honeycombs created by honeybees are different from those created by wasps—similar structure but different outcomes.

There are six major types of file systems used on Intel-compatible PCs today, as seen in Table 1.9.

◄◄◄

Swap partition: A section of space on a hard drive used by the computer as auxiliary RAM. When a program or process uses more memory than RAM exists on the computer, the swap partition provides additional memory for the process to use.

◄◄◄

TABLE 1.9 FILE SYSTEM TYPES (INTEL PCs)	
File System	**Used By**
FAT	Windows 95, Windows 98, Windows NT
FAT32	Windows 95b, Windows 98, Windows ME, Windows NT, Windows 2000
NTFS	Windows NT, Windows 2000
ext2	Linux
os2	OS/2
swap	All operating systems

Different types of partitions typically do not work with other operating systems. Thus, in order to install Linux on your PC, you will need to create an ext2 partition on your hard drive. Unfortunately, if your PC contains a typical installation of Windows, your Windows file system is contained within one big partition that covers your entire hard drive. This leaves no room for a partition and a new file system. Remember, even if you have gigabytes of empty space on your drive, this space, like files and directories, may be scattered throughout the drive.

The easiest method to add a partition to your existing hard drive file system is to use a third-party application. This shoves all of your data into a single collection of data blocks, leaving truly contiguous empty and unstructured (unformatted) space elsewhere in the drive where you can install a partition.

CAUTION   Before you use any tool to manipulate and/or create partitions, back up or save your data to an alternate physical drive.

PartitionMagic 5.0

Of all of the partitioning software out on the market today, PartitionMagic is arguably the easiest to use and certainly the most time-tested. PartitionMagic enables you to create partitions on your hard drives with ease. It even comes with BootMagic, a multi-operating system boot utility.

What makes PartitionMagic so great to use is that it will actually create a Linux ext2 partition without potential loss of data. Using PartitionMagic to create a native Linux partition saves you a lot of steps in installation.

For more information on PartitionMagic, surf to **http://www. powerquest.com/partitionmagic**. There you will find detailed product information. I heartily recommend this product for your use.

TIP If you run a search for "linux" on the PartitionMagic Web site, you will find detailed instructions on how to specifically install Linux partitions and mount points. You will learn about mounts points tomorrow morning when you actually install Red Hat Linux.

fips

If you do not want to plunk down the cash for PartitionMagic, never fear. Red Hat Linux has thoughtfully provided fips, a utility that can resize and create FAT (either FAT16 or FAT32) partitions in Windows systems.

The fips utility will reduce the size of your current FAT partition and create a new FAT partition. You'll then need to delete the new FAT partition. Because Linux will only sit inside an ext2 file system, created only from unformatted space during the installation process, you'll need to run the DOS fdisk utility to remove the new FAT partition.

NOTE The fips utility is located in the \dosutils directory on the Red Hat Linux/Intel CD 1. Documentation for fips is located in the \dosutils\fipsdocs directory on the same CD. I strongly agree with Red Hat that you read the fips documentation before using the application.

When to Use fdisk

You may have heard somewhere out in computer legends and lore that eventually you will have to use the DOS utility fdisk on your PC. The fdisk utility is used when you have to completely wipe the data from your hard drive.

NOTE This section is referring to the DOS fdisk utility, not the Linux version of fdisk, which sometimes has trouble with Windows partitions.

CAUTION

◆◆

All kidding aside, be very careful when you use fdisk. One wrong move and you *will* lose all of your data.

◆◆

For the purposes of Linux installation, there are really two instances where you will need to use fdisk. The first instance is if you plan to install Red Hat Linux by itself on the PC. The fdisk utility is the preferred method to use should you want to completely wipe the hard drive clean and install Linux.

The second opportunity to use fdisk is to eliminate any partitions a third-party partitioning utility might have created for you (such as fips). The fdisk utility can wipe these non-ext2 partitions off the hard drive.

Here's how to use fdisk to remove partitions on your hard drive.

1. Using Windows Explorer, format a floppy disk. Make sure the Create System Disk option is checked.

2. Copy the fdisk.exe file from the \Windows\Commands folder to the floppy disk.

3. Reboot your computer, leaving the floppy disk in the drive. The floppy disk is bootable because you copied the system files to it.

4. When the DOS prompt appears, type **fdisk,** then press Enter. A message regarding large disk drives will appear (see Figure 1.18).

5. Enter **N** so that large drive support is not enabled.

6. In the FDISK Options screen (see Figure 1.19), type **3** to start the Delete Partition or Logical DOS Drive option.

7. In the Delete DOS Partition or Logical DOS Drive screen (see Figure 1.20), type **1** to activate the Delete Primary DOS Partition option.

8. In the Delete Primary DOS Partition screen, type the number that identifies the partition you want to delete (see Figure 1.21). Refer to the disk size listings and file system types to help you identify which partition number you want to remove, if there is more than one.

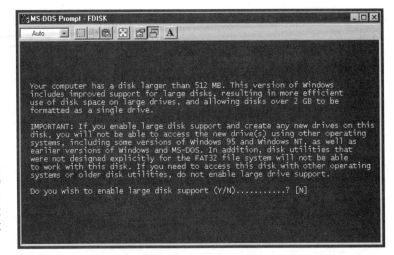

Figure 1.18

Starting fdisk will display important information about large disk drives.

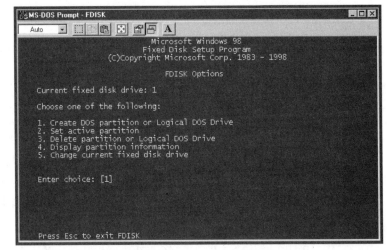

Figure 1.19

Your FDISK options—potentially deadly unless in the right hands.

CAUTION Remember to make sure you are modifying or deleting the right partition when you take these actions. The simplest way is to check the file system type and disk size against the known size of your partitions. If you have a 2 GB Windows partition that you want to remove, for example, be sure the partition you select is a 2 GB FAT32 partition.

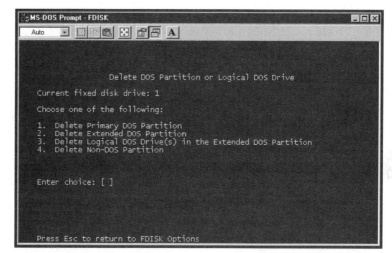

Figure 1.20

Choose which partition you want to delete in this screen.

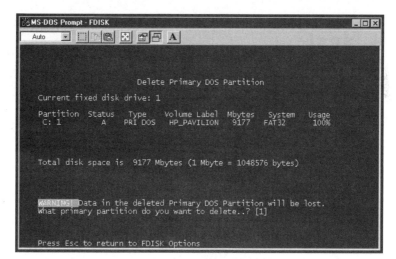

Figure 1.21

The last step before the partition deletion occurs.

9. Type the Volume Label of the partition you are deleting. A confirmation line will appear.

10. Verify that you do want to delete the partition, then type Y in the confirmation line. The partition you chose will be deleted.

11. When complete, press the Esc key until you return to the DOS prompt.

NOTE If you're wondering why the deletion of the partition only took a second or two when it seems to take longer to erase just a portion of the hard drive, it's because only the *partition* definition is deleted, not the data within. Without the partition and its file system, however, the data within is now a jumbled and worthless mass of data blocks. Like honey would be if the honeycomb suddenly vanished. Eliminating this partition essentially erases the data, since you'll never get to it again.

Tonight you have an idea of how to make room for a Linux partition. Tomorrow morning you'll examine just how to set up your Linux partitions. That's right. Partitions—plural. Not to fear, Linux will do a lot of the work for you.

What's Next?

This evening we delved into some of the major considerations and information you need to gather prior to installing Red Hat Linux 7 on your system.

Tomorrow morning this preparation will be put to work while installing Red Hat Linux 7 on your PC. Specifically, you'll:

✪ Start and use the Red Hat installer

✪ Set your partition options

✪ Configure user accounts

✪ Configure the X Window system

✪ Start and use the text installer, if need be.

And that's all before lunch! For now, set your journal notes where you can find them, grab your favorite beverage, and go watch some *Letterman*. You've earned it!

Installing
Red Hat Linux 7

- ✿ Starting the Red Hat Installer
- ✿ Running Your Installation
- ✿ Other Installation Concerns

Good morning! I hope you slept well last night, because you have a busy day ahead of you. Everything should go well, though, so it should be a fun day, too. In fact, by the end of this morning, you should have Red Hat Linux 7 installed on your PC.

Bold statement? Hardly. The plain fact is that installation is not that big of a deal anymore—*if* you did your preparation in last night. That's the real key to installing any distribution of Linux.

It is important that you gather all of the information specified last night because you are going to need it to double-check what the installation program does this morning, entering the information yourself if need be. By the end of this morning, you will have:

- ✪ Installed the Red Hat Linux operating system
- ✪ Dealt with any unusual installation issues
- ✪ Configured your PC to boot to Linux and Windows

Three words of advice before you begin: do not panic. If you read the instructions carefully and have the right information, little can go wrong.

Starting the Red Hat Installer

There are various ways to install Red Hat Linux 7. The easiest way is to use the official Red Hat 7 CD-ROMs that you can buy with the official boxed sets in most software stores.

Red Hat Linux 7 is available in three flavors: The Standard, Deluxe, and Professional editions. The Standard edition contains the Red Hat Linux Installation Guide and Reference Guide, as well as a boot disk. You'll find out more about this important disk in the next section, "Creating a Boot Disk".

In the Deluxe and Professional editions, a CD-ROM set of Linux workstation applications, PowerTools, is included for your use. The Professional edition also includes a bonus pack of server applications and additional Web building tools.

Since Red Hat Linux can be obtained from sources other than a boxed Red Hat Linux set (including the CD-ROM that came with this book), you may need to get some of these additional resources in some other fashion. If you can't get a boxed copy, or don't want to lay out the cash, there are some methods you can use to get the tools you need.

NOTE   A great place to learn about downloading Red Hat Linux is **http://www.redhat. com/download/howto_download.html**.

The documentation included in the boxed set is freely available in HTML or Acrobat PDF format on the Web at **http://www.redhat.com/ support/manuals/**.

You will not find the additional software packaged together all in one place as you will in these boxed sets, but a quick check of Linux-related Web sites will point you to the same tools and more. For example, you can find StarOffice, a very robust office suite application that's fully compatible with Microsoft Office, at **http://www.sun.com/staroffice**.

The final component needed to duplicate any of the boxed sets is the boot disk, which will be detailed in the next section.

Creating a Boot Disk

The most important resource you'll need besides the Linux program CD-ROMs is the boot disk. Without your own copy of the boot disk, you could have difficulty installing the software.

◄◄

Boot disk: A floppy disk that contains Linux system files that allow users access the Red Hat Linux CD-ROM *before* any other operating system is loaded.

◄◄

The reason a boot disk is required is that Linux cannot be installed from within another operating system, and must be run beginning right after a PC starts, before anything else loads. Many PCs cannot start directly from a CD-ROM drive, but can start from the floppy drive. Have you ever noticed the sound of the floppy drive rattling when your computer powers up? That's the BIOS looking for a boot disk in the drive.

• •

NOTE If you are fortunate enough to have a bootable CD-ROM, then you do not need a boot disk. Simply insert the Red Hat Linux CD 1 into your CD-ROM and restart the computer. The installation program will then begin automatically.

• •

The boot disk contains just enough Linux commands to start a mini-version of Linux, including the instructions that enable Linux to recognize and run your CD-ROM drive. At that point, you can "jumpstart" the full installation program into action.

Procedure

Use this procedure to make your own boot disk:

1. Format a 3.5-inch disk and leave it in the floppy drive.

2. Insert the Red Hat Linux CD 1 into the CD-ROM drive.

3. Start an MS-DOS window by selecting Programs, MS-DOS Prompt on the Start menu.

4. Type *<drive letter>*:\, where *<drive letter>* is the letter of your CD-ROM drive.

5. Type **cd \dosutils**. You should now be in the dosutils directory on the CD.

6. Type **rawrite**. The rawrite application will start.

7. When prompted for a disk image source, type **..\images\boot.img**.

8. When prompted for the target diskette drive, type *<drive letter>*:, where *<drive letter>* is the letter of your floppy drive.

9. Press the Enter key when prompted. The Red Hat Linux boot instructions will be copied to your floppy disk.

 TIP If you later chose to use the Custom installation path, you'll be prompted to create another copy of the boot disk. Since having more boot disks is safer, you'll want to go ahead and make a second one at that time.

Navigating the Installer

You're ready to begin now. You have all your information gathered, disks ready, and a cute stuffed penguin for luck sitting on your desk. It's time.

Insert the Red Hat CD-ROM 1 into your CD-ROM drive and then shut down your computer. If you do not have a bootable CD-ROM drive, insert the boot disk into the floppy drive while the computer is off, then turn it on again. Your computer will begin the boot process, starting from

either your CD-ROM or floppy drive. It will boot using the instructions on the CD-ROM or floppy disk rather than continuing to your hard drive and consequently loading your usual operating system.

Once the computer recognizes the bootstrap code from the floppy disk or CD-ROM drive, it will start Anaconda, the Red Hat installation program. The very first screen of Anaconda is shown in Figure 2-1. As you can see, it's rather plain, but it prompts you to make a significant decision.

You can choose from three installation options (sometimes termed "installation classes") when installing Red Hat Linux 7. The first is the graphical mode, which is a Windows-like installation that is certainly the easiest to use. The second option, text mode, is slightly less robust than the graphical mode. It will also get the job done.

The final option is the expert mode. For now, I suggest that you stay away from this one. You should really only use expert mode if Linux has trouble detecting the hardware you need to run the installation program such as the CD-ROM drive and the hard drive. Such an event is rather rare. You should be able to press Enter at this screen to start the graphical installation mode.

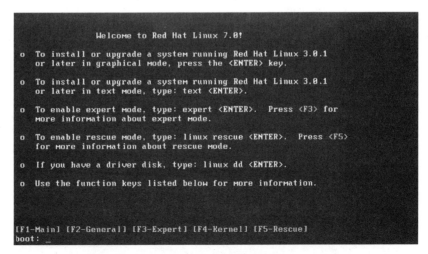

Figure 2-1

Choose the type of installation program to use.

TIP

After leaving the first screen, more hardware detections will occur. If Red Hat's installation program does not recognize your video card, your screen may appear all white or black. If this happens, restart the PC again, this time typing **text** at the opening installation prompt. Text installation mode is less fussy about display drivers. You can configure the graphic display after Linux is installed.

The graphical mode of installation will begin. The next sections will detail each step of a typical workstation installation.

Running Your Installation

As the installation progresses, you will see a sequence of installation screens that will present choices to you based on the type of installation class you chose. These screens are organized in the same manner throughout the entire installation process, as seen in Figure 2-2.

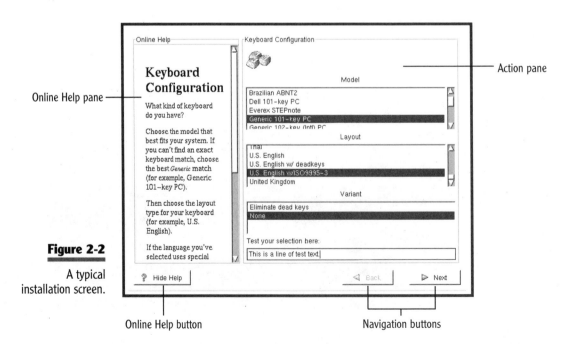

Figure 2-2

A typical installation screen.

On the left side of the screen, you will see the Online Help pane. This pane contains general help pertinent to the current installation screen. Although it takes up some screen space, I recommend that you leave it on throughout the entire process. This enables you to quickly find help for a term or option you may not understand. If you really think you don't need the Online Help, you can turn it off by clicking the Hide Help button.

The pane on the right side of the screen is where all of the action happens. The action pane displays the options appropriate to the current task from which you make your installation choices. Each time you complete a selection, click the Next button to move to the next screen. Conversely, if you need to reverse a decision you made, you can click the Back button and return to the screen you want to change.

NOTE In some cases, the Next button is disabled (indicated by its gray appearance) until you have made all of the necessary choices, a helpful safety feature.

NOTE You can step backward through the Anaconda screens up to the About to Install screen. Once past this point of no return, you cannot change your mind.

Determining Language, Keyboard, and Mouse Settings

Early in the installation process, Red Hat Linux gathers important information so that it can continue smoothly. This information is centered around input—specifically, how you will input data into both Anaconda and, later, into Linux. You'll need to select the language, keyboard, and mouse device you want to use.

The very first screen of the installation path requires you to select the Language you will use. This will be the language used during the installation process, not necessarily within Red Hat Linux. From the language list, select your preferred language and then click the Next button.

The Keyboard Configuration screen, shown in Figure 2-2, now appears. There are three categories here used to define your keyboard: Model, Layout, and Variant.

While keyboard models are currently fairly ubiquitous, there are some variations among styles. One example many Americans will recognize is the difference between "natural" (ergonomically designed) keyboards and the more standard (flat) 101-key keyboards. Check for your keyboard model and style in the Model list. If you do not see your specific keyboard model, select Generic 101-key PC.

Layout refers to the alphanumeric characters used by the selected keyboard. For example, someone using the German language will need characters such as ¨, and if you live in Great Britain, you might require characters such as £. In the United States, one of the U.S. English choices will be appropriate.

The dead keys option should be selected if you still want an English layout but you also use alternate characters that require the creation of dead keys. If you have a newer computer, choose the ISO-9995-3 option, as it will enable your keyboard to adhere to an international standard.

◄◄

 BUZZ WORD   *Dead keys*: Keys that allow the quick creation of non-English characters on an English keyboard.

◄◄

The options in the Variant category will change based on the Layout selected. Typically, the option is to have no variants on your keyboard model and layout versus one or more different variants, such as using dead keys. See your keyboard's documentation for help if you have an unusual typing situation. Once you have completed all your selections, click the Next button.

In the Mouse Configuration screen (see Figure 2-3), you will have the option to choose the type of mouse you use. As you can see when you go to the local computer store, not all mice are created equal. They all have to perform the same task, however—move the mouse pointer across the screen.

Three types of mice are available: bus, serial, and PS/2. Bus and serial mice are not as popular in the PC world, as most PC makers recognized that users would like to use their bus and serial ports for something other than a mouse. Thus, most PCs use a PS/2 port mouse. The latest PCs have USB-supported mice, which are still rather unstable when used with Linux.

If you are not clear on what type of mouse you have, refer to the documentation for your mouse to determine its connection. Again, if you cannot locate the specific type of mouse you own, choose one of the generic options.

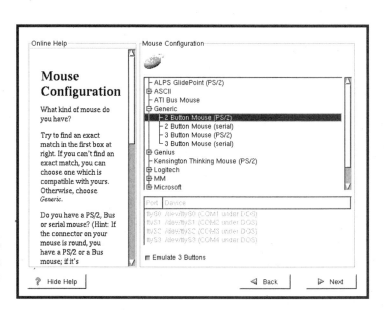

Figure 2-3

The Mouse Configuration screen.

TIP What? You don't religiously save the documentation for every piece of hardware you own? In that case, check the back of your PC. If the mouse is plugged into a little round 6-pin port, it's PS/2. If it's plugged into a trapezoidal 9-pin port, it's a serial port. Anything else is a bus port.

You will notice Linux offers options for three-button mice. These devices are not as familiar to Windows users but well known to UNIX users. Many UNIX and Linux X applications make use of the center button found on three-button mice, and mice used in Windows applications are usually of the two-button variety. Because Linux applications often use the center button, Linux can set a two-button mouse to emulate a three-button mouse (usually by clicking both mouse buttons at once). I recommend that you select the Emulate 3 Buttons option, because you will eventually find the need for a center button in Red Hat Linux—and it's less expensive than going out and buying a new mouse.

Use the expansion icons to explore the mouse options, select the mouse you need, and click the Next button to continue.

Choosing Installation Class

Before you move into the more critical areas of the installation process, you will get a brief break with the Red Hat Welcome screen, as seen in Figure 2-4. This screen is more than the official beginning of the System Installer. The Online Help pane contains some helpful information about where you can get the Red Hat Linux Installation Guide and other manuals.

Click the Next button to move to the Install Type screen. You must now decide what you are going to install.

You can select three primary installation options. These options are each discussed in more detail throughout this section. Be sure you read this section all the way through before deciding on an installation path—one wrong move could wipe your entire hard drive.

Figure 2-4

The Welcome
screen is the real
start of the
installation process.

Within the figure:
Online Help — Welcome

Welcome to Red Hat Linux

Welcome! This installation process is outlined in detail in the Red Hat Linux Installation Guide available from Red Hat, Inc.. Please read through the entire manual before you begin the installation process.

HTML and PostScript copies of the manual are online, at http://www.redhat.com.

redhat. **Linux**

System Installer

? Hide Help   ◁ Back   ▷ Next

✪ **Workstation**. This path will automatically install Linux with X and either the KDE or GNOME desktop environments, or both, should you so choose. You will decide the question of desktop environments later. This installation option will include the packages needed to run a standard PC workstation.

✪ **Server System**. This path will automatically install Linux with additional server packages, including the Apache Web server, perhaps the most-used Web server. With this choice, X is not automatically installed.

✪ **Custom System**. Custom enables the user to select exactly which packages to install. The user also gets the opportunity to configure settings that might otherwise be automatic in the other installation paths, such as placement of the LILO and partitioning of the hard drive.

A fourth option, Upgrade, appears on the screen, but it does not actually affect what is installed. Upgrade will let you keep your current Linux installation on your hard drive and will simply upgrade your current version of Red Hat Linux to 7.

When should you use each of these options? Well, like most computer-related installations, your specific situation will very likely differ from any scenario I could present here. Table 2-1 lists some basic guidelines you can follow when deciding which installation path to choose.

TABLE 2-1 INSTALLATION PATH GUIDELINES	
Path	**Issues**
Workstation	Simplest path to take. Good for a home PC with a single or dual operating system setup. Automatically installs X Window. Can be used if setting up a dual boot system with Windows 95/98, but not Windows NT or OS/2.
Server	Good for the more advanced user, particularly someone looking to create a network or Web server. Can be used if setting up a dual boot system with Windows 95/98, but not Windows NT or OS/2.
Custom	Must be used to install on a PC that will be shared with Windows NT or OS/2, so that LILO will be placed in the correct place on the hard drive. Not very complicated and gives users the ability to pick and choose between every application package, not just what Linux supplies in the other two installation paths.

TIP Make sure that you not only select each installation option's button but that you also select (click and highlight) the Install option. Otherwise, nothing will happen when it comes time to install packages.

When you've completed selecting all installation options, click Next to continue.

Selecting Your Partition Options

The Automatic Partitioning screen is the next to appear in the installation process. It is here that you will decide whether to partition your hard drive yourself or have Linux do it.

If Red Hat Linux will be the only operating system on your PC and you have eliminated all the other operating systems and their partitions, then you should allow Linux to perform the partition for you. Choose the Automatically partition and REMOVE DATA option.

You can also allow automatic partitioning if you plan to dual boot with Windows 95 or 98. In the Workgroup installation, only existing Linux partitions are replaced with new partition settings for Red Hat Linux 7. The existing DOS partition used by the Windows operating system remains unaffected.

Table 2-2 lists the partition settings you will have if you allow Red Hat to partition for you using either the Workgroup or Server installation choices.

If you're wondering why this wasn't all taken care of already, it's because the partitioning operations you performed last night were basically done to shove the Windows partition out of the way and make room for the Linux partitions. Today, during installation, you can fine-tune the big block of space you made for Linux with Linux's own partitioning tools.

TABLE 2-2: LINUX INSTALLATION PARTITIONS

Partition	Mount Point	Memory Allotment
Workstation		
Boot Partition	/boot	16MB
Swap Partition	None	64MB
Root Partition	/	The remainder of any unpartitioned space on the disk
Server		
Boot Partition	/boot	16MB
Swap Partition	None	64MB
Root Partition	/	256MB
Var Partition	/var	256MB
Usr Partition	/usr	Half of remaining unpartitioned space on the disk
Home Partition	/home	Half of remaining unpartitioned space on the disk

If you want to manually partition the Linux portion of the hard drive yourself, you have the choice of two tools: Disk Druid and Linux fdisk. Of the two, I *strongly* recommend you choose the Disk Druid option, because Linux fdisk (quite different from DOS fdisk used yesterday) is very capable of partitioning the hard drive, but it is not a very intuitive application and therefore could irreparably harm your drive's partitioning.

When you select the Manually partition with Disk Druid option and click Next, you will see the Disk Druid screen, as shown in Figure 2-5.

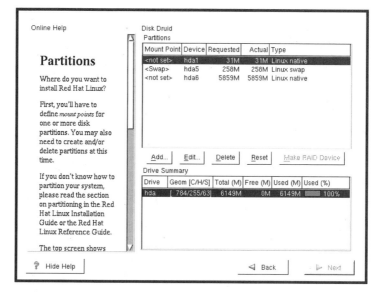

Figure 2-5

Control manual partitioning with the Disk Druid tool.

The fundamental operation of the Disk Druid tool is simple. You receive a list of existing drive partitions, either Linux or DOS. Below the Partition list is the Drive Summary list, which gives the details of the hard drives on your PC. Watch the Used (M) and Used (%) fields as you add or delete partitions. The percentage of used disk space will approach or move away from 100%. As long as the field displays less than 100%, unpartitioned space remains on the drive for you to use. Conversely, if the Used (%) field displays 100% usage and you still need to add partitions, you will have to delete some existing partitions to make room.

Use the following steps to manually create a workstation partition set on your PC. I recommend that you add the partitions in the following order: boot, swap, and root (/). Since the root partition will be set to fill all of the remaining space on the hard drive, you'll first want to specify exactly what share the other partitions will require.

If existing partitions were removed by DOS fdisk prior to the installation process, use the Disk Druid screen to create partitions for a workstation PC.

First, create the /boot partition using these steps:

1. Click the Add button in the Partitions section. The Add dialog box will appear.

2. In the Mount Point field, type **/boot**.

3. In the Size (Megs) field, type **16** (16MB is the recommended size for the boot partition on an Intel-compatible PC).

4. Confirm that the Partition Type is Linux native.

5. Select the hard drive where you want to place the boot partition (refer to last night's Table 1-12 to make sure the selected drive is acceptable).

6. Click OK. The Add dialog box will close.

Now create the swap partition:

1. Click the Add button again so that you can create the swap partition. The Add dialog box will appear.

2. Leave the Mount Point field blank.

3. In the Size (Megs) field, type **94**.

TIP   The value of the swap disk should be at least the number of MB of RAM memory you have on your PC. In this example, 94MB of RAM suggests a 94MB swap disk size.

4. Click the Partition Type list control and select Linux swap.

5. Select the hard drive where you want to place the swap partition.

6. Click OK. The Add dialog box will close.

Finally, create the root (/) partition:

1. Click the Add button again to create the root partition. The Add dialog box will appear.

2. In the Mount Point field, type **/**.

3. Leave the Size (Megs) field setting as 1 MB.

4. Click the Grow to fill disk? option. This option will increase the size of the partition to fill up any remaining unpartitioned or Linux-partitioned space without wiping out existing installations.

5. Confirm the Partition Type is Linux native.

6. Select the hard drive where you want to place the root partition.

7. Click OK. The Add dialog box will close.

You will now see the new partitions displayed in the Partitions list on the Disk Druid screen. The Used (%) value should be 100%.

If you want to change any of these values, simply select the partition to be modified and click the Edit button. The Edit Partition dialog will appear. If the partition was pre-existing on your PC, you can only change its mount point. To make other changes, delete the partition by selecting it, then pressing the Delete key. You can then create a new one to your specifications.

TIP The Next button on the Disk Druid screen will not activate until there is a Linux-compatible partitioning scheme set up, which is a handy way of knowing your settings are okay.

After partitioning is complete (using either the automatic or manual choices), click the Next button to advance to the Choose Partitions to Format screen.

This screen will let you decide which of the new Linux partitions you just created in Disk Druid will be formatted. The default option is for all of them to get formatted, and I suggest you let these stand. I also recommend you select the Check for bad blocks while formatting, which will allow Anaconda to scan your hard drive for physical defects on your hard drive while the partitions are formatted. This is a good idea, because a lot of people don't do this very often and every little bit of disk maintenance helps.

Click the Next button to advance to the Time Zone Selection screen.

Networking Your Computer

If the installation program detects that you have a network card, you will need to provide the pertinent information about your computer.

If you are on a large network, it's a good idea to get the requested data from your network administrator. If that's you, then you should have the information from the data gathering process you performed before installation.

If a network card is indeed detected, the Network Configuration screen will appear, as shown in Figure 2-6.

1. Click the Configure using DHCP option if you have a dynamic IP address or know that your Internet Service Provider (ISP) uses Dynamic Addressing.

◄ ◄

BUZZ WORD

Dynamic IP address: Every computer on the Internet must have its own IP (Internet Protocol) address. To share an finite and increasingly limited number of available addresses, many private networks and ISPs distribute temporary or dynamic IP addresses from a pool of IP addresses.

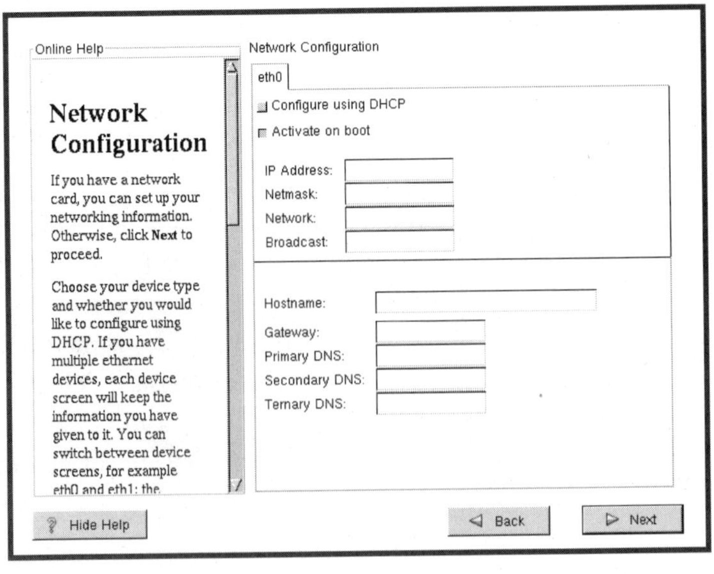

◄ ◄

Figure 2-6

You can enter networking options during installation.

2. Click the Activate on Boot option if you want the network to start automatically when you start Red Hat Linux.

3. Enter your IP address in the next field. This is your own IP address assigned by your ISP or possibly your system administrator.

NOTE If you want to use only a private LAN and have no direct Internet connection, then you can use the group of IP addresses that has been reserved for this purpose. Probably the most common group used is 192.168.1.1 through 192.168.1.254.

4. Linux will attempt to automatically assign a Netmask setting according to your IP address. Check to see that it matches the one you are assigned.

◄◄

BUZZ WORD *Netmask*: Also known as a Subnet Mask, a netmask is used to determine what subnet an IP address belongs to. For example, with the IP address 150.216.019.031, the first two numbers indicate the address is part of the Class B sub-network on the Internet.

◄◄

5. Linux will automatically attempt to fill in an address here, based on information it gleans from your network. This will be part of your assigned information if you are part of a large system.

6. The Broadcast field will need to be filled in if your PC is a broadcasting component of your network.

7. If you are connecting directly to the Internet from your computer, you will be assigned a Hostname by your ISP or system administrator. Enter that information in the Hostname field.

8. Enter your gateway or router IP address in the Gateway field.

9. The Primary DNS address may or may not be your gateway IP address; enter whatever your ISP gives you.

10. If you have an alternate nameserver IP address, enter it in the Secondary DNS.

11. Some networks provide access to more than two nameservers. Enter the address of any additional DNS, if you have it, in the Ternary DNS field.

12. Click the Next button to continue with the installation process.

Your initial networking configuration is now complete.

Setting the Time Zone

You might think the subject of time zones would not be rocket science. 24-hour day, divide the Earth into 24 parts, and there you have it, right?

Wrong. Several nations around the world have set their clocks based on reasons that are more political than geophysical. Even here in the United States, a couple of states don't adjust their clocks to Daylight Savings Time. So, even time settings can get tricky. Looking at Figure 2-7, it's clear that the Red Hat developers considered this matter carefully.

Dominating the screen is a map of the world with several areas highlighted. Since the cities are so small at this scale, click the View drop-

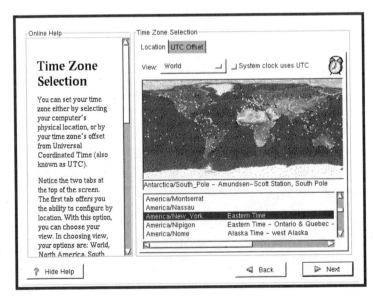

Figure 2-7

Does anyone have
the time?

down list, and select the region you live in. A larger scale map of your region will appear.

To set your time zone, simply click on the city/region closest to you on the map. Alternately, you can select your city/region from the list that appears below the map. Your choice then appears in the field immediately below the map.

If you wish, you can set the time based on the Universal Time Clock (UTC) (an unchanging standard time based on the Greenwich Mean Time). To do so, click the option labeled System Clock Uses UTC, entering your time based on the number of hours offset from UTC.

When complete, click the Next button.

Configuring Your Accounts

Whenever a Linux system is created, the root account must be created as well. The root account is the administrator account for the Linux PC. Since you use the root account to make modifications to the operating system settings, it's the most powerful account on the system. All you need to do to set up the root account is to enter the same password in both the Root Password and Confirm fields. The Confirm field entry ensures that you have not made a typographical error in the password.

If you will have additional users on the system, it's a good idea to create additional user accounts for them now. User accounts are analogous to user profiles found in Windows. They allow certain users to have customized access to a Linux system and provide the additional security of knowing who's doing what on the system.

As you can see in Figure 2-8, to create a user account, type a user ID in the Account Name field, supply a password, and the user's full name. Similar to creating the root account, you'll need to type the password twice to ensure that no typos occur. Clicking the Add button will finish the process.

TIP Passwords within Red Hat Linux are case sensitive.

TIP Even if you are the sole user of the PC, it's a good idea to make a regular account for yourself. Using the root account all of the time can lead to potential errors, where using a regular account limits the amount of damage.

After you have added users on the system, click the Next button to continue.

Selecting Package Groups

At this point in Anaconda, you get to decide what packages will be installed on your Linux machine. It's like a birthday celebration!

Packages in Red Hat Linux are synonymous with application installation programs. Inside each software package are most or all the files a

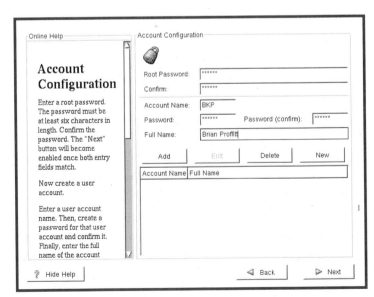

Figure 2-8

Adding users to your Linux system.

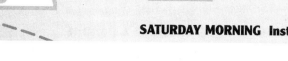

given application needs to run. Opening a package will automatically install the application within onto your PC.

The first package selection screen, and really the only one you need, gives you what appears to be three measly choices: GNOME, KDE, and Games. But what choices they are! Each option represents large sets of the packages needed to run a GNOME or KDE workstation, with another set of packages reserved strictly for games.

GNOME and KDE are different desktop environments that run on top of X. Truthfully, there are little operational differences between the two, just different approaches in the interface. If you have a lot of space on your hard drive, I recommend selecting both and seeing for yourself. If you have a preference, just select the one you like.

Whether you select Games is also up to you, of course, but if you have the room, go ahead, yield to the temptation. Everyone needs a break now and then.

On the bottom of the screen is the Select individual packages option. You would select this if there was a certain package you wanted to install that you knew would not be a part of one of the three pre-determined package sets. Since you will likely get everything you will need from the default package sets, I suggest you skip this option and click Next to continue to the Unresolved Dependencies screen.

If you want to really delve into the various package choices, go ahead and click on the Select Individual Packages option at the bottom of the Package Group Selection screen. Once selected, clicking Next will take you to the Individual Package Selection screen.

On the left side of the Individual Package Selection screen is a structure similar to a directory tree that lists all of the package groups. Selecting any group will cause a list of its individual packages to display on the right side of the screen.

To select a package for installation, double-click the package name. A red check mark appears on the package icon indicating its readiness for installation. Click Next to continue to the Unresolved Dependencies screen.

The Unresolved Dependencies screen addresses packages that may need additional files within other packages in order to work. Recall that some packages don't always contain every file an application needs for installation. Many times they rely on the presence of other packages to work correctly. That's what a dependency is. An unresolved dependency is when a needed package is absent. Anaconda checks all the package sets you selected in the previous screen and makes sure that every package in the sets have all of their dependencies resolved.

If a few unresolved packages appear in the screen, don't worry. Click the Install packages to satisfy dependencies option and then click Next. All of the needed files will be added to the installation set automatically.

Configuring the X Window System

In the Workstation installation path, the next two screens are the X Configuration screens. These screens are important because they determine how X coordinates with your graphics card and monitor to generate graphic displays. Recall that the Linux OS is based on textual command lines and requires X server to run graphic-based interfaces.

Unlike Microsoft Windows, X must be carefully configured to work with your video hardware. Does this mean that Windows is more flexible? Not at all. It's just that monitors and graphics cards in recent years have been designed to comply with Windows. Linux is a relative newcomer to hardware vendors, so manual configuration is still required for most equipment.

Before you even get to the first X Configuration screen, the Linux tool, Autoprobe, has attempted to identify the type of monitor you have. If it finds it, the identity will appear at the top of the first screen, which is the Monitor Configuration screen.

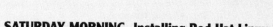
On the Monitor Configuration screen, Anaconda will display the type of monitor it thinks you have. Check this very carefully, because Autoprobe could guess wrong. If it's correct, click Next to continue.

If Autoprobe can't decide what monitor type you have, it will select the Unprobed Monitor category. At this point, you will need to make sure you have the right values in the Horizontal and Vertical Sync fields at the bottom of the screen. Be careful here. You don't want to use a monitor setting that will damage your monitor. Erroneous sync rate settings can lead to the monitor *overclocking*, a fancy term that basically means making the monitor run beyond its display tolerances.

The best place to locate your monitor's sync rates is in the manual that came with the monitor. Barring that, try the manufacturer's Web site for the monitor. After you get your sync rate values entered, click on Next to continue.

In the next screen, Anaconda will reveal what video card Autoprobe has found. The video card determination is important because it will determine what X Window server will actually be used to run X later.

Confirm the card selected, or, if need be, select a value that better matches your card. Just below the video card list are eight options for the amount of video memory your card has, in kilobytes. Click on the appropriate value.

When the video hardware has been determined, click the button labeled Test This Configuration. The screen will probably flicker. If all goes well, you should see a blue-green screen with a small dialog box asking if you can see the message on the dialog box. Click Yes. You will always have a successful test if Autoprobe has located your hardware for you.

If you cannot see the message, you will need to change the settings for the graphics card and monitor.

Also on the X Configuration screen may be a list box field that allows you to choose which desktop environment you want to be the default during your work with Red Hat. I say "may," because it only appears if you selected both the Gnome and KDE packages groups to install. It will not appear if you just selected one of these desktop environments. Select the environment you wish to be the default.

Just below the Test button you'll see three options. If you select Customize X Configuration and then click Next, you will move to a screen where you can try out different color depths (number of colors on the screen) and screen resolutions.

The Use Graphical Login option is very important for new users to select, as it enables the appearance of the X login each time you start Linux.

CAUTION   ◆

There appears to be a glitch in the Linux program at this point. If you select the Customize option and go to that screen, the Use Graphical Login option (even if you selected it) will be cleared and X will not load on boot. For this reason, I suggest that you wait until later to change your video settings.

◆ ◆

An expert who wants to set up X manually should be the only person to click the Skip X Configuration option. New users should stay away from this option.

For maximum ease, I recommend that you click the Use Graphical Login option and then click Next to continue.

Finishing the Installation

All of the pertinent installation information has now been gathered by Linux and the installation program is ready to copy files to your computer. Figure 2-9 shows the About to Install screen warning you that this is about to happen.

Remember, after this point you will not be able to click the Back button to make changes to your chosen installation settings. Don't worry, though—if you've made it this far, you are likely okay; the hardware

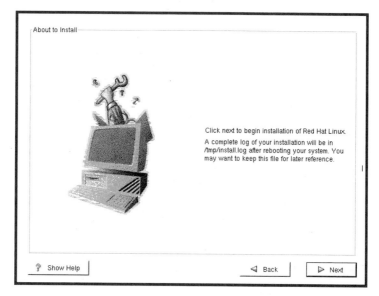

Click next to begin installation of Red Hat Linux.

A complete log of your installation will be in /tmp/install.log after rebooting your system. You may want to keep this file for later reference.

Figure 2-9

Ready to begin?

configuration to display graphics was the trickiest part of the installation. So, take a deep breath, exhale nice and easy, and click the Next button to continue.

You will now see the Installing Packages screen. Before any packages are actually installed, however, the partitions you have set up will be formatted. You'll know this is happening by the appearance of a progress message (see Figure 2-10).

Formatting the partitions can take anywhere from 5 to 15 minutes depending on the amount of formatting required. If you had selected the option to check for bad blocks while formatting, the formatting will take a longer amount of time. The Linux installation will then gather all of the information obtained in the first part of the installation program and build its file copy list. A progress bar appears on the screen (see Figure 2-11) so that you can monitor the process.

Now the bulk of the installation occurs. As seen in Figure 2-12, the Installing Packages screen displays the progress of the installation as it proceeds.

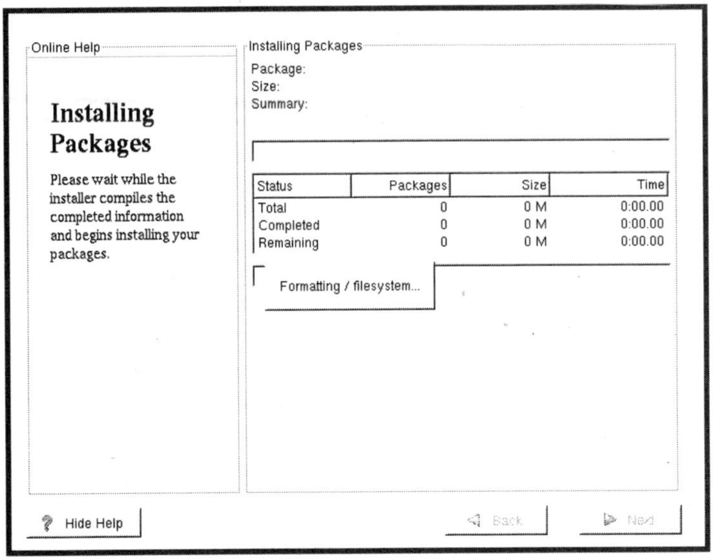

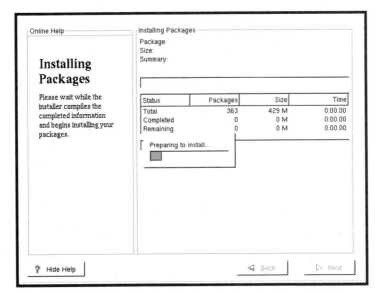

Figure 2-10

Formatting your
Linux partitions.

Figure 2-11

Getting ready to
copy files.

The top progress bar indicates the status of the package currently installing. The bottom bar shows the cumulative installation progress of all packages. You also get a time remaining value so you'll know if you still have time to go grab a sandwich.

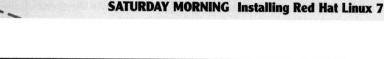

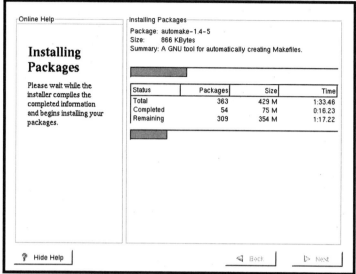

Online Help ────────────────

Installing Packages

Please wait while the installer compiles the completed information and begins installing your packages.

Installing Packages ────────────────

Package: automake-1.4-5
Size: 866 KBytes
Summary: A GNU tool for automatically creating Makefiles.

Status	Packages	Size	Time
Total	363	429 M	1:33.46
Completed	54	75 M	0:16.23
Remaining	309	354 M	1:17.22

Hide Help   Back   Next

Figure 2-12

The package installation process.

When everything is finished, the Boot Disk Creation screen will appear.

You may not have created a boot disk before installing Red Hat Linux 7, particularly if you have a bootable CD-ROM drive. If you didn't then, now's your chance—and I highly recommend you do. To make a boot disk, simply insert a blank floppy disk into your floppy drive and click the Next button. Anaconda will automatically build a boot disk that is completely up-to-date with your Linux installation.

When the boot disk is complete, the Congratulations screen will appear as shown in Figure 2-13. Remove the boot disk from the drive now.

Clicking the Exit button will close the installation program and restart your machine. Make sure you have removed the boot disk from the floppy drive (or the installation CD-ROM if you have a bootable CD-ROM drive) before clicking Exit.

Once the PC has restarted, you will see a bright blue screen displayed that contains a list of all of the operating systems on your PC. This screen, the graphical LILO screen, appears each time Linux begins to load. Use the arrow keys to select the operating system you want to boot up and press

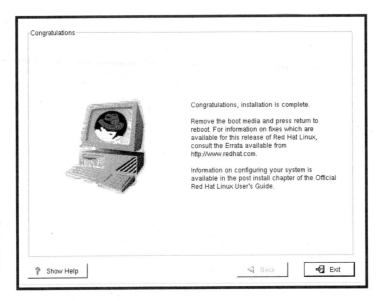

Congratulations

Congratulations, installation is complete.

Remove the boot media and press return to reboot. For information on fixes which are available for this release of Red Hat Linux, consult the Errata available from http://www.redhat.com.

Information on configuring your system is available in the post install chapter of the Official Red Hat Linux User's Guide.

Show Help · Back · Exit

Figure 2-13

You have now arrived in the strange world of Linux.

the Enter key to continue. If you want Linux to load, you don't have to do anything. LILO defaults to loading it first.

TIP

If you see "DOS" in the LILO list, and not Windows, don't worry. LILO recognizes operating systems, and on a Windows PC, DOS is the true operating system, while Windows is just the graphical interface, contrary to popular belief. Selecting DOS will start Windows . . . if you have to.

Unlike Windows, Linux likes to broadcast every little step it takes as it starts. Keep an eye on these messages (see Figure 2-14) so you become familiar with them. In time, this familiarity will enable you to identify any problems that occur as Linux loads just because you recognize a message that is out of the ordinary.

In a moment, you will arrive at the login screen for the desktop environment you selected in the X Configuration screen. Type in your account login name and password you created during the installation process.

```
 hda: hda1 hda2 < hda5 hda6 >
RAMDISK: Compressed image found at block 0
autodetecting RAID arrays
autorun ...
... autorun DONE.
VFS: Mounted root (ext2 filesystem).
autodetecting RAID arrays
autorun ...
... autorun DONE.
VFS: Mounted root (ext2 filesystem) readonly.
change_root: old root has d_count=1
Trying to unmount old root ... okay
Freeing unused kernel memory: 64k freed
INIT: version 2.77 booting
                    Welcome to Red Hat Linux
            Press 'I' to enter interactive startup.
Mounting proc filesystem                              [  OK  ]
Setting clock : Thu Nov  4 20:27:24 EST 1999          [  OK  ]
Activating swap partitions                            [  OK  ]
Setting hostname localhost.localdomain                [  OK  ]
Checking root filesystem
/dev/hda5: clean, 34880/250880 files, 130805/500968 blocks
                                                      [  OK  ]
Remounting root filesystem in read-write mode         [  OK  ]
-
```

Figure 2-14

Watching Linux
start up.

You'll then enter the desktop environment and begin your Red Hat Linux journey.

Other Installation Concerns

If you've successfully installed and started Red Hat Linux 7, congratulations, you've pretty much accomplished everything you needed to this morning! You can take an early lunch break, or skip ahead to this afternoon's lesson, "Initial Configuration Issues."

Some of you, though, may need additional information about other installation modes and paths, because sometimes things do not always go according to plan. If that's you case, stick around—the rest of this morning's session will examine text installations, custom install options, and dual booting.

Text Installation

If you had some trouble with the graphical mode of installation, you should now use the text installation mode. While not as robust, the text mode is just as effective as the graphical mode.

Navigating the text screens is done without a mouse, but it is fairly simple. You move between objects on the screen by pressing the Tab key (or Alt+Tab to move backward). Press the spacebar to select or clear check box options. Press Enter to activate a selected function. Not too hard, right?

All the same installation information is gathered during text installation as was done during graphical installation. One exception occurs, however, in that text installation asks for permission before starting to probe your system's video hardware (which you should do).

By comparing Figure 2-15 to Figure 2-4, you can see that, other than mere aesthetics, not many differences exist between the two interfaces.

The text installation mode is a great fallback to use if you experience initial display problems.

Configuring LILO

Since you plan to use more than one operating system on your Red Hat Linux PC, you will need to make sure the Linux Loader (LILO) is installed in the correct location. If it isn't, you may run into trouble.

Dual Booting Explained

When a system with a single operating system boots, the BIOS looks at a special section of the hard drive called the master boot record (MBR or *boot sector*) to see what operating system will be loaded.

When a system has two or more operating systems, a special multi-boot application must reside in the boot sector that temporarily halts the boot process and allows the user to choose which operating system to load. LILO is just such a program.

How to Dual Boot with Windows 95/98

To configure LILO to run Linux and another operating system, you will need to use the Custom installation path. However, if you are installing Linux on a system preconfigured with Windows 95 or 98, you can just

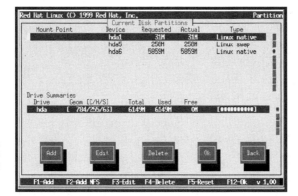

Figure 2-15

The text version of
Disk Druid.

run the Workstation installation path. The default LILO settings provide all you need to run both operating systems.

LILO is then installed in the MBR and the Linux boot sector is given the default priority to load. You can change these settings later from within Linux using a utility called linuxconf; for now use the Workstation settings.

How to Dual Boot with Windows NT

Quite simply, the easiest way to get Linux and Windows NT to work together is to install NT first on your machine (which is a likely scenario for anyone reading this book). Then, when you install Linux, make LILO boot to the Master Boot Record (MBR). Finally, edit your /etc/lilo.conf file and add an "nt" option that points to the device NT resides on (for example, /dev/hda1).

If you want to run Linux with Windows NT or Windows 2000 installed later, you will need to take some special steps during the installation.

The most important thing to remember is that you *must* run the Custom installation path, for it is the only method that enables you to configure LILO to meet your needs.

Basically, the problem is this: the Windows NT OS Loader does not recognize Linux as a valid operating system (imagine that) because Linux does not produce the type of file the NT OS Loader needs to read before starting an operating system. In addition, the NT OS Loader will not function from anywhere other than the boot sector. Since only one boot loader can be in the boot sector at a time, you will have a problem if LILO sits in the MBR.

The Custom install path gives you access to the LILO Configuration screen from where you can elect to have LILO either installed on the MBR (the default setting) or on the first sector of the Linux boot partition.

If you select the latter option, there will be no conflict between LILO and the NT OS Loader. Unfortunately, the NT OS Loader will still not see Linux and it won't present Linux as a boot choice. Now comes the chicanery.

There is a way to create a file in Linux that the NT OS Loader *can* use to boot Linux, but creating it takes a bit of time. I recommend that you obtain a little third-party program called Bootpart, which is available at **http://www.winimage.com/bootpart.htm**. This program will quickly create the Linux boot file for NT OS Loader and place it where NT OS Loader can use it. I highly recommend this application if you plan to use either Windows NT or Windows 2000 with Linux.

For more information about configuring Windows NT and Linux, read the mini-HOWTO document at **http://www.linuxdoc.org/HOWTO/mini/Linux+NT-Loader.html**.

Conclusion

This morning's work got you where you wanted to be: the owner of a PC running Red Hat Linux 7. Now that you have completed this task, it's time to configure and customize your newly installed OS to meet your qualifications.

This afternoon, you'll learn about the underpinnings of the graphical interface: configuring the X Window System.

Initial Configuration Issues

- ☼ Understanding Gnome and KDE
- ☼ Configuring X Window
- ☼ Customizing the Desktop

You've had a pretty productive morning, having installed Red Hat Linux on your PC on your own. You should now have a nice desktop displayed on the screen, all ready for you to work or play. You should spend some time looking around the desktop and getting familiar with its interface.

By the end of this afternoon, you will have:

- ✪ Examined the Gnome and KDE interfaces
- ✪ Configured X Window to work with your system
- ✪ Created a customized desktop
- ✪ Explored the Linux filesystem

Seek Out and Explore Strange New Desktops

One of the things you'll notice right off the bat is how similar your desktop looks when compared to Microsoft Windows. This is no accident. Most GUIs (graphical user interfaces) follow a set paradigm when presenting tools to the user. GUIs all have windows, menus, and dialog boxes, because that is what most users already know.

◄◄◄

GUI (Graphical user interface): Any computer interface that uses visual rather than textual information to convey information and accept commands.

◄◄◄

One of the unique benefits of Linux is that, while DOS can use only Windows as its desktop environment, Linux can use a myriad of desktops, making it very user friendly. After all, if you don't like Windows, there's not much you can do about it (save install Red Hat Linux). If you don't like your Linux desktop, just switch it out.

We'll cover the Linux desktops in a bit more technical detail later this afternoon. Right now, let's look around the two big desktops included with Red Hat Linux 7: Gnome and KDE.

Exploring Gnome

Gnome is a desktop environment that has been associated with Red Hat for quite some time. Developed by the Gnome Project, developers are constantly examining and tweaking Gnome to ensure it is as user-friendly as possible.

Understanding Desktop Elements

Like every GUI, Gnome has a ubiquitous set of controls for users to manipulate their work onscreen. Figure 3-1 shows a typical Gnome screen and lists the main desktop elements.

- The **desktop** is the background for all of the elements you see on your screen.
- Desktop icons are called **Launchers**. Launchers open applications, files, or directories quickly. You can place icons on your desktop for those programs and files you use frequently.
- **Windows** are framed areas that contain menus, buttons, and scroll bars. Applications and files appear inside windows.

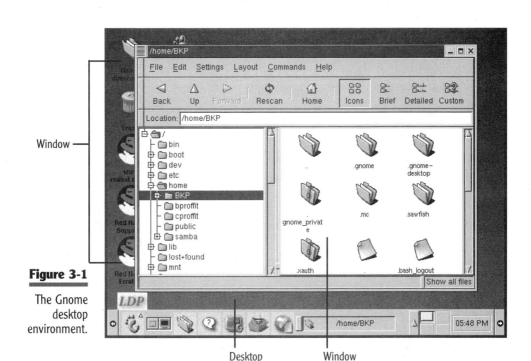

Window ─

Figure 3-1

The Gnome
desktop
environment.

Desktop   Window

The Gnome Panel, shown in Figure 3-2, resides at the bottom of your screen. The Gnome Panel contains a number of tools to help you work, including the Main Menu button, a number of panel applets, and the Gnome Pager.

○ The **Main Menu button** opens a menu of all the applications, utilities, and actions you can perform with Gnome. To display the menu, click on the Main Menu button (it's the foot at the far left). To close the menu, click on the Main Menu button a second time or click on an empty area of the desktop.

○ Panel **applets** are small programs that you can start easily by clicking on the applet icon. You can add and delete applets from the panel.

○ The **Pager** displays all open tasks or applications currently running on the displayed desktop.

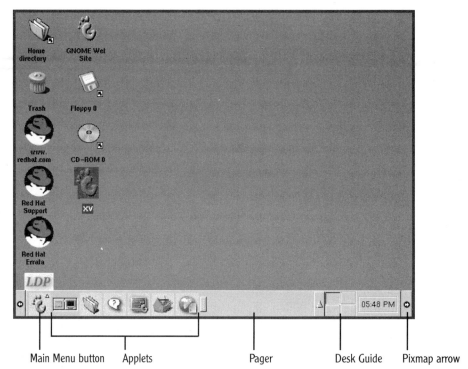

Figure 3-2

The Gnome panel.

Main Menu button   Applets   Pager   Desk Guide   Pixmap arrow

- ✿ The **Desk Guide** shows you which applications and files are open on your computer and where they are located on the virtual desktops.

- ✿ At each end of the Gnome Panel are the **pixmap arrows**. These arrows, when clicked, hide and display the Gnome Panel.

Starting Programs from the Main Menu Button

Now it's time to take a look at some of your software applications and get a quick overview of how to use the common window interface elements. The next few sections will show you how to use the basic elements of a Linux application by using the Gnome Calendar.

First off, let's go through the steps you need to take to get the Calendar application (or any other application for that matter) started.

1. Click on the Main Menu Button. The Main Menu will appear as shown in Figure 3-3.

2. Move the mouse pointer over the Programs menu item. The Programs menu will appear.

3. Move the mouse pointer over the Applications menu item. The Applications menu will appear.

4. Click on the Calendar option. The application window will appear on your screen (see Figure 3-4).

This is pretty straightforward and likely not much different than you're used to.

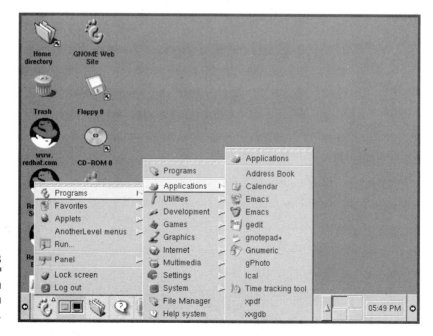

Figure 3-3

Using the Main Menu to launch applications.

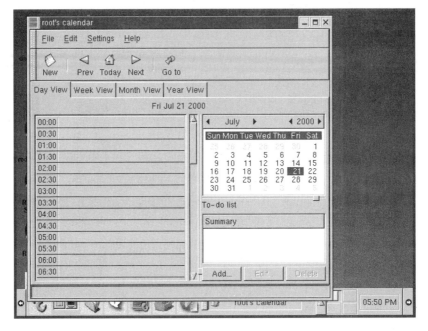

Figure 3-4

The open Calendar application.

Using Buttons, Menus, and Dialog Boxes

You've successfully opened a Linux application and now you're ready to see how it works. Program windows contain elements such as menus, command buttons, resize buttons, and a host of other elements. Spend a few minutes to explore the different menus to see what is available. This section will show you how to use buttons and menus to execute commands.

1. Place the mouse pointer over a button on the toolbar. The button will be highlighted and a tip will appear telling you what function the button performs.

2. Click on a button. The command associated with the button will be executed. Either the command will be executed automatically or a dialog box will appear allowing you to make choices about the command you wish to execute.

NOTE If you've opened a dialog box, click on the Close button. The dialog box will close and any choices you made in the dialog box will be ignored.

3. Click on a menu item to open a menu. A list of menu commands will appear.

4. Click on a command. A dialog box will open or a function will be performed, as shown in Figure 3-5.

   Dialog boxes contain buttons that display secondary dialog boxes, buttons that let you select options, lists that let you select a number of predefined options, and tabs that group several dialog boxes into one.

5. Click on OK. The dialog box will close, the options will be applied, and you will be returned to the program window.

TIP Click on Close or Cancel if you don't wish to apply any of the changes you made to the dialog box or you decide that you no longer want to execute the command.

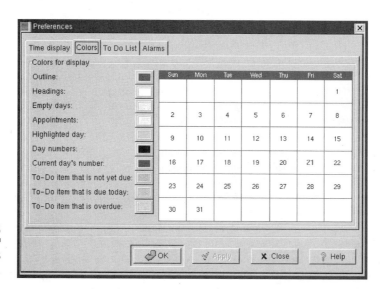

Figure 3-5

Using dialog boxes
is a piece of cake.

When you are finished with an application, the fastest way to close it is to click on the Kill button at the top right of the program window (see Figure 3-6). The application will close and you will be returned to the Gnome interface.

 NOTE If a window refuses to close, right-click on the Kill button. A pop-up menu will appear, from which you can select Destroy. The Destroy option is the ultimate utility to stop applications that are stuck.

Exploring KDE

If you set KDE as your default desktop, you can explore it here.

KDE (which stands for the K Desktop Environment), is a lot like Gnome, in that it too has menus, dialog boxes, and windows. Red Hat Linux 7 ships with KDE and the beta version of KDE2, the second edition of this desktop environment. KDE is the version that is installed by

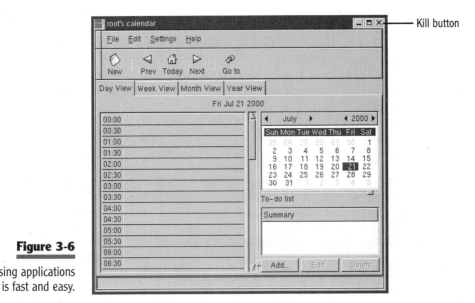

Figure 3-6

Closing applications is fast and easy.

default. There are some subtle differences from Gnome, mostly in the descriptions of the KDE environment, not in the behavior.

Understanding Desktop Elements

In Gnome, you had a pretty easy time getting around the desktop. You will find a lot of familiar controls in KDE, though they may not have the same names (see Figure 3-7).

- ✿ The **desktop** is the background for all of the elements you see on your screen.

- ✿ Desktop icons are called **Nicknames** in KDE. As in Gnome, nicknames open applications, files, or directories quickly. You can place icons on your desktop for those programs and files you use frequently.

- ✿ **Windows** are framed areas that contain menus, buttons, and scroll bars, just like other graphic interfaces.

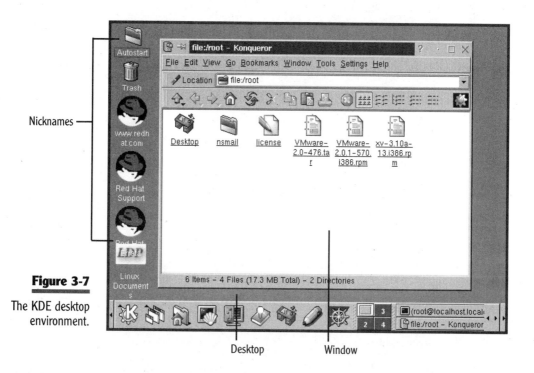

Figure 3-7

The KDE desktop environment.

The Kpanel resides at the bottom of your screen, as shown in Figure 3-8. The Kpanel contains the Application Starter button, a number of panel applets, and the desktop manager.

○ The **Application Starter button** opens a menu of all the applications, utilities, and actions you can perform with KDE. To display the menu, click on the Application Starter button. To close the menu, click on the Application Starter button a second time or click on an empty area of the desktop.

NOTE   Pressing Alt+F1 will open the Application Starter menu.

○ The **icon bar** contains small programs that can be started easily by clicking on the, er, icon.

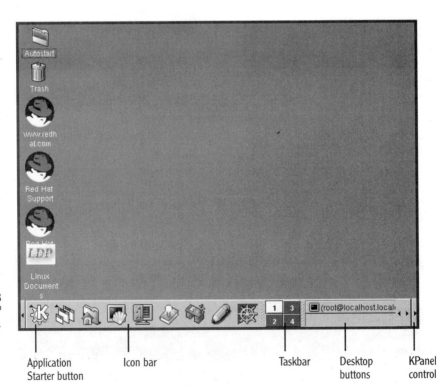

Figure 3-8

The Kpanel.

Application
Starter button

Icon bar

Taskbar

Desktop
buttons

KPanel
control

- ✿ The **Taskbar** displays all open tasks or applications currently running on the displayed desktop.

- ✿ The **Desktop Buttons** manage the virtual desktops on your system.

- ✿ This textured bar is the **KPanel control**, which regulates the hide and show feature of Kpanel. Click this bar to remove or display the Kpanel on your desktop.

Starting Programs from the Application Starter

When you want to start applications in KDE, you use the Application Starter, what else? Just follow these steps to get an application going in KDE.

1. Click on the Application Starter Button. The Application Starter Menu will appear.

2. Move the mouse pointer over the Games menu item. The Games menu will appear.

3. Click on Reversi. The Reversi window will appear on your screen.

Go ahead, have a little fun! When you've played a game or two, you'll be refreshed and ready to start learning about the inner workings of the Linux/GUI relationship.

What Is X?

Before we start configuring X, let's take a few moments to learn just what X is. Start by imagining an onion in your hands. Peel away the brown, crinkly stuff on the outside. What's left? A peeled onion. If you pull off another layer, you are left with . . . ? That's right, a smaller peeled onion.

While not exactly the most stunning comparison, in some ways it's applicable to the relationship between Linux, X server, and a Window Manager on a Linux system. They are all layers of a big onion of an operating system—except they don't make you cry.

Non-Linux users are often a bit confused at first about which components make up X. In the Microsoft Windows environment, you have the DOS operating system with the Windows operating system interface running on top of it, as illustrated in Figure 3-9. Running on top means that Windows is essentially one big program that runs from the DOS platform—really no different than running a program like Doom. The upshot of this is that you must have DOS running in order to run Windows.

For Windows NT users, it's a bit more simplified. Windows NT and Windows 2000 are true graphical user interfaces that run on their own. The advantage here is that you really do get what you see. You can still run DOS when you have to, but in Windows NT and 2000, a DOS emulator runs within Windows. One disadvantage to Windows NT is that your PC must have a lot more memory and speed to run as efficiently as a comparable Win98 system.

◄ ◄

BUZZ WORD *Emulator.* A program that can mimic the look and feel of another operating system.

◄ ◄

As mentioned earlier in the book, the Linux system you have just installed is most analogous to the DOS/Windows system. Like DOS, Linux is a text-based command line operating system (albeit a *much* more sophisticated one). You can perform a great many functions using just the Linux operating system, and many people do. Many more people, however, have been bitten by the GUI bug and are accustomed to using windows, menus, and dialog boxes to get things done.

Figure 3-9

The DOS/Windows relationship.

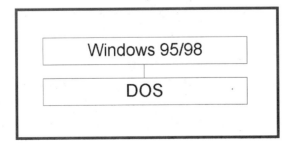

In 1986, an international consortium of UNIX programmers began putting together a graphical operating system, based on the GUI research done by the Xerox Palo Alto Research Center. Thus was X born.

After Linux was introduced in 1991, it was not long before X found its way to the Linux desktop. When Linux began appearing on Intel-based PCs, a new version of X, XFree86, helped make the transition.

XFree86 is the heart of any GUI that runs on Red Hat Linux. Also referred to as the X server, XFree86 is where video output and PC input comes together to form one cohesive interface. PC input is obtained from the two basic input devices: the keyboard and the mouse. Then video output is sent through the graphics card to the monitor.

While this sounds like the entirety of the GUI, it's not. That's because the X server is only a network-transparent display layer that provides the "home" for GUI to operate.

To generate the actual windows and menus that make up a traditional GUI, you need a window manager running on the X server display layer.

◄◄◄

Window manager. The application that gives X server its "look" and determines how graphical applications will be displayed.

◄◄◄

Several windows managers come with Red Hat Linux: AfterStep, AnotherLevel, Enlightenment, fvwm, fvwm95, KVM, olvm, Sawfish, and tvm, to name a few. The two big ones you'll need to work with in Red Hat 7 are Gnome and KDE.

KDE—the K Desktop Environment—is an award-winning environment that is packaged with Red Hat Linux 7. Often referred to as a window manager, in fact it is not. KDE usually runs over a window manager called KWM (K Window Manager). As KVM enhances the look and feel of XFree86, so KDE enhances the look and toolsets of KWM.

A similar relationship exists when running the Gnome (GNU Network Object Model Environment) desktop. Gnome is not a true window manager, either. Gnome is an enhancement for a window manager running on XFree86. By default, Red Hat 7 installs the Sawfish window manager with Gnome. Confused yet? Take a look at Figure 3-10, which displays a simplified representation of the relationship between all of these components.

Note that just because a certain combination of window managers and desktop environments have been installed, it doesn't mean that you are locked into that combination. For example, you can run Gnome on top of fvm95 if you want to. That's one of the great things about Linux's open platform philosophy: you have real choices on how to run your PC.

A big question that's often asked, though, is what do all these choices mean? For what is each of these components responsible? In the installation you did this morning, I recommended that you install the Gnome desktop environment. With that in mind, Table 3-1 breaks down the different responsibilities of each of the Linux components in a Gnome installation.

Now that you have a better idea of just how all of the different components fit together, it's time to examine how to configure X Window. Notice in Table 3-1 that certain components of X have different responsibilities. The responsibilities handled by XFree86 will focus on its video output, keyboard, and mouse responsibilities.

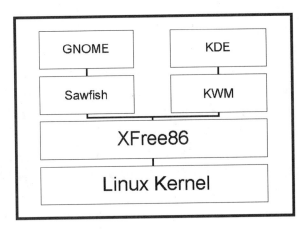

Figure 3-10

The components of a Linux GUI system.

TABLE 3-1	COMPONENTS OF A LINUX/GNOME SYSTEM
Component	**Responsibilities**
Linux	The base on which everything runs. Handles all basic file system and device tasks, as well as translating commands into the PC's rudimentary machine language.
XFree86	The heart of the GUI. Generates a display layer that allows the creation of graphics and then marries those graphics to input from the keyboard and mouse.
Sawfish	The window manager responsible for the look of all windows, dialog boxes, and menus that are generated from XFree86.
Gnome	Enhances the Sawfish window manager by providing additional interface tools and appearance. Additional controls provided for input device configuration.

Using Xconfigurator

Within Red Hat Linux 7, there are two tools designed to manage XFree86: Xconfigurator and xf86config. Each tool focuses on a different aspect of XFree86, and should be used accordingly. Table 3-2 reveals the capabilities of each tool.

Although it appears that xf86config is the best program to use because of its greater capabilities, in actuality I recommend that you split the usage of these programs. Xconfigurator has an easier-to-use interface for making changes to your display parameters, while xf86config uses a multiple choice linear interface that's a bit more difficult to follow.

One great use for Xconfigurator is changing the video resolution of your display. When Red Hat first installs, it may default to a resolution you don't like, such as the 640 X 480 resolution shown in Figure 3-11.

TABLE 3-2 COMPARISON OF XFREE86 CONFIGURATION TOOLS	
Xconfigurator	xf86config
Video monitor	Video monitor
Video card	Video card
Video resolution	Keyboard
	Mouse

◄◄◄◄◄◄◄◄◄◄◄◄◄◄◄◄◄◄◄◄◄◄◄◄◄◄◄◄◄◄◄◄◄◄◄◄◄

BUZZ WORD

Video resolution: The number of pixels arranged across a display. The smaller the resolution, the larger the pixels, and the less information that can be displayed on a screen.

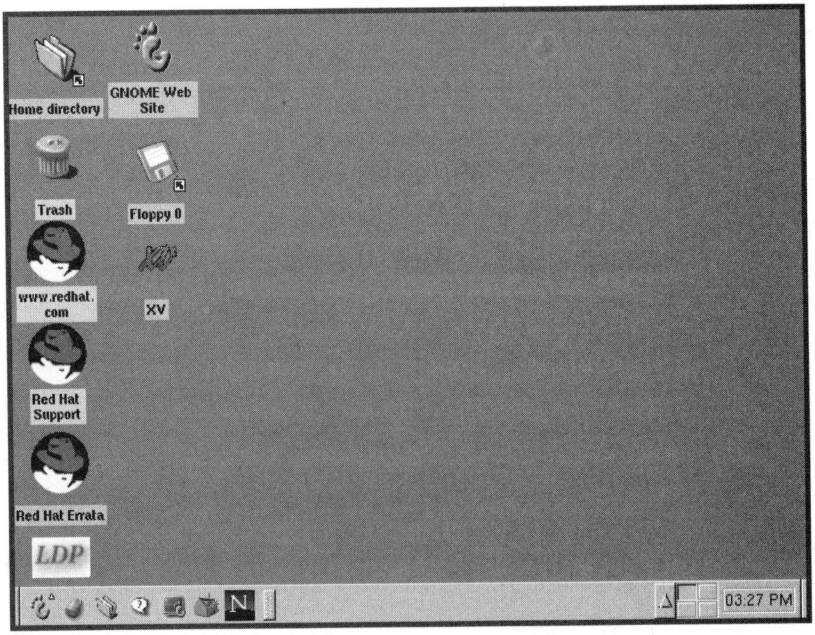

◄◄◄◄◄◄◄◄◄◄◄◄◄◄◄◄◄◄◄◄◄◄◄◄◄◄◄◄◄◄◄◄◄◄◄◄◄

Figure 3-11

There's not a lot of real estate in this screen resolution.

Xconfigurator is a text-based application, so to use it you need to use the command line interface after logging in using the root account. You can access the command line with a terminal emulation window, or just Terminal for short. A Terminal is not the real Linux interface, but it can be used as such for most operations. To start the Terminal, click the Terminal icon (which is the little monitor icon) on the Gnome taskbar. This opens the Terminal window (see Figure 3-12).

Now that the Terminal is up and running, the following steps will guide you through using Xconfigurator to modify your video resolution.

1. In the Terminal, type **Xconfigurator**. The Xconfigurator tool will start in the Terminal window (see Figure 3-13).

NOTE No, I wasn't fibbing when I said Xconfigurator was text-based. All of the color and lines are just individual text characters put together to give the appearance of a graphic interface.

2. By default, the OK control on the Welcome screen of Xconfigurator is selected. Press the Enter key to accept the OK selection and continue.

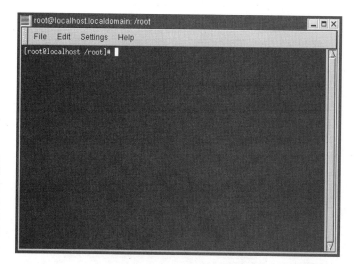

Figure 3-12

The terminal emulation program is a gateway to the Linux operating system.

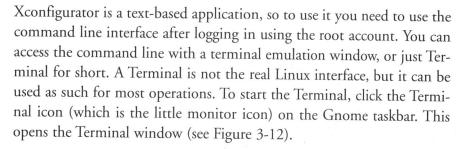

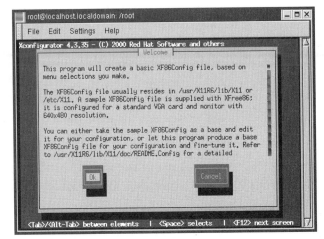

Figure 3-13

Running
Xconfigurator.

3. The next screen (see Figure 3-14) shows the results of the PCI
   Probe Xconfigurator started when you reached the second screen.
   PCI is a type of add-on card for PCs, a category into which graphics cards sometimes fall. If the result matches the card you have
   (and it should), press the Enter key.

   If the PCI Probe is unsuccessful, a screen displaying a list of
   graphics card choices will appear from which you can make an
   alternate choice.

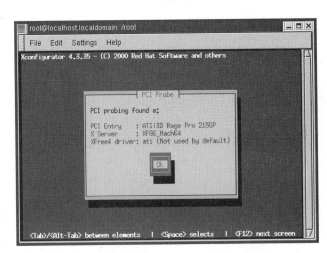

Figure 3-14

Confirming the
graphics card on
your machine.

4. The Monitor Setup screen appears next (see Figure 3-15). Select your monitor from the list using the up and down arrow keys.

TIP If you cannot locate your monitor, select the Custom option that appears at the top of the list. You should also choose Custom if you want to verify the synchronization (sync) rates with your monitor's settings.

5. Press the Tab key to select the OK control and then press Enter. If you selected Custom, proceed to Step 6. If you selected any monitor, skip ahead to Step 15.

6. In the Custom Monitor Setup screen, you should read the lengthy message that describes the importance of the horizontal and vertical refresh rates. Make sure you know this data for your own monitor (ideally obtained when you went through the steps last night in "Before You Install Red Hat Linux 7") and then press Enter to continue to the next screen.

7. The second Custom Monitor Setup screen (shown in Figure 3-16), lets you set the type of monitor based on a horizontal sync rate. Select a monitor type that has a higher resolution (such as

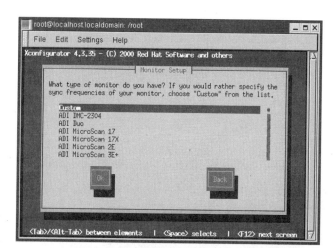

Figure 3-15

Choosing your monitor.

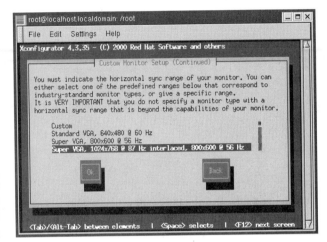

Figure 3-16

Choosing the
horizontal
sync rate.

800 X 600) and still has a sync rate within your monitor's horizontal sync rate parameters.

8. Press the Tab key to select the OK control and then press Enter.

9. The third Custom Monitor Setup screen requires you to specify the vertical sync range of your monitor (see Figure 3-17). Select the appropriate range using the up and down arrow keys.

10. Press the Tab key to select the OK control and then press Enter.

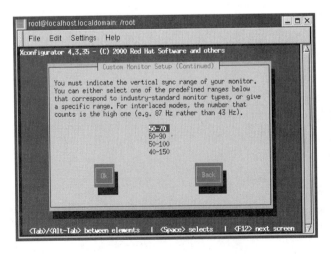

Figure 3-17

Selecting the
vertical sync rate.

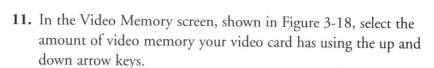

11. In the Video Memory screen, shown in Figure 3-18, select the amount of video memory your video card has using the up and down arrow keys.

12. Press the Tab key to select the OK control and then press Enter.

13. Many older video cards have specific clockchip settings, which appear in the Clockchip Configuration screen (see Figure 3-19). On the off chance your card has an active clockchip, select the type of clockchip using the arrow keys. Since most newer cards do not have clockchips, you will likely need to select the No Clockchip Setting.

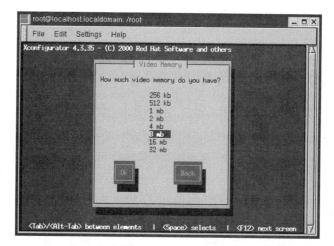

Figure 3-18

Choosing the amount of video memory.

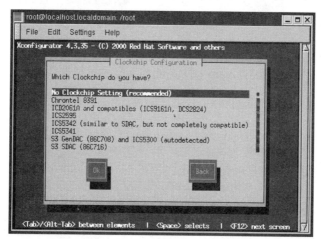

Figure 3-19

Setting up the clockchip.

14. Press the Tab key to select the OK control and then press Enter.

15. You will now see the Select Video Mode screen (shown in Figure 3-20). Use the Tab key to navigate to the appropriate column, the up and down arrow keys to move within the color depth columns, and then press the spacebar to select any option.

TIP Select more than one resolution in this screen. If they are all successful, you will be able to quickly cycle through each configured resolution by pressing Ctrl+Alt+Plus Sign within X.

16. Press the Tab key to select the OK control and then press Enter.

◄◄

BUZZ WORD ***Color depth***: Expressed in bits per pixel, color depth can be translated into the number of available colors by raising 2 to the power of N, where N is the number of bits per pixel. Thus, an 8 bits per pixel color depth would have 2^8, or 256 colors, 16 bits per pixel = 65,536 colors, and 24 bits per pixel = 16,777,216 colors.

◄◄

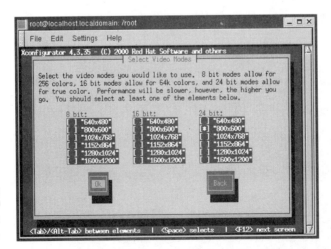

Figure 3-20

The results of the video probe.

17. You will arrive at the Starting X screen (see Figure 3-21), which simply informs you that another session of X will be started to test your settings. Press Enter to continue.

18. If your settings are okay, your will see a message on screen indicating your success. Click Yes to continue.

    If any other kind of message, or if no message is seen, use the Back controls to move back to a previous screen. You can then change your settings.

19. A message will appear asking you if you want to start X when you reboot. Click Yes.

20. Yet another message will appear informing you where the changes to your system were recorded. Click OK to continue.

21. Xconfigurator will close. Restart your X Window session by clicking Log Out on the Gnome Control Menu.

22. Select the Logout option in the Really Log Out dialog box and then click Yes.

    Upon returning to the graphical login screen, the new default video resolution will be set. You will see this most dramatically after logging into X again (see Figure 3-22).

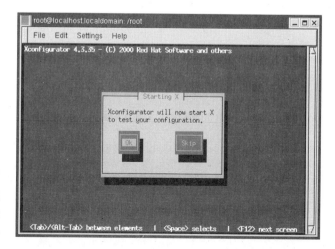

Figure 3-21

Preparing to test your settings.

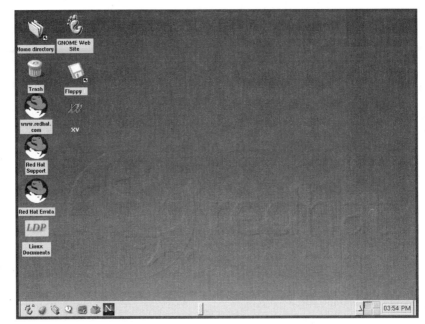

Figure 3-22

A higher resolution gives you more screen real estate.

Starting Up the xf86config Tool

When you have significant changes to make to your system's input devices, you should use xf86config to reconfigure X. You can also use it to make monitor and display setting changes; if that's all you need to do, however, I suggest that you use Xconfigurator.

TIP   Be sure you're logged in using the root account screen when you make any configurations to XFree86.

Like Xconfigurator, xf86config is located in the /usr/X11R6/bin directory. However, all you need to do in a Terminal window is type **xf86config** and the program will begin. .

> **TIP** If at any point you need to leave xf86config, press Ctrl+c. The changes will be cancelled and the program will end.

Configuring the Mouse

In the first xf86config screen, you will see a text message detailing what changes will be made to your system (see Figure 3-23). Press Enter to continue to the next screen.

The second screen reveals a list of nine possible mouse types. To select an option, type its number and then press Enter (see Figure 3-24).

If you selected a mouse type other than the Mouse Systems (3 button protocol), you'll next be asked if you want to start the Emulate3Buttons option. Since a number of Linux programs still use three buttons, I recommend that you type y, and then press Enter to continue.

Next, Linux asks the device name of the port to which the mouse is connected. Unless you are using a non-standard port, press Enter to accept the default.

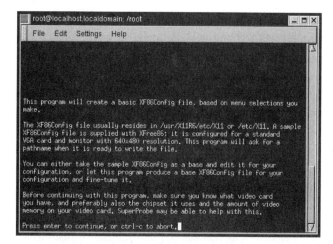

Figure 3-23

The opening message for xf86config.

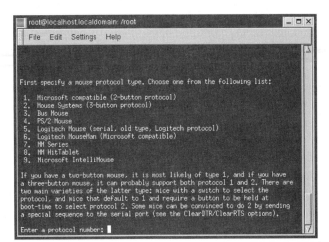

Figure 3-24

Selecting a
mouse type.

The mouse portion of xf86config is now complete and you are ready to answer questions about your keyboard.

Configuring the Keyboard

After your mouse type is selected, you will see a list of keymaps, which apply to different types of keyboards.

◀ ◀

Keymap: A configuration setting designed to match the keys of a keyboard to the correct electronic characters. Each type of keyboard has a different keymap.

◀ ◀

This keymap list is nothing overly dramatic, as you can see in Figure 3-25. It's just a list of twelve keymaps. Most keyboards in the United States fall into the first keymap category. Type the number associated with your keymap and press Enter to continue to the next screen.

After selecting the keymap for your keyboard, you will see a list of languages that you can use in X. As you can see in Figure 3-26, only 18 appear at first, but if you want to continue to look, just press the Enter key

```
root@localhost.localdomain: /root                        _ □ ×
  File   Edit   Settings   Help




Please select one of the following keyboard types that is the better
description of your keyboard. If nothing really matches,
choose 1 (Generic 101-key PC)

    1  Generic 101-key PC
    2  Generic 102-key (Intl) PC
    3  Generic 104-key PC
    4  Generic 105-key (Intl) PC
    5  Dell 101-key PC
    6  Everex STEPnote
    7  Keytronic FlexPro
    8  Microsoft Natural
    9  Northgate OmniKey 101
   10  Winbook Model XP5
   11  Japanese 106-key
   12  PC-98xx Series

Enter a number to choose the keyboard.
```

Figure 3-25

A dozen of the most commonly used keyboards.

```
root@localhost.localdomain: /root                        _ □ ×
  File   Edit   Settings   Help

    1  U.S. English
    2  U.S. English w/ISO9995-3
    3  Belgian
    4  Bulgarian
    5  Canadian
    6  Czech
    7  German
    8  Swiss German
    9  Danish
   10  Spanish
   11  Finnish
   12  French
   13  Swiss French
   14  United Kingdom
   15  Hungarian
   16  Italian
   17  Japanese
   18  Norwegian

Enter a number to choose the country.
Press enter for the next page
```

Figure 3-26

Sprechen Sie Deutsch? Get X to speak your language, too.

to see more options. Once you locate a language you want, simply type the number that corresponds to the language and press Enter to continue.

Configuring the Monitor

After the keyboard and mouse are configured, xf86config moves into the video settings. Because of their importance, xf86config spends a lot of

time and screen space working with every aspect of video configuration, beginning with the monitor.

As you might expect, the first screen of the monitor section (shown in Figure 3-27) warns the user about the importance of having the correct horizontal and vertical synchronization rates for your monitor.

TIP

The monitor information you gathered Friday evening will be used repeatedly. Be sure to save it where you can easily refer to it.

Press Enter to continue into the monitor section, which displays a list of the possible horizontal sync ranges for a monitor. There is also an option to enter a custom range, as seen in Figure 3-28. Type the number of the range category you want and press Enter to continue.

After you enter the range, a smaller list of potential vertical sync rates appears (see Figure 3-29). Again, use care in selecting your range to avoid overclocking and damaging your monitor.

Unlike the installation program and Xconfigurator, xf86config gives you a chance to assign a name to your monitor. You can describe an overall

Figure 3-27

Make sure you know your monitor's sync rates.

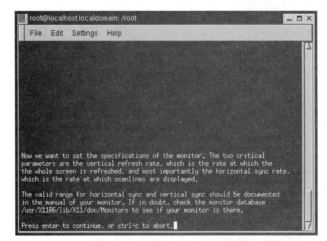

Figure 3-28

Choose the horizontal sync rate range very carefully.

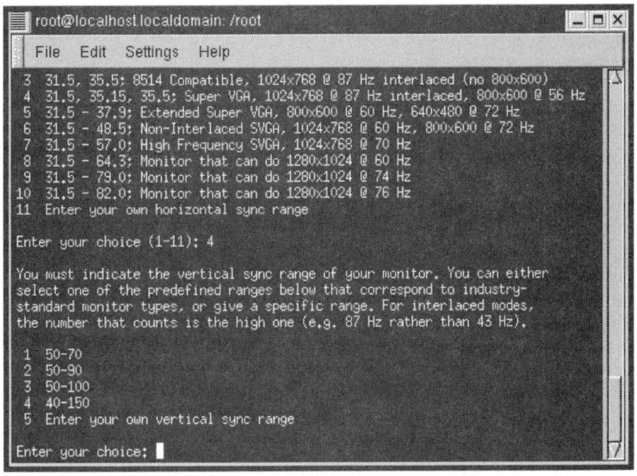

Figure 3-29

Choose the vertical sync rate range with equal care.

designation, the vendor name, and the model to this monitor configuration. Type the designation you want to use and press Enter, as shown in Figure 3-30.

Once the monitor settings are made, xf86config will move to the graphics card section, the last, and most detailed, portion of xf86config.

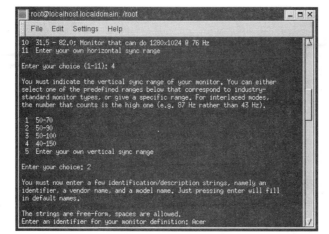

Figure 3-30

Assigning a name
to your monitor
settings.

Configuring the Graphics Card

If you ever need to modify your graphics card settings, you can use xf86config to do so. As you have seen, you must first navigate through the entirety of the program to get to this point.

The first screen (see Figure 3-31) discusses the value of using the current database of graphics cards that are accessible by xf86config. I recommend that you try to find your card in this database; but as the message says, you must be very careful about selecting your card. Similarly named cards may not be compatible with each other and if you try to fake it with a card that looks close to yours, you might inadvertently damage your monitor.

If you choose to check out the database (and you should), type **y** and press Enter to continue. The beginning of a lengthy list of graphics card models and manufacturers, complete with chipset information, appears (see Figure 3-32). Scroll though the list by pressing Enter to see the next batch. Be careful not to scroll past your card, since there is no "back" option. When you locate your card, type the number of the card and press Enter. Whether you use the card database or not, the next step will be the video RAM settings screen.

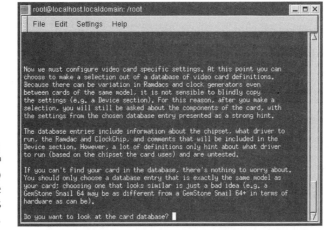

Figure 3-31

Take the time to
read this message
about the graphics
card database.

Figure 3-32

The list of graphics
cards.

In this screen, Linux asks how much video RAM memory your card has.
It's important to get this right, since you will be cheating yourself out of
all of your card's capabilities if you underestimate your VRAM. Type the
size of your video RAM and press Enter.

The program will now ask you to supply a plain English designation for
your card's configuration just as you did for the monitor. Type the name
you want to use.

In the next screen, you will specify the color depth you want the X server to use, as shown in Figure 3-33. I recommend you use at least 16-bit color depth, to get a good range of colors on your screen.

Finally, you are informed that xf86config is about to save your settings to the all-important XF86config file. If you are in any way unsure of any settings you have made, you should type **n**, because there is no way to back up and fix a particular setting. If you think everything is in order, type **y** and press Enter to finish the program.

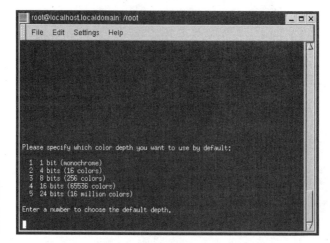

Figure 3-33

From 2 to 16,000,000 colors!

Using the Control Panel

Although the settings for the keyboard and mouse are primarily the function of the X server, it is possible to make certain setting changes from the window manager, too. You can make these changes from the Control Center. While these settings are not major, they are the type of little things that can make your life easier.

You can use either the GNOME or KDE control panels to make these settings. Just remember that any changes you make will be exclusive to the environment you are configuring.

Configuring the Keyboard

To access the Control Center application in the Gnome environment, click on the Gnome control menu and choose Settings, Peripherals, Keyboard (or Mouse). Choosing the Keyboard option will open the Control Center directly at the Keyboard settings pane, as shown in Figure 3-34.

If you are not satisfied with the performance of your keyboard, you can adjust the slider controls to change the values of repeating keys or keyboard clicking. You can also change the tone of the keyboard bell, something that in past versions of Gnome was handled in the Sound section of the Control Center. After making a change, click the Try button and then test your new settings in the Test setting field provided near the bottom of the dialog.

Once the settings are to your liking, click OK to close the Control Center window.

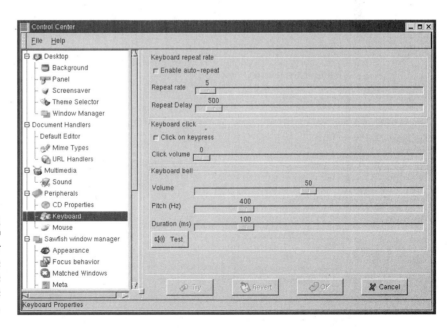

Figure 3-34

Keyboard user settings can be modified from the Gnome environment.

Configuring the Mouse

As noted in the previous section, you can also tweak your mouse settings a bit in the Control Center. Again, these are not earth-shattering changes, but sometimes these little things really matter. In Figure 3-35, you can change the button orientation on your mouse and change its responsiveness to motion—both very handy features.

When you're finished experimenting with the settings, click OK to close the window.

Properly Logging Out of X

Before we continue with desktop work, you may be curious by now as to how you turn Linux off. Not that you're going anywhere, right?

Windows and Mac users are accustomed to the fact that they simply can't just turn off their PCs. Instead, they must Shut Down first.

Figure 3-35

Lefty? You'll love this pane of the Control Center.

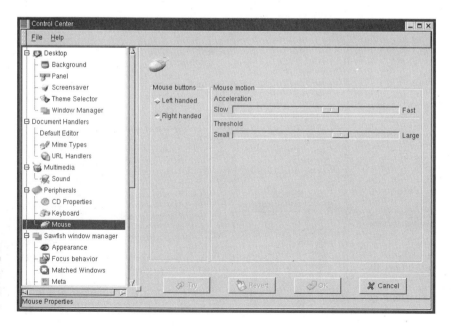

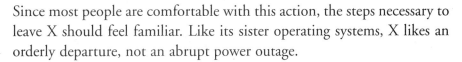

Since most people are comfortable with this action, the steps necessary to leave X should feel familiar. Like its sister operating systems, X likes an orderly departure, not an abrupt power outage.

To leave X, you must first log out and close your account. In Gnome, click the Main Menu icon and select Log Out. A message box will ask you whether you want to Logout, Halt, or Reboot.

If you just want to log out leaving the computer on for the next user, click the Logout option and then click Yes. The X session will close and the screen will return to the graphical login screen if the Workstation installation was the option you selected. If you installed Red Hat as a server, you'll be returned to the command-line interface.

If you want to reboot the system, click Reboot, then Yes. X will close, the Linux system will halt your PC and then reboot itself, returning to the graphical login screen.

Finally, if you just want to turn the computer off and go home to watch TV, click the Halt option before clicking Yes. X Window will close and Linux will close all running processes down as part of its halt sequence.

If you change your mind, simply click No to resume your X Window session, which you will need to do now so we can start looking at configuring your desktop environments.

Choosing a Desktop Environment

So far this afternoon, you have learned about the components that make up the X environment and found out which components handle specific aspects of your PC. The procedures to configure video and input devices at the X server level were also reviewed.

Now you will explore X even further at the window manager and desktop environment level. You will also start to learn the ways you can make configuration settings at that level.

Not only is Linux a viable alternative to Microsoft Windows as a work-station platform, the operating system itself contains several choices on which to operate.

For example, with Microsoft Windows you can change the look of the desktop by manipulating the colors and fonts of the menus and windows. There are even prepackaged themes available to unify the desktop into a cohesive look.

You can accomplish the same thing in X Window and go way beyond that point. Not only can you manipulate the look of a desktop environment such as Gnome, you can also change the entire desktop environment to something else entirely! This complete ability to customize your system makes X Window a much friendlier tool to use than the static Microsoft Windows.

There are two other advantages to moving across desktop environments: you have the ability to access environment-specific tools you might not otherwise see; and you can also decide which desktop approach you prefer to use, since each environment has a different presentation and work method.

Now let's learn how to move between environments.

Login Options

The first place you can choose which environment you will use occurs at the login screen. You now have the ability to pick the environment for the account into which you're logging. For instance, if I log into KDE as root and set KDE as the default, KDE will only be set as the default for the root account. Any other accounts into which I may log will use their own default environment.

The Session menu command appears in the login screen. When clicked, the menu opens to reveal the available environment options. If you originally installed using the KDE Workstation path, your options will be:

- **Default**. The default environment is set by either the original installation or the Gnome Desktop Switching application
- **Failsafe**. The Failsafe command line interface is used when there is difficulty getting an environment to run, as might occur when an incorrect video setting was made in Xconfigurator or xf86config that needs to be adjusted
- **Gnome**. The Gnome desktop environment

If you have added any other desktop environments to your system, they will appear here as environment options as well. Once selected, the choice is confirmed by a message just below the Login field. After you complete your login procedure, the environment of your choice will appear.

Switching Desktop Environments

Once inside your environment (let's assume it's Gnome for now), you can quickly switch to another environment, as you will discover in the following steps.

1. Click the Main Menu icon to open the Main Menu.

2. Choose Programs, System, Desktop Switching Tool. The Desktop Switcher window will open, as shown in Figure 3-36.

3. Click the KDE option (see Figure 3-37). The KDE logo appears.

Figure 3-36

The Desktop
Switching Tool.

NOTE The Change Only Applies to Current Display option should only be enabled if your Linux PC is networked to other PCs and you want to just make changes to your own workstation.

4. Click OK. A message will appear reminding you that these changes will not take effect until you log back into the X Window system (see Figure 3-38).

5. Log out of the environment and return to the graphical login screen.

6. Login using the same account. You will see the new default environment, KDE. (See Figure 3-39.)

TIP If you want to reset Gnome to be the default environment, simply open the Desktop Switching Tool once more. The application can be found on KDE's Application Menu (akin to Gnome's Main Menu) under Red Hat, System, Desktop Switching Tool.

Figure 3-37

Picking the KDE environment.

Figure 3-38

Environment changes occur after logging out of the current environment.

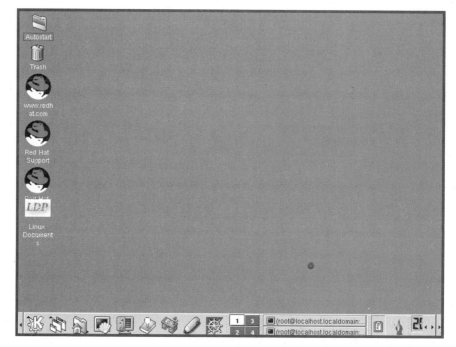

Figure 3-39

The KDE desktop environment.

Failsafe

As indicated in the Login section earlier today, the Failsafe login option is a command line interface setting. If selected during login, a small terminal emulation window will open in the lower right corner of the screen.

Note the description of the window in the previous paragraph: this is a terminal *emulation* window. X is still running, even if a desktop environment isn't. This may appear to be a fine point, but it's necessary to illustrate this distinction.

Some programs are not meant to run from within X, such as sndconfig, which we'll examine this evening in "Configuring Printers, Sound, and Other Devices." If you were to try to run sndconfig in the Failsafe mode thinking it's the true Linux command line (which I actually tried way back in my novice Linux days), bad things may happen to your system, such as a system lockup.

Basically, most applications that can run from the console (the true command-line mode) can also run in Failsafe mode. Any that can't will warn you that they won't run within X. At that point, you should heed the warning and exit the application.

TIP

To access the Linux console while in any X mode, try pressing Ctrl+Alt+F1. To return to X from Linux, press Alt+F7.

The best use I have found for using Failsafe mode occurs when I make a mistake while experimenting with video settings. By logging into X in Failsafe mode, I can start Xconfigurator up and easily repair the error.

Now that you are familiar with the different login modes, a quick examination of the methods to configure your desktop is in order.

Configuring Your Desktop

After you have taken the grand tour through the desktop and all that it has to offer, you may find some aspects of the desktop you want to change. For the remainder of this afternoon, placement of the tools that are available to you within the desktop will be discussed as well as another important aspect of desktop customization: desktop themes.

Menu Customization

What if you don't like digging through three or four menu levels to launch one of your most-used applications in Gnome? In a situation like this within Gnome, you can place the application launcher somewhere on the desktop so that you can start the program much more quickly.

BUZZ WORD

Launcher. A menu item or icon that starts an application.

The Main Menu is a prime place to place your favorite application's launcher. If it's buried four levels down in a tiny little submenu, then follow the steps below to place the launcher on the second level of the Main Menu, with the Favorites submenu.

1. Click the Main Menu icon to open the Main Menu.

2. Navigate to the menu launcher you want to relocate (see Figure 3-40).

3. Right-click the menu launcher.

4. Select the Add This to Favorites Menu option. The launcher is copied to the Favorites Menu of the Main Menu.

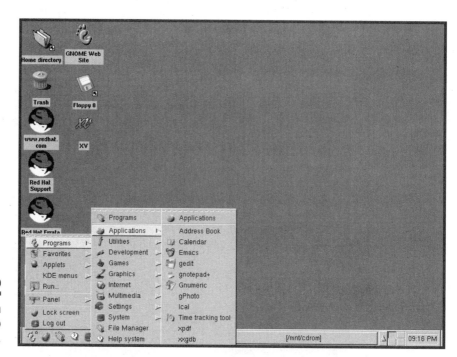

Figure 3-40

Choosing an application to move.

Desktop Icons

If you want to place a launcher on the desktop itself for even faster access, it's a simple drag-and-drop exercise.

1. Click the Main Menu icon to open the Main Menu.

2. Navigate to the launcher icon you want to move.

3. Select the application launcher icon, then drag the icon out to the desktop area.

4. Release the mouse button. A copy of the launcher icon appears on the desktop (see Figure 3-41).

5. You can drag the icon to another location for aesthetics, if need be.

 TIP You can automatically arrange icons on the desktop by right-clicking any blank area of the desktop and selecting one of the Arrange Icons options.

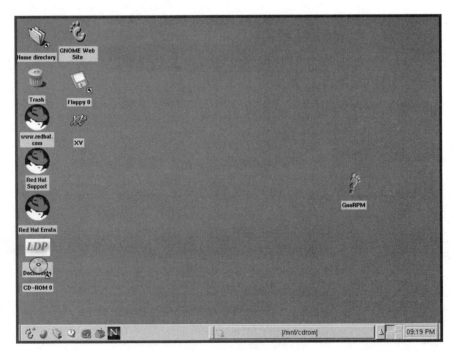

Figure 3-41

Placing a launcher on the desktop.

6. To remove the icon, right-click the icon and choose Delete from the control menu. Click Yes when asked to confirm.

Panel Icons

A launcher can also reside on the Gnome Panel. The next steps detail how to accomplish this goal.

1. Click the Main Menu icon to open the Main Menu.

2. Navigate to the launcher icon you want to move.

3. Right-click the application launcher.

4. Select the Add This Launcher to Panel option.

5. The launcher is copied to the Gnome Panel (see Figure 3-42).

6. If you want to move the icon's position on the panel, right-click the icon and select Move Applet.

The new ———
launcher icon

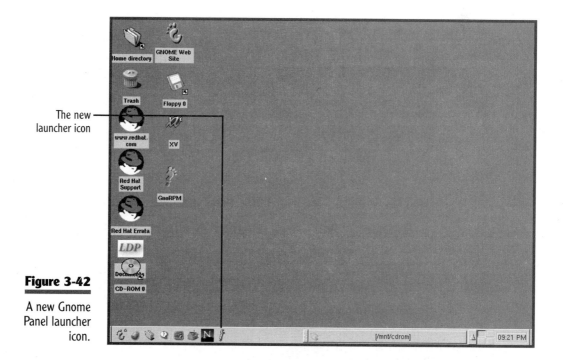

Figure 3-42

A new Gnome
Panel launcher
icon.

7. Without clicking the icon, move the multi-directional pointer along the panel. The selected launcher icon will follow.

8. When the icon is in the appropriate position, single click the icon to lock its position.

9. To remove the icon from the panel, right-click the icon to open the control menu. Now choose Remove From Panel.

Desktop Themes

If you could wear clothes that reflected your true personality, people would likely look at you very strangely.

Why let your uniqueness get buried in a wave of peer pressure? Throw off the chains of mediocrity, and get ready to strut your stuff. You can start with your Linux desktop.

Themes are a desktop environment's way of packaging unique looks and textures of desktop objects into one (ideally) coherent design. The themes of a KDE or Gnome desktop are managed within the Control Center. For our example today, we'll look at Gnome's themes.

Changing Themes

You may not realize it, but the combination of colors and textures that appears on your Gnome desktop after installation is itself a theme. This is Gnome's Default theme, which looks suspiciously like the look of a certain other operating system's default desktop.

Be that as it may, you are certainly welcome to try one of the other themes Red Hat provides. As you might expect, this is accomplished using the Control Center.

1. Click the Gnome Configuration Tool button. The Control Center window will appear.

2. Click on the expansion icon next to Desktop, then click on Theme Selector. The Theme Selector pane will appear, as shown in Figure 3-43.

3. In the Available Themes field, you can view a list of the 16 themes installed with Red Hat Linux. Click on any of the themes in the list and view a preview in the display near the bottom of the Pane (see Figure 3-44).

4. When finished, click Try to see the changes to your desktop instantly (see Figure 3-45).

5. If you approve of the change, click OK to close the Control Center.

When you activate the change, you will notice that the theme changes only applied to the interior of open windows and the Gnome Panel. Screen components such as the window borders and title bars were not affected at all.

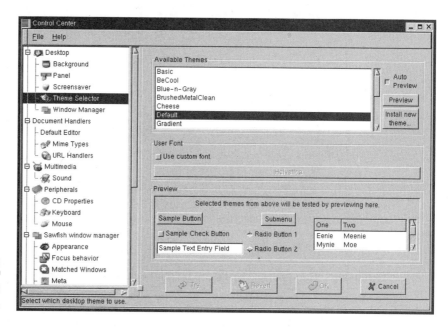

Figure 3-43

The Gnome Theme Selector.

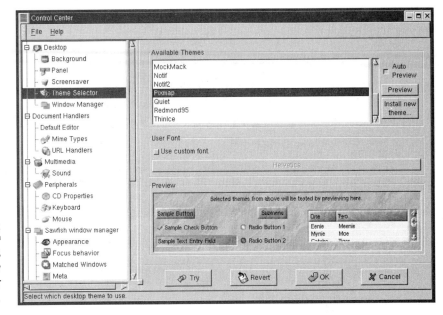

Figure 3-44

Check out themes
before you apply
them to your
desktop.

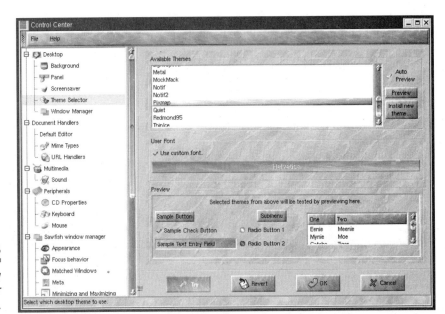

Figure 3-45

A new theme now
graces your
desktop.

You are seeing a clear example of how the desktop environment (Gnome) and the window manager (Sawfish) each controls different aspects of the display. If you want to change the other elements on the screen, you will need to configure Sawfish, as shown in the following steps.

1. Click the Gnome Configuration Tool button. The Control Center window will appear.

2. Click on the expansion icon next to Sawfish window manager, then click on Appearance. The Appearance pane will appear, as shown in Figure 3-46.

3. Click on the drop-down list for the Default frame style (theme) field. A list of available themes will be displayed.

4. Click on the theme you want to try.

5. When finished, click Try to see the changes to your desktop instantly (see Figure 3-47).

6. If you approve of the changes, click OK to close the Control Center.

Figure 3-46

The Sawfish window manager can control aspects of the display as well.

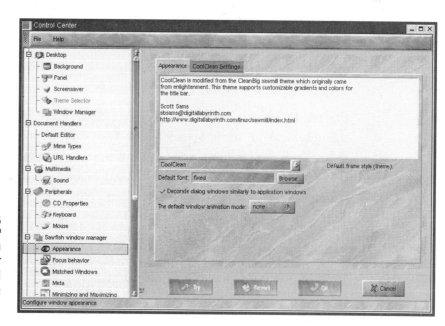

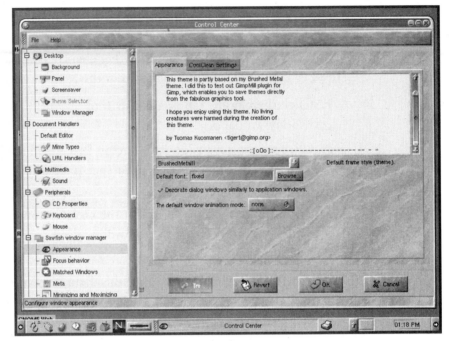

Figure 3-47

The BrushedMetalIII theme of Sawfish applied to the Gnome Pixmap theme.

Getting a New Theme

Don't be fooled by the availability of just 16 themes for the Gnome desktop. There are a lot more themes available, just a hyperlink away.

On the Internet is a fantastic Web site designed to provide ready-made themes for your desktop for free. The site, located at **http://www.themes.org**, is the home of a large collection of **theme.org** Internet sites that provide themes for the major window managers and desktop environments. For most users of Red Hat Linux, the KDE site (kde.themes.org) will be the one you want to visit, as well as sawfish.themes.org and gtk.themes.org.

The latter site is the home of themes Gnome can use directly. GTK stands for Gimp Tool Kit, which is the application Gnome uses to manage themes.

At any of these sites, you will be asked to login with a predetermined username and password. If you have not gotten this yet, do so. It is free of charge, and you really shouldn't download a theme without one. You can, but it's rather impolite.

Once you have registered on a site, you can explore the Theme Gallery, which displays themes by category or by the total number of downloads, as shown in Figure 3-48.

When you locate a theme you want to use, click on the hyperlink within the theme's description and save the download to your hard drive, wherever you prefer. Now you can tell the theme manager in your desktop environment to use the new theme, once you point it to the right location on the hard drive.

1. Click the Gnome Configuration Tool button. The Control Center window will appear.

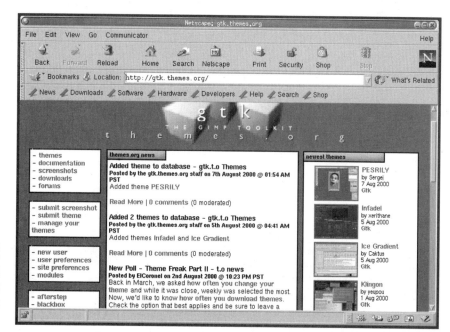

Figure 3-48

A smorgasbord of new themes from which you can choose.

2. Click on the expansion icon next to Desktop, then click on Theme Selector. The Theme Selector pane will appear.

3. Click the Install New Theme button. The Select a Theme to Install dialog box will appear, as seen in Figure 3-49.

4. Select the theme you want to install and click OK.

 NOTE You do not have to uncompress the theme files you download, even though they are *.tar.gz files. In fact, the Theme Selector won't pick up a theme unless the theme is compressed in this manner.

5. Click on the new themes in the preview list and view the preview in the display within the Preview area of the Theme Selector.

6. When finished, click Try to see the changes to your desktop instantly (see Figure 3-50).

7. If you like your new theme, click OK to close the Control Center.

Now that you know how to beautify your desktop, it's time to dig a little deeper and learn the basics of how your Linux machine organizes its files.

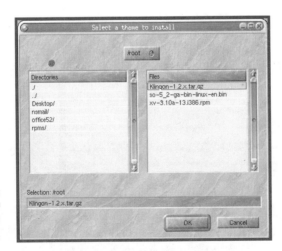

Figure 3-49

Adding a new theme.

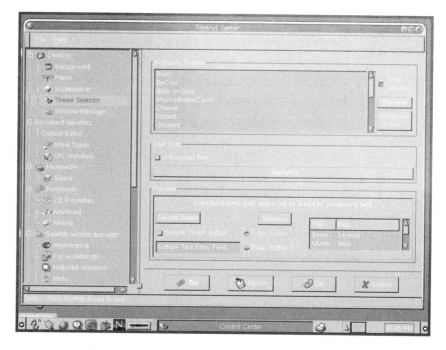

Figure 3-50

A new theme fresh
from the Internet.
Qapla!

Configuring Your File System

A file system is the way any operating system organizes its files. Most modern file systems use a hierarchical system. That is, a main or root directory that contains files and subdirectories. Each subdirectory contains additional files and subdirectories. This hierarchy makes it easier to organize and arrange files.

Using the Linux File System

Linux uses a single root directory. DOS, on the other hand has multiple root directories (\)—one for each disk (actually each disk partition). Each disk is assigned a letter followed by a colon, (C:, D:, E:, . . .). Linux mounts one disk as the root directory (/) and subsequent disks are mounted anywhere in the file system as subdirectories. In English, this means that if you mount your CD-ROM drive in Linux, it may appear in the directory as /mnt/cdrom, as opposed to D:.

◄◄

Mounting is another way of saying "connecting." In DOS (and Windows), you do not concern yourself with mounting, as all disks and their partitions are connected at the same time. This is not the case in Linux, though Red Hat 7 makes it very easy to have disks automatically mount whenever a disk is inserted.

◄◄

An important benefit of this flexibility is that branches on the directory tree are scalable. If a branch of a directory tree becomes so large that it fills up its disk, you can assign a new disk to this branch. This frees up space on the drive containing the parent directory—without changing the directory structure of the filesystem. It is possible that Linux may start on one disk and grow to reside on several disks but still have the same core directory structure.

This is a great benefit to have, particularly if some of your Linux applications need files in certain directories. With this system, you can move directories and their files to any device on your system and still use all of your applications. Those of you familiar with trying to move application directories in the Windows environment are familiar with just how difficult this particular task can be.

Another big difference between Linux and DOS is that Linux is case sensitive. Capital letters appear different to Linux from lowercase characters. A directory can contain files named Notes, NOTES, and notes. This can be confusing. You are encouraged to avoid this situation by choosing a naming convention for your files and directories and sticking to it.

Linux uses the forward slash (/) to separate subdirectories. MS-DOS uses the backslash (\); don't confuse the two. A file will then have a path that looks something like `usr/src/linux/Makefile`.

Linux has some other special characters: ~ points to the user's home directory; / points to the root directory; MS-DOS and Linux share the use of . (current directory); .. (parent directory); * (wildcard); and ? (placeholder). Like Windows 95/98 and Windows NT, Linux requires you to surround file names containing spaces with quotation marks.

Functions and Permissions

There are hundreds of distinct Linux commands that you could learn. Most of the time, however, you won't use more than a score of those commands. Some of the more common commands you will need to know are included in this section. Appendix A, "The Linux Primer," lists these functions in even detail.

This section also includes some of the most common switches used to modify these commands. Switches follow the command and are preceded by a dash (-) symbol. These switches can be combined behind one dash (as in, `ls -1R`). There are many switches available for these commands, but the ones included are just those that are most commonly used.

- ls. The list command is probably the most used command. It corresponds to the DIR command in DOS. It lists the files, links, and subdirectories in the current directory. Used without switches, ls displays a list of files in the current directory using a short format.

- -l. The -l switch (short for long) is probably the most often used switch. It displays detailed information about each file in a long format. The output from this command is important because Linux uses much of this same information to determine how it treats the files. For example, using the command `~$ ls -1` returns a list of files similar to:

```
~$ ls -1
total 47
-rw-r--r--    1 root     root       1560 Dec 10 14:12 Application_Notes
-rw-r-- r--    1 root     root        911 Dec 10 14:12 Daemon_Notes
drwxr-xr-x    5 guest    guest      1024 Nov 11 09:09 Desktop
-rw-r--r--    1 root     root       2253 Dec 10 14:12 Disk_Notes.txt
-rw-r--r--    1 root     root       1104 Dec 10 14:12 Hardware.Specs
-rw-r--r--    1 root     root        477 Dec 10 14:12 Initialization_Scripts
-rw-r--r--    1 root     root      33792 Dec 10 14:12 Master ICC TOC.sdw
-rwxr-xr-x    1 root     root        573 Dec 10 14:12 StarOffice
-rw-r--r--    1 root     root        149 Dec 10 14:12 Startup-files
-rw-r--r--    1 root     root        773 Dec 10 14:10 notes.txt
```

This option displays the file type, privileges, links, owner, group, size, last modification date and time, and file name associated with each file. The file type, privileges, owner, and group fields will be discussed later this afternoon.

- -a. Shows all the files in a directory, including the hidden files. File names for hidden files begin with a period (.).

- -R. Shows the contents of the subdirectories recursively.

- —color. This is a special switch that makes it easy to differentiate between files and directories. —color displays executable files differently than regular files. Directories, links, and device files also have separate colors. This is extremely valuable when displaying files in the short format.

  To avoid having to retype this option each time, place it in an alias. Type:

  ```
  $ alias ls='ls —color'
  ```

  To use this option each time you log in, use your favorite text editor (emacs, vi, pico, or whatever) to edit. ~/.bashrc. Add the following line:

  ```
  alias ls='ls —color'
  ```

  Save the file. Now, each time you log in, this script will run.

- cd. This command is like the DOS cd (change directory) command. It, likewise, changes the current working directory.

  For example, to change the working directory to the root directory, use cd /.

  To change the working directory to the user's home directory, (the directory he or she starts in after logging in), use cd ~.

  To return to the previous working directory, use the cd - command. This is convenient when switching back and forth between two directories.

Directory paths can be expressed in either relative or absolute terms, using commands such as `cd ../../etc or cd /etc`. This command is equivalent only as long as the reader is not more than two levels deep in the file system. For instance, if the current directory is /usr/local/bin then the first command will take you to /usr/etc.

✿ `pwd`. This command displays the current working directory. For example, the command line `~$ pwd` displays `/home/guest`.

✿ `cp`. This command corresponds to the **Copy** command in DOS. For example, use this command to copy the file named `test` into the new file named `test2`:

```
cp test test2
```

You can include paths in the file names. Notice that several periods are allowed in Linux file names:

```
cp /etc/lilo.conf lilo.conf.copy
```

`cp` does not normally check to see if the target file already exists before overwriting it. To make `cp` always display a prompt before overwriting a file, edit the file `.bashrc` in your home directory. Add the following line if it doesn't already appear in `.bashrc`.

```
alias cp='cp -i'
```

Later, if you want to override the prompt, use the `-f` switch.

✿ `mv`. Similar to `cp` is `mv`. This command moves the file to the new directory or file name, leaving no copy in the original location. This command is most often used to move files from one directory to another. It is also used to rename a file. DOS users often find the use of such a powerful command in place of their **REN** command startling.

For example, the following line renames the file `test` to `test2`:

```
mv test test2
```

Like `cp`, `mv` normally doesn't check before overwriting a file. Therefore, add the following line to the `.bashrc` file in your home directory if it doesn't already appear there.

```
alias mv='mv -i'
```

To override the prompt at a later time, use the `-f` switch.

✿ `rm`. Removes (deletes) a file or directory. You must have write privileges to a file to delete it.

`rm` doesn't prompt before deleting a file. Also, files aren't as easily restored in Linux as they are in Windows. To give yourself a second chance to not make a mistake, add the following line to the `.bashrc` file in your home directory if it doesn't already appear there. As with other commands, you can override the prompt whenever you want using the `-f` switch.

```
alias rm='rm -i'
```

✿ `-r`. When combined with `rm`, the recursive switch removes the directory and all its files and subdirectories.

For example, to remove the directory `testdir` and any subdirectories it contains, use the command `rm -r testdir`. Likewise, the command `rm -r tt` removes the directory `tt`. Alternatively, use the command `rmdir tt` to remove an empty directory.

✿ `rmdir`. Removes an empty directory. If the directory `testdir2` happened to be empty, then the following two commands would be equivalent:

```
rmdir testdir2
rm -r testdir2
```

✿ `mkdir`. Makes a new directory. You can specify the directory in either absolute or relative references. For example, use the command `mkdir testdir` to make a new directory within the current directory.

⚙ `ln`. The link command is one final command that you may use frequently. Use it to make symbolic links to another directory or file. Use the following format:

```
ln -s <filename> <linkname>
```

For example, the following creates a link to a file:

```
~$ ls -l test*
-rw-r--r--    1 guest     guest         1560 Dec 01 12:44 testfile
~$ ln -s testfile testlink
~$ ls -l test*
-rw-r--r--    1 guest     guest         1560 Dec 01 12:44 testfile
lrwxrwxrwx    1 guest     guest            8 Dec 01 13:06 testlink -> testfile
```

Use links as temporary shortcuts to directories buried deep in the file system structure.

Permissions are used because Linux is a multi-user operating system. That means different people can use the computer at the same time. Some files and directories you will want everyone to be able to access. Others, you will want to be private. Linux organizes access to files and directories into three groups: owner, group, and other.

The user is usually the owner of the files he creates. When you create a user account, it is assigned to a group. Some examples of group are sys (system processes), root (the super-user root), and user (the group to which most users are assigned).

The owner can set his files to be readable, ratable (and deletable), and executable by himself, his group, or all others. The root user always has full access to every file and directory.

Working with Non-Linux Partitions

While another file partition is not exactly a peripheral, it certainly is another device on your PC that can be exploited like any other. If you have another partition on your computer, such as a Windows partition, you can easily access its file system from Linux.

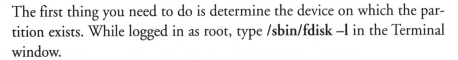

The first thing you need to do is determine the device on which the partition exists. While logged in as root, type **/sbin/fdisk –l** in the Terminal window.

You will see a list of all logical and actual hard disks on your PC, including a line that includes "Win95." At the beginning of that line will be a /dev/hda*X* value. There should also be value such as FAT32 or FAT16. Keep these values in mind for later.

You will need to create a mount point directory from which the Windows partition can be accessed. Type **mkdir /mnt/win** or **mkdir /mnt/windows**, naming the directory something that you can remember.

Now, all you need to do is mount the partition by typing **mount –t vfat /dev/hda*X* /mnt/win**. Remember to replace the *x* with the correct drive number. Your Windows file system can then be accessed like any other file directory.

TIP   To remount the partition after a halt or reboot, simply type the mount command once more.

Conclusion

You accomplished a great deal of tasks this afternoon, and learned a lot about the background of how Linux works under the hood.

By getting your desktop and working environment established up front, you will make Red Hat Linux a physically and mentally soothing tool to work with. In these hectic times, the easier the better.

Now you should grab something to eat. When you come back this evening, you'll learn how to start connecting your computer to other devices, be they PCs or printers. You'll also learn how to get sound pouring out of your speakers so you will have a multimedia Linux PC.

Playing Well with Others

- ✿ Setting Up Your Internet Account
- ✿ Configuring Networks and IP Addresses
- ✿ Installing Printers
- ✿ Setting Up Sound
- ✿ Using ISAPNPTOOLS Utility

Now that you have run through some of the basic configuration of your PC, its time to take a look at how you can get your PC talking to other devices.

There are a myriad of ways that your Linux machine can communicate with other machines, the most popular way being through the Internet. This is not the sole way, nor is it the most common way. This evening, you will learn how to:

- Create an Internet account
- Configure your network settings
- Add a printer to your PC
- Set up your sound card
- Add additional hardware to your PC

After some of the earlier sessions, all of these tasks may seem completely over your head. Don't worry, they're pretty straightforward, even for beginners. Just follow along in this session to learn how to get some configuration work done.

Setting up Your Internet Account

A great deal has been said about the Internet this past decade. Although much hoopla and hype has been associated with the Internet—the largest of all public computer networks—it should be noted that the Internet is not even close to being finished.

The growth of the Internet (thus far) is in many ways similar to the growth of the telephone in the United States in the late 19th Century. For the first five years of its commercial existence, the telephone was in about 10 percent of U.S. households. In five more years, it was in 50 percent of American homes. And in another five years, it was in 90 percent of all U.S. homes.

The Internet matches this growth pattern closely. By 1994, five years after the Internet broke out of its pure academic setting, connection to the Internet could be found in about 10 percent of U.S. homes. Now, a little over five years later, the pervasiveness of Internet access in the United States has reached nearly 50 percent. Incredible as it may seem, the United States is only at about its halfway mark toward full Internet usage. (The Internet's presence in other nations is behind in terms of percentages but perhaps only because the U.S. had a head start; the pattern of the growth remains the same.)

Whether you are one of the new kids on the Internet block or have been surfing since the days of Lynx, you will find the Internet is becoming less of a place to play and more of a place to work. More and more people are turning to the Internet to handle banking needs, shop for holiday gifts, and even check up on their kids at daycare via Web cameras.

The history of Linux and the Internet is an intertwined one. Linux's predecessor, UNIX, was *the* operating system upon which the Internet was built. In fact, much of the syntax of the Internet ("http://," FTP commands, forward slashes for directory separators) is directly derived from UNIX line commands.

Thus, it should come as no surprise that Red Hat Linux 7 provides a rich set of Internet tools for access. All you have to do is get yourself connected.

Getting an Internet account is simple these days. Many of us seem to get a CD-ROM in the mail with connectivity software almost once a month. However, with Linux, you will need to make sure you are using the right type of account.

The "language" of the Internet is called TCP/IP. This language (called a protocol) is how data is sent from your computer to a Web server computer in, say, Durham, North Carolina.

◄ ◄

TCP/IP (Transmission Control Protocol/Internet Protocol): A suite of communications protocols used to connect hosts on the Internet. TCP/IP is a product of the UNIX operating system and is used by the Internet.

◄ ◄

Even though TCP/IP is a UNIX-based product, Red Hat Linux needs additional protocol help connecting to the Internet through a dial-up connection. TCP/IP, after all, does not transmit the IP (Internet Protocol) data packets through serial lines very well—serial lines like those in modems, for example.

To get all of the data packets through a modem, an additional protocol, PPP, is used. The irony of this is that PPP is not a UNIX invention—it and its predecessor, SLIP, was developed to connect Windows computers to the Internet.

◄ ◄

PPP (Point-to-Point Protocol): A communication protocol used to deliver data packets through modem lines during a dial-up call to the Internet.

◄ ◄

PPP works on Linux systems—Red Hat (RH) being no exception. The RH PPP Dialer program manages connection of your PC to the Internet. You must first configure the Dialer so that it can communicate properly to the computers at your Internet Service Provider.

Configure the PPP Dialer

Red Hat Linux 7 comes with the Dialup Configuration Tool, an automated method of setting up your Internet connection. For most ISPs, using this application is enough to create a routine connection. There may be instances where more control over a connection's configuration is needed—which is why this section will also examine the manual editing of a connection using the Dialup Connection Tool.

Using the Dialup Connection Tool is directly analogous to the Internet Connection Wizard used within the Microsoft Windows operating systems. The idea is to step though the application, providing the snippets of information needed by Red Hat to create a new PPP connection.

Before you begin the next task, which will demonstrate the creation of a connection, you should gather the following information:

- Domain name of the ISP (e.g., earthlink.net)
- The user name for your account
- The password for your account
- The phone number for the ISP

You should also confirm what communications protocol your ISP requires. A vast majority of the ISPs will require PPP; but some may use alternate protocols, such as SLIP or PLIP.

TIP Many ISPs provide connection information in a single Web page or Web-accessible document. If you have access to the Internet from another PC or a Windows partition, visit the Web site of your ISP to see if yours has provided this information. A good place to check can be the "technical support" or "FAQ" sections.

Once this information is gathered, it is a simple matter to enter it into the Dialup Configuration Tool, as shown in the following steps.

1. Click the Main Menu icon to open the Main Menu.

2. Choose Programs, Internet, Dialup Configuration Tool. The application window will open in the foreground, with a window of existing Internet Connections visible in the background (see Figure 4-1).

3. The first window is an introductory message. Click Next to continue.

4. If you have not yet configured your modem, the Select Modem screen will appear (see Figure 4-2). Click Next to have the application automatically search for all modems connected to your PC.

Figure 4-1

Starting your new Internet connection set up.

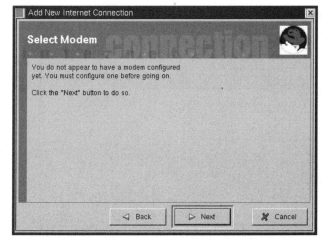

Figure 4-2

If the Dialup Connection Tool does not have a record of your modem, it will ask to configure it for you.

CAUTION Be sure you have turned your external modem on and that it is properly connected to the computer before the application searches for the device.

5. A list of modems currently connected to your PC will appear, as displayed in Figure 4-3. If the displayed list of modem(s) is correct, click the modem you want to use. Then click the Keep This Modem option. Finally, click Next to continue.

6. In the Phone Number and Name screen (displayed in Figure 4-4), type a descriptive name for the connection as well as the phone number your modem will need to dial. Click Next when finished.

CAUTION Don't enter prefix or area/country code data in their respective fields unless needed. The RH PPP Dialer does not have a setting to turn off area code dialing, for example.

7. Every ISP account includes a user ID and a password. This data will be input on the next screen. (See Figure 4-5). Click Next to continue.

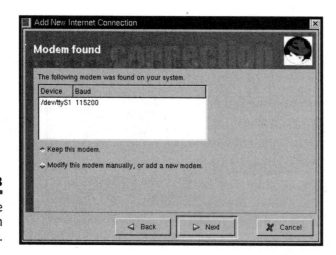

Figure 4-3

Confirming the found modem choice.

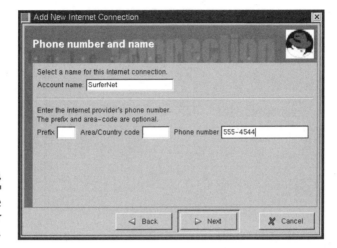

Figure 4-4

Entering telephone information for the connection.

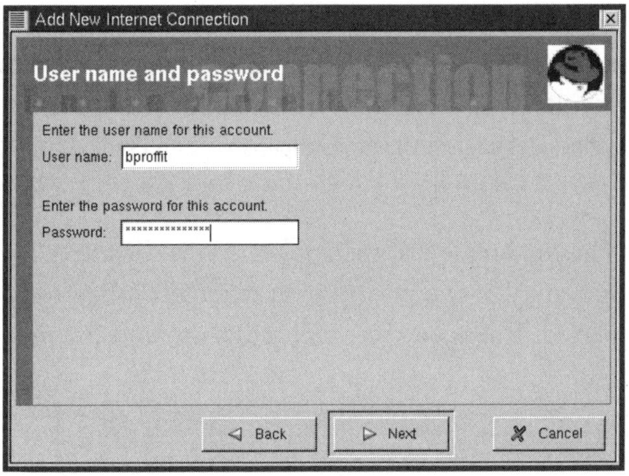

Figure 4-5

The user name and password screen.

TIP

To protect your account from unwanted use, the password field substitutes asterisks for each character in your password. The upshot of this is that you need to use care while typing your password to avoid typing miscues.

8. Red Hat Linux can access two types of ISPs: the AT&T Global Network Services and regular nonproprietary ISPs. Select from one of these two categories (see Figure 4-6) and click Next to continue.

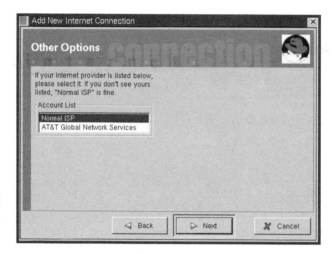

Figure 4-6

Choosing your
ISP type.

NOTE   "Proprietary" ISPs are those online services that use their own communications protocols. They also typically provide their own content over and above Internet access. These
services include America Online, CompuServe, and Prodigy, to name a few.

9. The final screen of the application is shown in Figure 4-7. A brief
   summary of the information entered in the previous screens is displayed. If it is correct, click Finish to end the program.

Figure 4-7

Wrapping up the
Dialup Connection
Tool process.

The Add New Internet Connection dialog box will close, and you will be returned to the Internet Connections window. Your new connection will appear in this screen, as shown in Figure 4-8.

Though the Dialup Connection Tool is by far the most intuitive method of creating Internet connections, there may be times that you will need a bit more control over your connection. For example, your ISP may require you to enter DNS information. For this type of detail, you will need to use the Dialup Connection Tool again to manually fine-tune a connection.

◄◄

BUZZ WORD **Domain Name Service (DNS):** A network of specialized servers within the Internet that translates alphabetic domain names into IP addresses. All Internet servers have a unique IP address, such as 198.105.232.95. Since these are more difficult to remember than plain-language domain names, the DNS translates domain names into its corresponding IP address. Many ISPs have a default DNS that is queried first when a request to connect to a Web server is made.

◄◄

Now you will learn to add or confirm the modem port for your modem device. Similar to hard drives, modems are also mounted on the Linux file system. Modems are, after all, just another type of device with which Linux exchanges data. Like other PC devices, modems appear in the /dev

Figure 4-8

The new Internet connection.

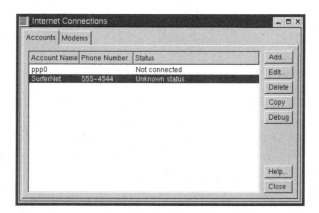

directory of the file system. Table 4-1 lists the available modem ports and their DOS equivalents.

▴▴▴

Alias: A term describing a secondary name for an object in Linux. An alias is equivalent to a Windows shortcut. For instance, a PC's sole modem at /dev/ttys1 can have an alias of /dev/modem.

▴▴

The following steps illustrate how to use the Dialup Connection Tool to edit an Internet connection.

● ●

Be sure you are logged in as root for these steps.

● ●

1. Click the Main Menu icon to open the Main Menu.
2. Choose Programs, Internet, Dialup Configuration Tool. The Internet Connections window will open.
3. Click on the Modems tab. The Modems pane will appear in the window, as seen in Figure 4-9.

TABLE 4-1 MODEM FILESYSTEM PATHS	
Path	**DOS Equivalent Port**
/dev/ttyS0	COM1
/dev/ttyS1	COM2
/dev/ttyS2	COM3
/dev/ttyS3	COM4
/dev/modem	The alias for any configured modem

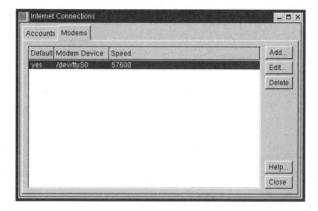

Figure 4-9

Configured
modems are listed
in this pane.

4. Click Add to start the process of configuring a new modem. The Edit Modem Properties dialog box will open (see Figure 4-10).

TIP

To save some time, click the Auto Configure button and have Red Hat get the correct settings for you.

5. Change the properties you need to change and then click OK. The settings will be saved and the Edit Modem Properties dialog box will close.

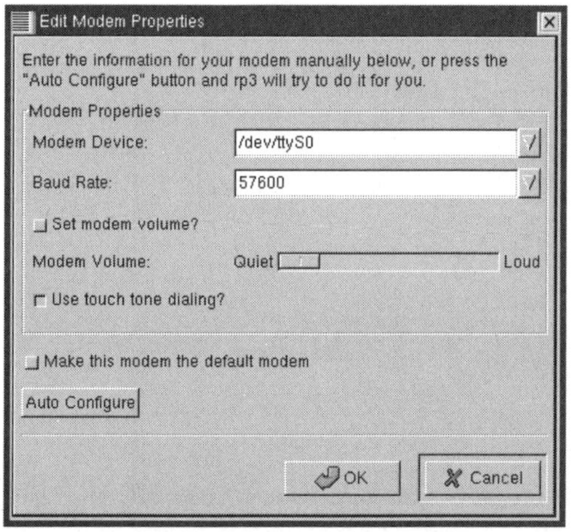

Figure 4-10

You can change
your modem
options from this
dialog box.

6. Click on the Accounts tab. The Accounts pane will appear.

7. Select an account to fine-tune and click on Edit. The Edit Internet Connection dialog box will appear, as shown in Figure 4-11.

8. Click the Advanced tab. The Advanced pane will appear (see Figure 4-12).

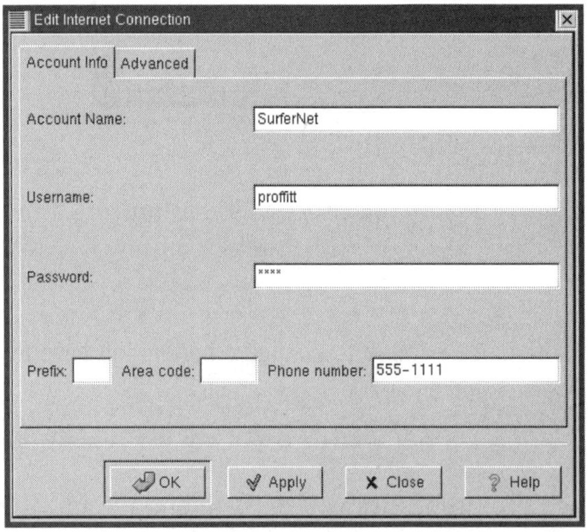

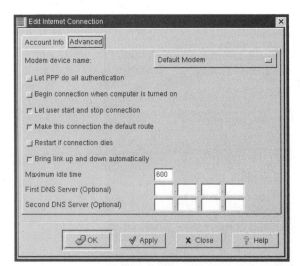

Figure 4-11

This dialog box allows you to modify your connection settings.

Figure 4-12

Fine-tune your connection.

9. To enter the DNS information, type the IP address sections in each of the four First DNS Server fields. Use the Tab key to quickly navigate the fields.

10. Prevent some hang-ups by setting the Maximum idle time value to more than the default 600 seconds. Try 1200 seconds, which will give you 20 minutes.

11. Click on OK. The Edit Internet Connection dialog box will close.

12. Click on Close. The Internet Connections dialog box will close and your new setting saved.

Connect to the Internet

Now that you have set up a connection to the Internet, it's time to start that connection and see what it can do!

Connecting to the Internet on a Linux PC used to be a combination of voodoo and science, much like picking who the number one-ranked college football team is today. No longer. All you need to connect to the Internet is the RH PPP Dialer application, called "RP3" for short.

In the next steps, you will see how to access the Internet on your PC, as well as how to configure RP3 to suit your needs.

1. Click the Main Menu icon to open the Main Menu.

2. Choose System, RH PPP Dialer. The Choose dialog box will open (see Figure 4-13).

Figure 4-13

Select the PPP
connection you
want to start.

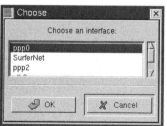

TIP If you frequently connect to the Internet, you might consider adding an icon for RP3 to the Gnome Panel using the technique described in this afternoon in "Configuring Your Desktop."

3. Click the connection you want to use and then click OK to continue. The Change Configuration Status dialog will appear (see Figure 4-14).

4. Click Yes. RP3 will begin the dial-up and login process, all the while displaying the Waiting dialog (see Figure 4-15). Click Cancel at any time if you want to stop the connection.

5. Once connected, the main RP3 window will appear. Although not much to look at, this window displays quite a bit of information, as shown in Figure 4-16.

6. When you want to disconnect from the Internet, simply click the Connection button in the RP3 window. The Change Connection Status dialog box will appear once more, this time asking if you want to stop the connection (see Figure 4-17).

Figure 4-14

Confirm that you want to start the connection to your PPP account.

Figure 4-15

One ringy-dingy . . .

Figure 4-16

The RP3 application window.

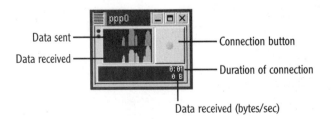

Data sent

Data received

Connection button

Duration of connection

Data received (bytes/sec)

Figure 4-17

Confirm stopping
your Internet
connection.

7. Click Yes to confirm this action. All of the RP3 windows and dialog boxes will close.

I find RP3's default method of asking for confirmation every time you
want to start or stop and Internet connection a bit annoying. While useful in preventing the accidental log off of an Internet connection, it certainly is bothersome when you're trying to connect.

Despite the apparent lack of interface within the RP3 application, there
is a way to adjust some of the program's settings. To do so, right-click in
the application window used to start the RP3 menu. Select Properties to
open the RP3 Properties dialog box (see Figure 4-18).

You can now turn off the confirmation messages that appear at the start
and end of RP3 sessions, as well as determine whether you want the
application to monitor the time or cost of the connection, based on a per
hour, minute, or second rate. This latter option is especially useful when

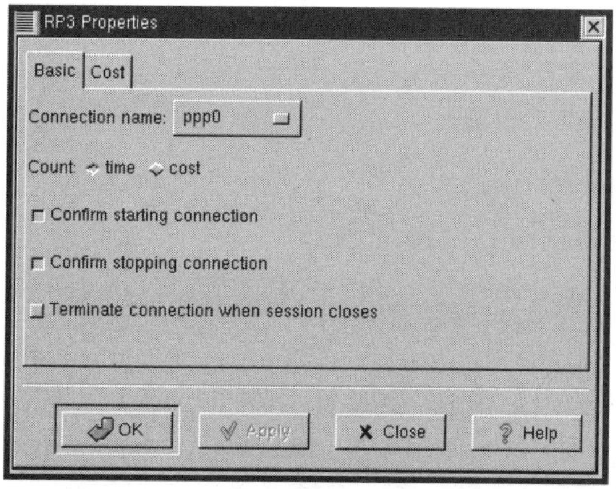

Figure 4-18

Configuring your
RP3 settings.

you have an ISP that bills you for connection time or should you have a toll charge for local telephone calls.

Networking and IP Addresses

TCP/IP is the standard protocol of the Internet, and most of the world's networks use this protocol to communicate as well. Your home or office network is no exception.

First off, you should know that all computers that use TCP/IP protocols have a unique address. No two computers can share the same address on the same network. The system used to assign an address to a computer is known as the Dotted-Decimal Address, usually referred to as an IP Address, or just an IP. The Class A, B, and C addresses are assigned to certain functions.

Class A addresses are normally used for loopback communications and for very large organizations. Usually 127.nnn.nnn.nnn IP addresses are used for applications and processes that communicate with other applications and processes on the same computer.

Class C addresses are the most commonly used, especially for networks that are not part of a widespread organization. Class C addresses are discussed here. Most Class C addresses are part of a LAN. A LAN can consist of any number of computers, (from two computers to 254 computers, or *hosts* as they are known in networking jargon). There are three sets of IP addresses assigned for use by LANs that are not part of the Internet. These sets are:

- 10.0.0.0 to 10.255.255.255
- 172.16.0.0 to 172.16.255.255
- 192.168.0.0 to 192.168.255.255

These blocks of addresses are used for LANs and will not be assigned to Internet addresses. Since they are not connected to the Internet, any of these blocks can be used as IP addresses for your private network. Probably the most commonly used block is the 192.168.nnn.nnn group. More discussion of these blocks of reserved addresses for LANs can be found in a bit. First, however, verify that you are communicating with the world using the Internet.

Begin by assuming that you are setting up a single computer and want to connect directly to the Internet through your organization's network, which has its own Internet connection. This section will show you how to add a LAN, and then discuss other complications that can occur after the first computer is connected correctly. Of course, if you have a system administrator to call, he or she has probably already taken care of everything. If not, read on.

While Red Hat Linux 7 was being installed this morning, the installation program asked for information concerning your network. Specifically it asked for:

- ✿ **Configure using DHCP**. A DHCP server on a network assigns a different unused IP address each time your PC connects to your network. If your network uses DHCP, press the button.
- ✿ **IP address.** This is the static IP address of your computer or host, if DHCP is not used.
- ✿ **Netmask**. The installation script attempted to enter this; be sure it is correct.
- ✿ **Network**. The installation script attempted to enter this also.
- ✿ **Broadcast**. The installation script attempted to enter this also.
- ✿ **Hostname**. This is the name your ISP assigned your computer or host.
- ✿ **Gateway IP**. This is the IP address assigned by your ISP for a gateway/router.
- ✿ **Primary DNS**. A nameserver that may or may not be your gateway IP address.
- ✿ **Secondary DNS**. A name server; at least one will be assigned.
- ✿ **Ternary DNS**. A name server.

If all the above entries were made correctly during installation, you should be able to connect to the Internet with a Web browser such as Netscape Navigator or Lynx. If you cannot connect, check to make sure the entries were made correctly.

The most common reason for networking to fail is that the network configuration information is incorrect. To see what entries were made in the initial configuration, log in as root, and then go to a terminal window and type **Netconfig**. You can then re-enter the entirety of your network information just as though you were configuring your network at the initial installation.

Network Configurator is another tool that you can use to re-enter your configuration information. Network Configurator is very easy to use and understand. It can be started in one of three methods:

- ☼ By selecting Programs, System, Network Configurator in the Main Menu.

- ☼ From the Control Panel (which under Programs, System, Control Panel). The icon for the application is shown in Figure 4-19.

- ☼ By typing **netcfg** in a terminal window.

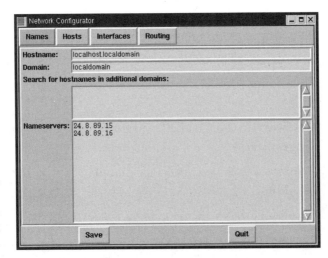

Figure 4-19

The Control Panel is a fast way to start the Network Configurator.

In the Network Configurator, clicking on the tabs Names, Hosts, Interfaces, and Routing, will allow you to check and change any information on your network configuration (see Figure 4-20).

If you want to modify any information in the Hosts tab (shown in Figure 4-21), first click the line to be changed, then click Edit. The Add button works similarly, allowing you to add information for a newly added Network Interface Card, for example.

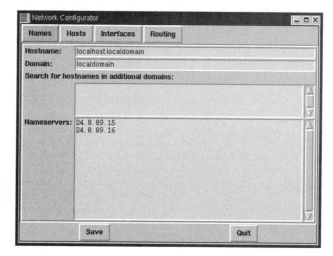

Figure 4-20

The Names tab of the Network Configurator.

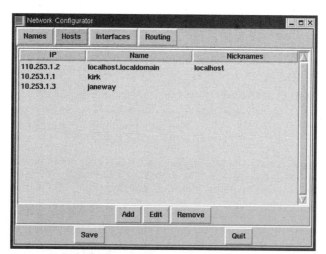

Figure 4-21

The Hosts tab of the Network Configurator.

The Interfaces tab, displayed in Figure 4-22, will allow you to check on settings for your Gateway Device (your NIC, or Network Interface Card). If you believe your card is not being activated, check the Active area. If the card is active, it will say so under this heading. If not, you can set a card to Active.

The Routing tab will allow you to set your Gateway IP address and your NIC, as seen in Figure 4-23. Red Hat will usually enter `eth0` as your

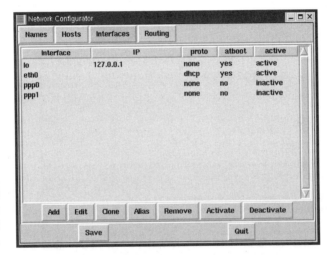

Figure 4-22

The Interfaces tab of the Network Configurator.

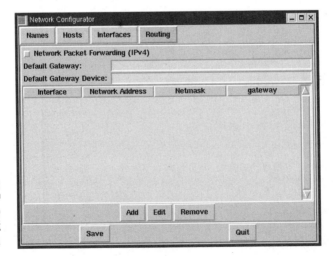

Figure 4-23

The Routing tab of the Network Configurator.

gateway device. You can, however, change or add a gateway device here. Verify that the Network Packet Forwarding button is selected.

When you are finished with Network Configurator, click Save.

There will come a time in the future when you will want to configure all of your PC's networking attributes in one fell swoop. Fortunately, there's a tool just perfect for this, known as Linuxconf. Linuxconf has become the most popular configuration tool in Red Hat Linux, and is used for making and changing settings for the entire Linux installation. Now you will see how to use Linuxconf to configure networking. Linuxconf is started by typing **linuxconf** in the terminal window. If you are using Linuxconf for the first time, you will see some initial information describing how to use Linuxconf. After the initial dialog box, you can use Linuxconf to configure your networking.

Once you open Linuxconf, click the Client Tasks, Basic Host Information tab to show the screen in Figure 4-24.

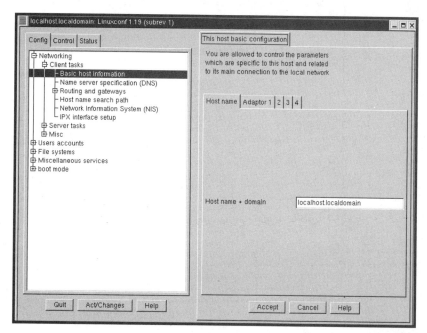

Figure 4-24

The Host Name can be verified and edited on this screen.

Check to see that the Host Name is correct. Clicking the Adapter 1 tab will open a screen similar to Figure 4-25.

Notice that the basic network information is easy to see and to change. Click any box and modify or enter the desired information.

You can tell, from the presence of the eth0 device, that I am using a PCI NIC card. Also note that I/O and IRQ address information is not entered. Red Hat quite capably handles the PCI bus. If you use PCI cards, you do not usually need to enter these parameters into your configuration. Likewise, the pcnet32 kernel module for your NIC is usually already chosen by Linux. If necessary, however, you can select a module for your NIC from the drop-down list.

Be sure that the Enabled checkbox is selected, along with your method of IP address selection. If you have a static IP address, click Manual. If you have dynamic IP addressing, as I do on my network, click DHCP.

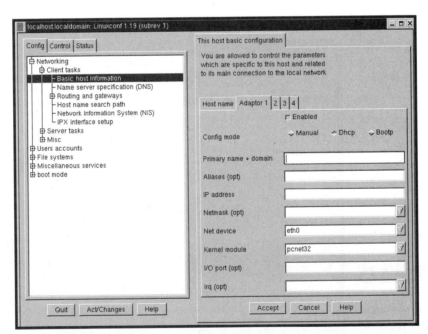

Figure 4-25

Your network card's information can be found here.

The Help button will give you access to information about a box you are configuring. Select the box in question, then click Help. A Help window will open and offer insights on that particular area (see Figure 4-26).

To exit the Help screen, simply click the Kill button.

In the Linuxconf application, when you are satisfied with the selections you have made, click Accept.

If you click the Name Server Specification option on the left side of Linuxconf, it will open a screen that will allow you to enter your DNS IP addresses, as shown in Figure 4-27.

The screen name, Resolver Configuration, gives you an idea as to what these lines do in the configuration of your Network. These parameters enable your system to access the Internet via your network.

Click the checkbox next to DNS for normal operation. An interesting fact about the Default domain line is that it will blank out if you enter a Search domain a few lines down. This is perfectly normal; if it happens, it means your configuration is using a search domain instead of a default domain.

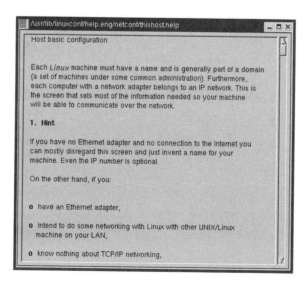

Figure 4-26

You can get specific help on any of the fields in Linuxconf.

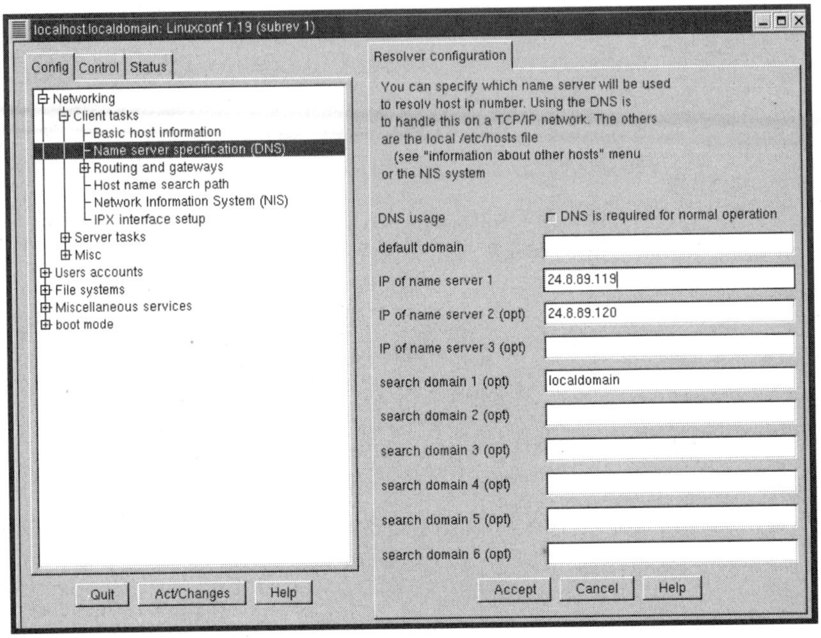

Figure 4-27

Domain
nameserver
information is
entered here.

Nameserver 1 is usually your gateway IP address. If you have been given additional name server IPs, enter them into the boxes below Nameserver 1. Having more methods for your computer to access the Internet increases the speed and reliability of your connections. This helps balance the loading of your ISP's servers and system. When you are satisfied with your entries, click Accept. Then close Linuxconf. You will be asked to activate the changes you have made as the application shuts down.

If you have entered the correct information in Linuxconf, you should now be able to connect to the Internet and to the other TCP/IP computers on your network.

Now that you have gotten connected, it's time to show you how to install other types of peripherals on you PC, beginning with the most ubiquitous peripheral of all: the printer.

Printers

Early computers did not communicate well. The first digital calculating device that could safely be called a computer was the Harvard Mark I, a five-ton, 750,000-component device that read its programming code from paper tape and its data from punch cards. Data was output on a similar medium.

Multimedia was a bit of a wash as well. The only sound the Mark I generated was the internal clicking of its components, which sounded a bit like a "roomful of ladies knitting." Hardly multimedia.

For those of you old enough to remember the Apple I and II microcomputers released in 1973, you'll recall that they weren't big on multimedia, either. Little beeps and clicks were about all the sound they emitted. Printing was coming along, though, as dot-matrix printers wound out reams of perforated paper.

Today, the number of communication devices that can be connected to PCs is phenomenal. Printers, speakers, television tuners, cameras, alarm systems . . . even cars.

Well, you might get me on stating that cars act as peripherals for PCs—but how long until it no longer becomes a joke? Commercially available GPS signals can place you within about 50 yards of your true location. (Military signals are a lot more defined, so the technology is farther along than you might think.) Video devices can see and process digital input faster than you and I can think, and the proliferation of information that's available now to assist motorists can be harnessed with ease—tying traffic, weather, and construction reports together to assist the driver's route from point A to point B.

In the meantime, you can focus on more immediate concerns, such as getting your own peripheral communication devices hooked up to your Linux PC.

For example, think about this: you can make a book on your PC. Right now. All you need are some good typing skills and about three cases of soda and you're set. Believe me, I know.

This may not seem like such a big deal to you, because you are likely accustomed to the PC/printer combination. But a mere two decades ago, there would have been little chance that you could find software and printers capable enough to perform such a feat. Thirty years ago, you would not have had a chance.

Again, what's the big deal? It's just technological advancement, right? True, but it is also a huge shift in social dynamics as well. No longer is the ability to distribute and publish information in the hands of a select few. Now almost anyone with the will can generate published works. This decentralization is aided by the nature of the Internet, which provides even more avenues of communication. Now a writer can generate work and send it electronically, letting the reader print it out as needed.

Linux, like any other operating system worth its salt, can use printers seamlessly from any application with a print function. First, though, you need be sure that communication occurs between Linux and your printer, whether connected directly or through a network.

Adding a Local Printer

Printers can either be local to your own PC or can exist on a network. Either way, accessing them in Linux is not difficult, especially where you work with a local printer.

Local printers are almost always connected to your PC's parallel port—the device known as lp in Linux. In DOS and Windows, the ports are named lpt1, lpt2, and so on; in Linux they are given the nomenclature lp0, lp1, etc.

It's important to remember that Linux handles devices as extensions of its file system. Any files to be printed are first converted to something the printer can use through Ghostscript, a utility that uses an additional printer filter to perform the conversion. Once the conversion is finished, the data is then loaded into the device's file system directory; i.e., the printer's file system directory. Finally, the data is automatically read by the device (in this case, the printer).

Now you will learn the steps necessary to connect a printer to your Linux system.

1. Click the Main Menu icon to open the Main Menu.

2. Choose Programs, System, Control Panel. The Control Panel will open (see Figure 4-28).

3. Click the printer icon to start the Red Hat Linux Print System Manager.

4. Before the Print System Manager starts the first time, an Error dialog box may appear warning you that ncpfs is not installed. If you do not intend to ever connect to printers through NetWare, click Ignore (see Figure 4-29).

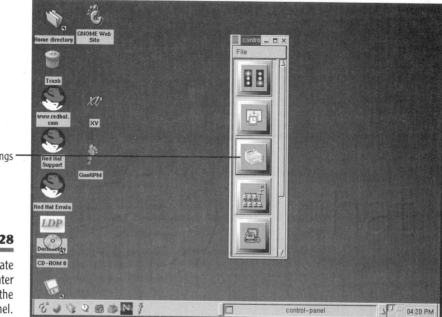

Printer settings

Figure 4-28

You can create and edit printer settings from the Control Panel.

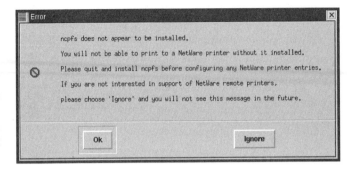

Figure 4-29

Print System Manager's cautious message about NetWare.

5. The Red Hat Linux Print System Manager will be displayed, as seen in Figure 4-30. Click Add to begin the printer connection process.

6. The first dialog box to appear is the Add a Printer Entry dialog box, as shown in Figure 4-31. Select the Local Printer option, then click OK to continue.

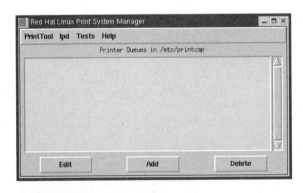

Figure 4-30

A list of all printers connected to your PC will be displayed in the Print System Manager.

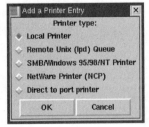

Figure 4-31

You can specify the type of printer you want to add.

7. A message box appears indicating what ports, if any, Linux was able to detect. Although not critical, it is important that Linux detects the port. Click OK to continue.

8. The Edit Local Printer Entry dialog box appears (see Figure 4-32). Linux typically auto-detects the active printer port, completing the Printer Device and remaining fields for you. If needed, however, type **/dev/lp**X in the Printer Device field, where X is the number of the device, starting with 0.

9. To select your printer device, click the Select button that appears adjacent to the Input Filter field. This opens the Configure Filter dialog box (see Figure 4-33).

10. Select your printer from the Printer Type list.

Figure 4-32

Many device parameters are entered in this dialog box.

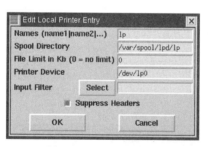

Figure 4-33

Choose your printer filter here.

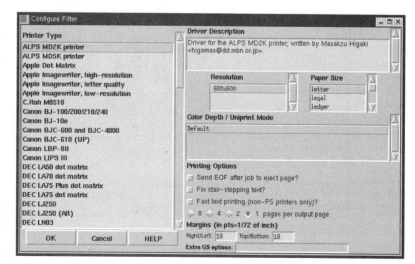

TIP

If your printer does not appear on the list, try getting the latest version of Ghostscript from the Red Hat FTP site, which lists additional filters.

11. Select the default resolution and paper size settings you want to use, as well as any available color depth settings (see Figure 4-34).

TIP

If you have a choice of printers to buy in the future and you're worried about compatibility, I recommend choosing a PostScript printer. No matter what the model, the printer language for PostScript printers is consistent.

12. Click OK to finish the filter settings. The Input Filter field in the Edit Local Printer Entry dialog now displays the selected filter (see Figure 4-35).

13. Click OK to continue. The Print System Manager now lists the new printer (see Figure 4-36).

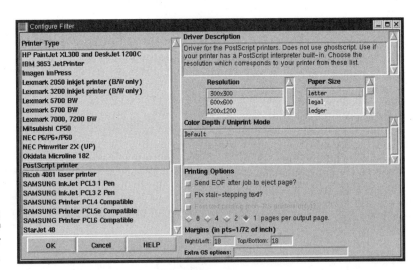

Figure 4-34

Fine-tuning your printer settings.

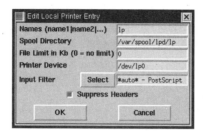

Figure 4-35

A completed set of printer parameters.

Figure 4-36

A connected printer.

Adding a Network Printer

Getting to a printer on a network is no big deal, either. There are three types of network printers that Linux can be configured to use:

- UNIX/Linux printers
- Windows printers
- Netware printers

Configuring these printer types is similar to configuring a local printer. However, rather than pointing the data to a device directory in the local file system, the data is directed to a remote printer's queue—the storage area where print jobs are held until printed.

Table 4-2 illustrates the information you will need to connect to a remote printer for each network type.

TABLE 4-2 REMOTE PRINTER SETTINGS

Network	Protocol	Other Values
UNIX/Linux	TCP/IP	Remote Host Remote Queue
Windows	TCP/IP	Hostname of Printer Server IP Number of Server Printer Name User Password Workgroup
Netware	Netware	Printer Server Name Print Queue Name User Password

When printing to a network printer, it is important that the network recognize the user name and password of the Linux user. In a UNIX or Linux scenario, this is a given; but you must make sure the incoming Linux user has access rights to the network print queue.

In Netware, the user must have rights to access a network printer. In Windows, the printer itself must be set to be "shared" first, as you will see in the following steps.

CAUTION The user names and passwords used to access a remote Netware or Windows printer must be different from any user names and passwords that access your Linux PC. The printer passwords are stored unencrypted before being used by Netware nprint or the Samba smbclient programs. Be creative!

TIP Connecting to a Windows printer, a common scenario, will entail the use of Samba, the tool needed to converse with Windows machines. While the configuration of Samba is a bit beyond the scope of this book, an excellent tutorial on Samba configuration can be found at **http://www.linuxnewbie.org/nhf/intel/network/samba/samba1.html**. Presuming your Samba settings are configured correctly, you should have little trouble connecting to a Windows printer.

1. Click the Main Menu icon to open the Main Menu.

2. Choose Programs, System, Control Panel. The Control Panel will open.

3. Click the printer icon to start the Red Hat Linux Print System Manager.

4. Click Add. The Add a Printer Entry dialog box appears.

5. Select the SMB/Windows 95/NT Printer option, then click OK to continue. A warning box will appear, emphasizing the point about password caution (see Figure 4-37).

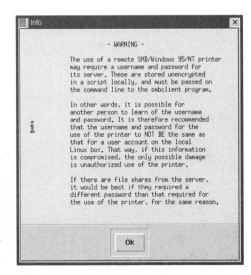

Figure 4-37

It can't be said enough: don't use passwords that can compromise your Linux PC.

6. Complete the Edit dialog box. Be sure to use the exact spellings of the names for your network devices.

7. Click the Select button (adjacent to the Input Filter field) to open the Configure Filter dialog box.

 TIP Be sure that your Windows printer is set to "shared."

8. Select the filter that matches the remote printer configuration.

9. Once the printer is selected, select the default resolution and paper size settings, as well as any available color depth settings.

10. Click OK to finish the filter settings. The Input Filter field in the Edit SMB/Windows 95/NT Printer Entry dialog will display the selected filter.

11. Click OK to continue. The Print System Manager will now display the new network printer (see Figure 4-38).

Sound

One of the most popular peripherals today is a sound device. No computer should be without one. Applications use sounds in increasingly creative ways to generate signals about what's going on. Games rely heavily

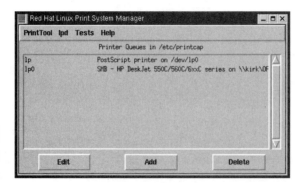

Figure 4-38

The new network printer.

on sound to put you into the action. And don't get me started on the Internet: entire radio and television broadcasts are now made available.

All of this sound content is worthless, though, without a decent sound device. Sound devices are typically composed of two sets of components: a sound card and a set of speakers. As you learned Friday evening, Red Hat Linux is able to support quite a few types of sound cards, which are the heart of a PC sound system.

 TIP Speakers will work with any sound card—the interface is pretty standard. This is not to say you should not give the purchase of speakers any thought. If you're going to get speakers, get mid- to high-quality speakers. This is one area where I think more investment is worthwhile.

When Red Hat is first installed, your sound card will likely be configured automatically. On the off chance that it is not configured, don't worry. Setting up a sound card is not hard to do.

Configuring Sound with the sndconfig Utility

The sndconfig application is used by Linux to configure sound. sndconfig is a command-line, text-based program and needs to run independently of X in the console. You cannot reliably run it from a terminal emulation window.

 NOTE For illustration and demonstration purposes, the sndconfig screens in Figures 4-39 through 4-43 appear in a terminal window. This is only for demonstration. Kids, don't try this at home.

 TIP To access the Linux console from any X mode, press Ctrl+Alt+F1. To return to X from Linux, press Alt+F7.

1. Click the Gnome Configuration Tool icon in the Gnome Panel.

2. Click the Sound category to open the Sound pane in the Control Center.

3. Make sure both Enable options are checked, especially the Enable Sound Server Startup option.

4. Click OK to close the Control Center.

5. Press Ctrl+Alt+F1 to go to the Linux command line.

6. Log in as root.

7. Type **sndconfig** to begin the application. The Introduction screen will appear (see Figure 4-39).

8. Press Enter to accept the selected OK button. The next screen should display the results of a probe of all of your computer's PCI devices. If any sound cards are displayed, the probe was successful (see Figure 4-40).

9. Press Enter to continue. A message appears advising that the conf.modules file will be overwritten.

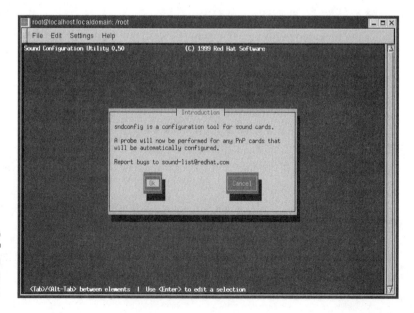

Figure 4-39

The first screen of the sndconfig utility.

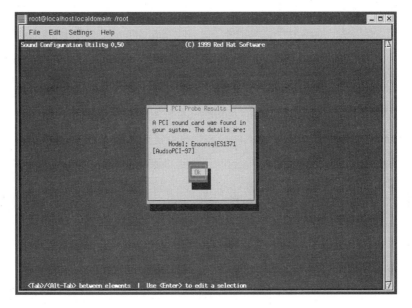

Figure 4-40

Finding your
sound card.

10. Press Enter to continue. sndconfig will inform you that it will now
    test the sound card by playing a sound sample (see Figure 4-41).

11. Press Enter to continue. A sample sound will play. (If you heard the
    sample, you will know the right way to pronounce "Linux," from
    the man himself, Linus Torvalds.)

12. If you heard the sound sample, press Enter to accept the selected
    Yes button. You can then proceed to Step 19.

13. If you did not hear the sample, press the Tab key to select the No
    button. Then press Enter. A message appears stating that autocon-
    figuration has failed.

14. Press Enter to continue to the manual configuration process. The
    Card Type window will be displayed (see Figure 4-42).

15. Scroll though the list to select your card. When selected, press Tab
    to select OK and then press Enter to continue. The next screen
    enables you to select the port and IRQ settings for the card (see
    Figure 4-43).

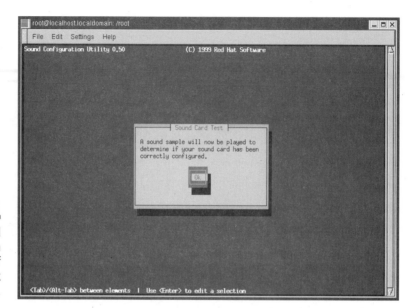

Figure 4-41

Testing your sound card and getting an answer to one of the great Linux mysteries.

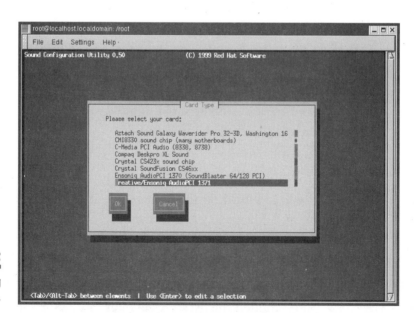

Figure 4-42

Manually selecting a card type.

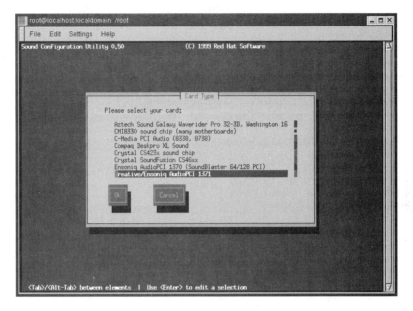

Figure 4-43

Selecting the sound card's port and IRQ settings.

TIP This should be information you acquired last night. However, if you are not sure of the settings, check your card's documentation. If your PC has a Windows partition, you might want to stop this process for now, boot to the Windows partition, and then check the settings used by Windows for the card.

16. Once again, press Tab until OK is selected, and then press Enter to continue.

17. The Sound Sample screen reappears. Select OK and press Enter to continue.

18. If the sample was heard, highlight Yes and press Enter to end the sndconfig program.

19. Log out of this X session and log back in to activate these changes.

Applying Sounds to Events

Once your sound card is configured, you can have sounds play at key events such as at an application's opening or closing. This capability will allow you to further personalize your PC.

1. Click the Gnome Configuration Tool icon in the Gnome Panel.

2. Click the Sound category to open the Sound pane in the Control Center.

3. Click the Sound Events tab.

4. Scroll through the list of events, selecting the one you want to change.

5. Click Browse to open the Select Sound File dialog box (see Figure 4-45).

6. Select the file name for the sound you want to use, and then click OK. You will be returned to the Control Center.

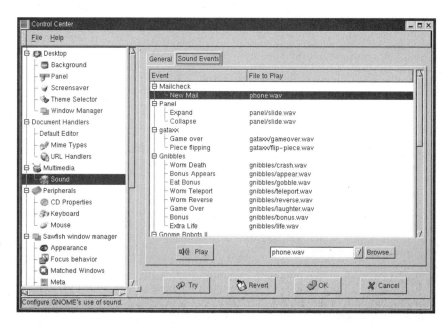

Figure 4-44

You can browse sounds before applying them to system events.

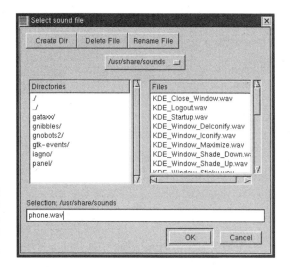

Figure 4-45

You can use
sounds from any
WAV file source.

7. Click Play to hear the sound sample. If you like the sample, click OK to save the configuration and close the Control Center.

TIP Don't go too crazy applying sounds to your events. You'd be amazed at how tiresome it becomes hearing Homer Simpson saying "Doh!" with every menu selection.

Plug and Play Using the ISAPNPTOOLS Utility

If you have a newer PC, then it is very likely that you have a PCI bus on your motherboard. PCI busses are nice for Linux users because Plug and Play technology is built into the bus itself. Any device connected to a PCI bus, therefore, is likely to be detected by Red Hat Linux.

Older PCs, however, have ISA busses, with which Red Hat Linux needs a little help. Linux must probe an ISA device more directly to determine whether it is Plug and Play.

◀◀◀

Plug and Play (PnP): The ability for expansion cards and peripheral devices to be automatically configured.

◀◀◀

◀◀◀

PCI (Peripheral Component Interconnect) Bus: a local bus standard developed by Intel Corporation. PCI is a 64-bit bus, although it is usually implemented as a 32-bit bus.

◀◀◀

◀◀◀

ISA (Industry Standard Architecture) Bus: The bus architecture used in the IBM PC/XT and PC/AT. Most computers made today include both an ISA bus for slower devices and a PCI bus for devices that require better performance.

◀◀◀

If your PC has an ISA device that is not recognized by Linux, you can use the isapnptools set of applications to help configure the device.

Performing a PnP Dump

The first thing you need to do is to perform a scan of all existing ISA PnP cards on your PC. This is done using the pnpdump application—an apt name for the program since it takes all of the PnP information and "dumps" it into the isapnp.conf file. From there, the isapnp application can configure the isapnp.conf file. Follow these steps to get the information you need:

◆◆

Because pnpdump will try to use real-time scheduling to get the right I/O port settings, all other programs will be locked while pnpdump runs. For this reason, do not run pnpdump from within X, as the terminal emulation window will be locked as well.

◆◆

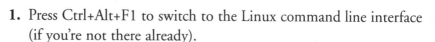

1. Press Ctrl+Alt+F1 to switch to the Linux command line interface (if you're not there already).

2. Log in as root.

3. Type **/sbin/pnpdump > /etc/isapnp.conf**.

4. Check and record the settings for all other devices so that you will avoid conflicts when setting up your ISA devices. Type the following commands, each on a separate line, to obtain other device information:

   ✪ cat /proc/dma

   ✪ cat /proc/interrupts

   ✪ cat /proc/ioports

   ✪ cat /proc/pci

Editing the isapnp.conf File

Now that the isapnp.conf file is made, you can use the isapnp utility to configure your devices, as seen in the following steps.

1. At the Linux console, while logged in as root, type **/sbin/isapnp /etc/isapnp.conf**.

2. isapnp will open and display the results of the pnpdump. If any ISA boards were found, remove the comment characters preceding the device listing. This will enable Linux to activate the board.

  NOTE   For more information on the format of the isapnp.conf file, see the isapnp Tools Home Page at **http://www.roestock.demon.co.uk/isapnptools/**.

3. Edit the values listed so that they match your card's exact specifications.

  TIP   If isapnp is not installed, you can use a text editor such as emacs to edit the file.

Conclusion

This evening's chapter led you through a lengthy exploration of how to configure your Linux system to connect to the Internet via a dial-up or network connection.

You also learned the finer points of connecting important peripheral devices to your computer. As Linux continues to grow, more and more devices will be included in the Linux world. Ideally, this will cause the Linux configuration methods to become more simplified. Until that day, I can only stress that you use patience and care when dealing with peripheral set up.

It's time to stop for this evening. Tomorrow morning begins with how to install additional software on your Red Hat PC, as well as additional techniques to install new hardware.

Adding to Your Linux System

✿ Installing Software Packages

✿ Using Setup Applications

✿ Adding New Hardware and Peripherals

Good morning!

Welcome to Sunday morning. If this is time you usually spend in bed, don't worry. This morning's chapter will be relatively painless.

It's time to talk about what you can do to add on to your Linux PC system. Linux, like every other operating system, does not come fully loaded with every application you can think of (though it does better than others). So, now is the time to learn how to add software to your new Linux system.

Now is also the time to learn more about expanding your PC's hardware. Admittedly, you may have all of your hardware needs set by this morning, but one trip to the computer superstore may change that in a hurry. And when you begin to drool over that Whiz-Bang 2000, you'll know how to get it installed onto your Linux system—or find out how to get help doing so.

In this morning's chapter, you'll:

○ Learn how to install software using RPM packages
○ Install software using archived setup files
○ Add hardware to your system
○ Help Linux auto-detect new hardware

After you master these skills, you will be able to add new applications and peripherals to your Linux system anytime you want.

Installing Software Packages

One of the biggest complaints heard about Red Hat Linux (and Linux in general) is its apparent lack of software applications. What good is an operating system that doesn't run anything useful?

First off, this is simply not the case. As experienced Linux users know, thousands of applications run on Linux. The misconception lies in the fact that many of these applications are either very, very specific in their performed tasks, or they are designed to run completely in the background from the command line. In either case, it becomes a case of "out of sight, out of mind." A Linux application is not perceived as "real" by an inexperienced observer unless that observer can see and manipulate the application. This novice mentality infuriates long-time Linux users— and for good reason, since there are thousands of perfectly good apps ready for the Linux platform.

When you install one of these many applications on Red Hat Linux, there are three ways of accomplishing the task: using packages, using the original source code, or using a third-party setup program. Each of these methods will be examined this morning.

Understanding Packaging

Nothing is more exciting than opening a new package. (Okay, well, a few things are more exciting.) You must admit, however, it's kind of cool to crack open that cardboard box and riffle through the Styrofoam peanuts to find that special item you've always wanted.

Packages are great ways of moving objects around. They keep items together and they keep the items protected from both the elements and postal workers. The idea of a package can be used electronically as well. Many of you have already used compressed files, such as Zip, gzip, or tar.

These compressed files are essentially packages of separate files that are all mashed together into one compact file, like that box of peanuts.

Red Hat has developed a methodology to package the open source code of Linux and its applications into packages as well. This method has proven so popular that many of the other Linux distributions have incorporated it into their toolsets as well. This method uses the RPM (Red Hat Package Manager) to track packages and their contents during application installation.

RPM comes in many forms. Within Linux, it is known simply as RPM; in Gnome, it is GnoRPM; and in KDE, it's referred to as Kpackage. Regardless of its form, the procedure the application follows is always the same: Linux examines a package and RPM determines whether all of the files necessary for the application to function are contained within the package or anywhere else on your Linux system. This procedure is called a dependency check, and it's one of RPM's great features.

The average application requires a lot of code to run, especially in a graphic environment. If all of the necessary code were included within every application, the executable files would be huge. To circumvent this, programmers often make use of code libraries, which are essentially redundant pieces of code necessary or useful to all applications. Why make a section of code to create a dialog box when a library of code already has the appropriate information? As a programmer, now all you must do is create a command in your program that references the necessary code in the correct library. Thus, your application is smaller, faster, and easier to install.

The catch in all of this is that the user's PC must have the correct type and version of the code library present for use by the application. This is where RPM comes in handy. RPM looks at the packaged application and determines what code libraries (or any other helper application) are required for the packaged application to work. The neat thing is that RPM will look at all packages on your PC. If something is missing, it tells you what you still need to perform a successful installation.

Finally, after the dependencies have been cleared, RPM will enable you to install new applications or upgrade existing ones. The next two sections will examine both ways to use RPM.

Installing a New Desktop Environment

On Saturday afternoon, you saw how simple it was to switch between the Gnome and KDE desktop environments. Upon installing Red Hat, however, you could choose both environments. For the sake of this example, let's say you only installed Gnome, and now you want to try KDE. Here's how you could go about it.

 NOTE Installing an environment usually requires more than one package. If you learn how to do this, then the installation of a single-package application will be a breeze.

1. Click the Main Menu icon to open the Main Menu.
2. Choose Programs, System, GnoRPM. The Gnome RPM window will open (see Figure 5-1).

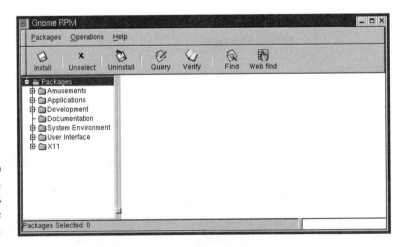

Figure 5-1

Installation typically begins with the Gnome RPM.

3. Click on the Install button. The Install dialog box will open and will begin to scan the Red Hat Linux CD-ROM for available RPM packages (see Figure 5-2).

4. To install KDE on your Gnome workstation, first expand the System Environment category, then expand the Libraries subcategory.

5. Select the kdelibs and kdesupport packages. Selected packages are indicated with check marks, as seen in Figure 5-3.

6. Expand the User Interface category and then the Desktops subcategory.

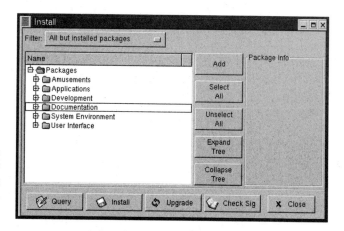

Figure 5-2

Pick and choose the applications you want to install.

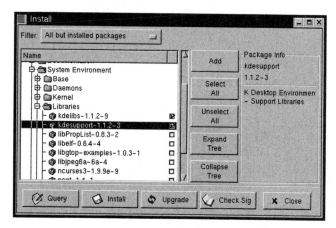

Figure 5-3

Selecting packages to install.

7. Select the kdebase and switchdesk-kde packages.

TIP

If your monitor does not display colors, be sure to select the kdebase-lowcolor-icons package as well.

8. Expand the Amusements category and then the Games subcategory.

9. Select the kdegames package.

10. Click Install to begin the installation process. A dialog box appears that displays the progress of the installation (see Figure 5-4).

NOTE

Don't worry if you miss a package when installing a multi-package set like the KDE desktop environment. If something is missing, a message box will appear informing you of dependencies that you need to add. Just select the necessary packages and click Install again.

11. When complete, click Close.

12. Click the Close application icon to close Gnome RPM.

Using the Update Agent

The need to fix what is broken and improve what works is a big driving force in human history, and software engineering is no different. Because we live in a universe of entropy and chaos, it should come as no surprise that the software in the nice white and red box has some flaws. It is, quite literally, a law of nature.

Figure 5-4

Monitor the process of installing your packages.

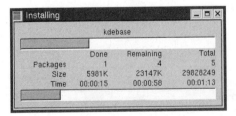

To combat these flaws and improve existing features, Red Hat has provided a great tool in this release of Linux: the Update Agent.

The Update Agent is an application that will monitor your installed applications and check the Red Hat FTP site for any newer versions of your programs that might be available. If any are found, the agent will present to you a Web-based list from which you can select the applications you want to upgrade. Update Agent will then coordinate downloading of the packages.

This procedure is outlined in the following steps.

1. Click the Main Menu icon to open the Main Menu.

2. Choose Programs, System, Update Agent. The Red Hat Update Agent window will open (see Figure 5-5).

NOTE When using Update Agent, be sure you are already connected to the Internet and have already registered your product with Red Hat at **http://www.redhat.com/now**.

3. To begin using the Update Agent for the first time, click Configure. The Configuration - Up2Date dialog box will appear (see Figure 5-6).

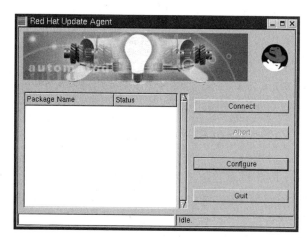

Figure 5-5

The Red Hat Update Agent, ready for action.

Configuration – Up2Date

User | Retrieval | Exceptions

Registration

User name: bproffit

Registration Key: 234dfg5678gaga33

E-Mail Addresses

Add new: authorboy@indiana.net   Add

Edit

Remove

OK   Cancel

Figure 5-6

User information is entered in the first panel of the Configuration dialog box.

4. Enter the name you used when you originally registered your Linux software with Red Hat. You'll need to also provide the registration key from the Personal Product ID card, found in the Red Hat Linux documentation.

5. Enter at least one e-mail address in the Add New field and click Add. You may enter additional e-mail addresses, if applicable.

6. When finished, click the Retrieval tab to open its panel, as shown in Figure 5-7.

7. Verify that the Package Server settings are set to priority.redhat.com.

TIP To retain control over the upgrading process, be sure to select Retrieve Packages, But Do Not Install.

8. Select Red Hat Linux 7 as the override version. Leave the default package storage directory as is, but make a note of the path for later use.

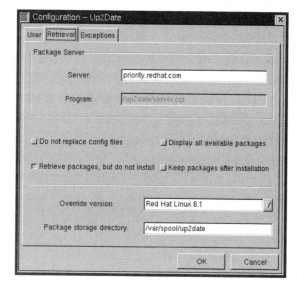

Figure 5-7

You must indicate from where the Update Agent will locate package information.

9. Click the Exceptions tab to open its panel, shown in Figure 5-8.

10. The Exceptions panel allows you to skip announced packages and files. To skip additional packages or files, click Add.

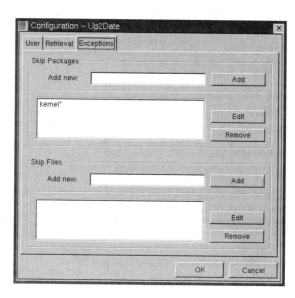

Figure 5-8

You can choose to skip downloading certain package types.

CAUTION

♦ ♦

It is not recommended you allow Update Agent to download and install kernel upgrades, so you should make sure that the `kernel*` exception is present in the Skip Packages section.

♦ ♦

11. When finished, click OK. Update Agent is now configured for future use.

12. Click Connect. Update Agent will poll the priority FTP site to determine whether needed updates are available.

13. If any packages are found for those included in the Exceptions panel, a list of those packages will appear in a Warning dialog box (see Figure 5-9). Click OK to continue.

14. The Update Agent will process and then display a Web page detailing what packages are available. You can select specific packages and then click Request Selected Packages. Alternatively, you can simply click Request ALL Packages.

15. The download process will begin, as shown in Figure 5-10. A red arrow indicates those packages that were successfully downloaded. When downloading is complete, click Quit.

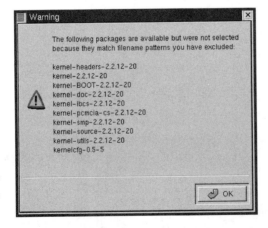

Figure 5-9

Package exceptions will be listed.

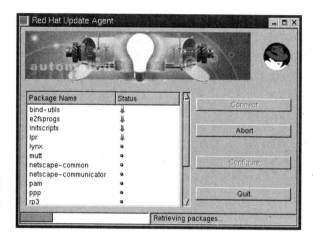

Figure 5-10

Downloading the selected packages.

Now that the updated packages reside on your local PC, you can install them using GnoRPM, as detailed in the previous section. The only difference in the procedure is that you will now need to locate the packages on your PC by clicking Add while in the Install dialog box. Once the packages are selected, you will then need to select the Upgrade option rather than Install.

Installing Software with Setup

As more applications are built for Linux, the size and complexity of the applications will increase. As this happens, developers will start using entire setup applications to install programs. Windows users are very familiar with these type of setup applications—virtually every application makes use of an installation program of some type.

Using similar installation programs in Linux is just as simple. The following steps demonstrate how to install StarOffice, a robust and free office suite, on Red Hat Linux.

NOTE You can download the StarOffice installation file from **www.sun.com/staroffice**. Follow the instructions on the Web site to get the file free of charge.

1. Open a Terminal window on your Gnome or KDE desktop and navigate to the directory where you saved the installation file.

TIP You may need to type **chmode 777 *.bin** on the command line before starting the setup in order to give yourself permission to run the downloaded file.

2. Type **./so-5_2-ga-bin-linux-en.bin**. This starts the installation program as shown in Figure 5-11.

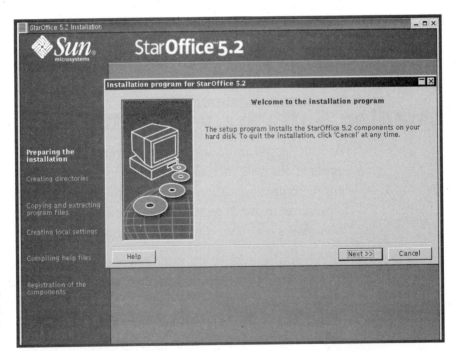

Figure 5-11

The StarOffice Installation Program.

3. The first dialog box welcomes you and tells you how to quit the program. Click Next to continue.

4. In the second dialog box (see Figure 5-12), you see the Important Information dialog box, which essentially displays the README file. Read the contents and click next to continue.

5. The next dialog box presents the Sun license agreement to you (see Figure 5-13). Read it carefully and click Accept if you agree to its stipulations.

6. In the fourth screen, enter your personal data and click Next.

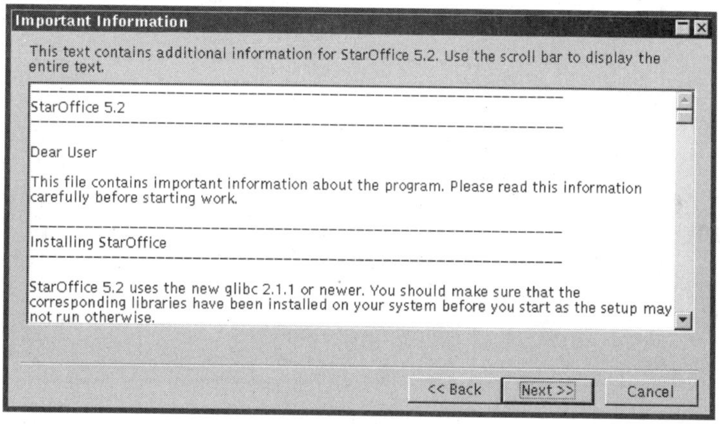

Figure 5-12

A good chance to read the README file.

Figure 5-13

Good reading? No, but important nonetheless.

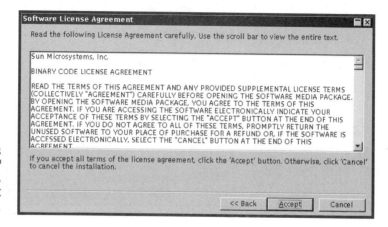

7. Choose which installation type you want, as shown in Figure 5-14. For now, select the Standard Installation choice and click Next to continue. Don't worry, you can always come back later to customize your settings.

8. Choose the directory to which you want to install StarOffice (see Figure 5-15). The suggested default directory is usually a safe bet. Click Next to continue.

9. When asked whether you want to create the directory name you entered or accepted, click Yes.

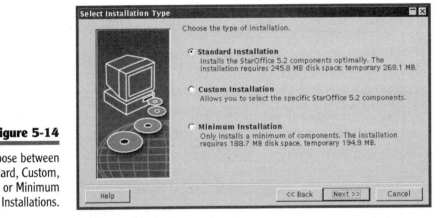

Figure 5-14

Choose between Standard, Custom, or Minimum Installations.

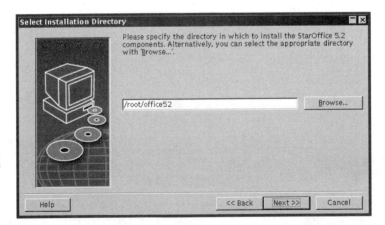

Figure 5-15

Select the installation directory.

10. You have reached the end of this section of the installation journey (see Figure 5-16). Click Complete, then sit back and relax while installation is completed.

TIP If the setup application cannot find a Java environment on your PC, it asks you what, if any, Java environment you want StarOffice to use. If you do not plan to use the StarOffice browser as your main Web browser—which I don't recommend—then there's no problem. Netscape or any other browser will contain its own Java capabilities. Just click No Support for Java or JavaScript and then click OK to continue. StarOffice now continues its installation, as shown in Figure 5-17.

11. Near the end of the installation process, a message box appears indicating that StarOffice was added to the KDE—Panel (even if KDE is not your default desktop environment). It also advises that you should restart KDE to complete the installation for that environment. Click OK to continue.

12. At the very end of the process, the Installation Complete dialog box appears. Click Complete to end the setup program.

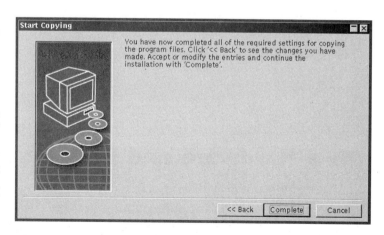

Figure 5-16

You have given StarOffice all the information it needs. Click Complete and let it do the work.

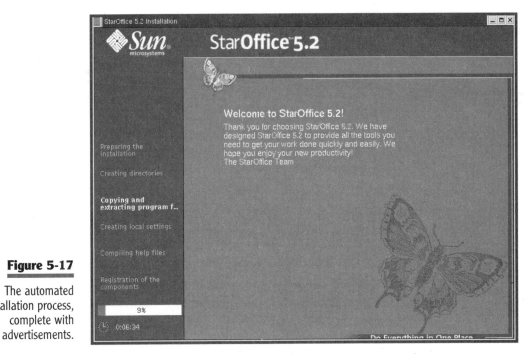

Figure 5-17

The automated installation process, complete with advertisements.

When you want to start StarOffice in KDE, you'll find it within the Application Starter menu. In Gnome, the fastest way to start StarOffice is to create a new Launcher in the Gnome window or panel, as you learned how to do on Saturday afternoon.

Now that you know how to install extra software, let's talk about adding new hardware to your PC.

Adding New Hardware and Peripherals

Last night, we dealt with some key hardware issues you might run across early in the initial Linux configuration process. After all, you typically need to get your printer, sound card, and any plug-and-play devices working right away.

This morning we're going to delve a little deeper into the hardware foray and examine what steps you need to take to ensure the success of any hardware installation.

Adding new hardware to a system consists of two phases: the hardware phase and the software phase. You need to add the hardware device to the system, and you need to tell your operating system how to manage it. The hardware phase is machine-dependent, and the software phase is operating system-dependent. Assuming you are working on a PC, regardless of its brand (AT, ATX, IBM, Compaq, etc.), installing new hardware is straightforward and is the same whether you are using Linux or some other operating system. The interface of the PC system is designed in such a way that any device can be accessed in a standard and documented method, and any operating system can then handle it. (We'll discuss a few exceptions to this rule later this morning.)

For the remainder of the morning, we'll discuss both phases. I'll put heavier emphasis on the second phase, because it is perhaps the most confusing. You may have installed new devices such as printers or sound cards in the past, but you may not be familiar with the way Linux handles them. First, you will see the various types of devices, including internal and external ones, with a warning about those devices you can safely install and those you should not touch unless you are a computer expert. Next, you'll explore the software phase. You will learn how the Linux kernel detects and configures hardware devices. Finally, you'll learn about the various configuration files and how you can change parameters for your new devices.

Similar to the steps you took on Friday evening before installing Red Hat Linux, before you begin any hardware installation you should check the hardware compatibility list to see if your device is Linux-compatible. In theory, any device conforming to the standards in PC technologies should work. However, in recent years many companies have started to make devices that were missing several important chips, and then using proprietary drivers to do their work. While making devices less expensive to the public, this strategy has resulted in two big side effects. The drivers are published for Windows 95/98 only, and, since the hardware device cannot work without the special Windows driver, it is incompatible with Linux or any operating system other than Windows. Secondly, the driver needs to do much more work, which means that your CPU will be busy doing what the chips were supposed to do. Hence, your system will feel much slower, even in Windows. The sad thing about this is that most of these components, commonly referred as *winmodems* and *winprinters*, are not identified as such on the packages. Contacting the manufacturer is often the only way you can be sure.

Adding New Devices

In this section, you will see the different types of devices that you can add to a personal computer, and how they differ from each other. Table 5-1

TABLE 5-1 COMMON HARDWARE DEVICES

Device	Internal/ External	Type of Plug	Auto-Detected?
Modems	External	COM port (/dev/cua0)	No, easy to set up
Modems	Internal	ISA or PCI	No, configuration needed
Monitors	External	VGA port	Yes
Video cards	Internal	PCI or AGP	In text mode: yes; in GUI mode: no
RAM	Internal	Sockets	Yes
Sound cards	Internal	ISA or PCI	No, configuration needed
Mice	External	COM port (/dev/cua0)	Yes, for standard models

lists a few common hardware devices and their specifications, which may help you to configure them.

Adding External Devices

External devices are the easiest to add because you simply plug them in. Further, because no vital system part is outside of the case, you don't risk corrupting your machine. You can install an external device even if you are still new to computers. For example, to add a printer, simply connect the printer cable to both the printer and the back of the computer, and then plug in the power supply.

There are many external devices. Most people who add components to their computer will add an external device since such devices are both simple to plug in and abundant in today's computer market. Specific devices exist for each of the ports on the back of your system, and, since they all have different socket sizes, you really can't connect the wrong device to the wrong port. For example, a standard parallel printer port is a female connection with 25 holes, and a mouse or modem serial port is a male connection containing either 9 or 25 pins. You already know how to connect a printer to your machine. Any other external device (keyboard, monitor, mouse, Zip drive, Ethernet-based cable modem) is just as easy.

While it will probably not damage your system to connect an Ethernet cable to the Ethernet socket in your system while the power is still on, it is generally recommended that you turn off the power before adding any new device. Most manuals also warn you of this fact. This will allow three things: The system BIOS will attempt to detect the new device when you reboot; the kernel auto-detect process will detect the device; and the device will benefit from a fresh system start. Some devices won't work right if they are plugged in while the power is on, especially external removable drives. Note that this does not apply to hot-swappable devices, such as special RAID arrays or rack-mounted servers, but most personal desktop systems don't use these device types.

Adding Internal Devices

Internal devices are more difficult to install only because they require you to work inside your computer case. Thankfully, very few devices still need to be added in this way. With the advent of external removable devices such as the Iomega Zip drive and the universal serial bus (USB), it isn't necessary to crack open the case of computers nearly as often. The most common internal devices are sound cards, network cards, and hard drives. In most systems, you can also add memory, change the motherboard, or even upgrade the CPU, although I would advise you against doing so unless you know exactly what you are doing. There are factors to consider when changing a CPU and memory such as bus speed, clock multiplier, and memory timing. For a fee, local computer stores will gladly install any internal device you require. This section will briefly show you how to add the three most common internal hardware devices yourself.

First, for your physical safety, you must turn off your computer's power. This warning is especially important when working with internal devices, since you can literally blow up your motherboard or CPU if you try to install internal hardware with the power still on. Once you have removed the screws on your system's case, you can add the device in an empty slot. If you want to add a device that has a standard card, you simply have to insert it next to the other cards in your system. Any slot on the PCI bus (the white ones) will work for a PCI card, any slot on the ISA bus (the black ones) will work for ISA cards, and video cards may go in the recently introduced AGP slot (the gray one). It's easy to determine the three types of slots because each has a different size and color. Just as you can't plug a square peg in a round hole, you can't plug one type of card into another type of slot by accident.

A hard drive is typically added near the front of the system, grouped with the existing hard drives and CD-ROM drives. After positioning the drive, you must connect the power cable and its ribbon. Ribbons connect the drive to its controlling card. (If working with a SCSI hard drive, the SCSI

controller is either on your main board or on a slotted card.) Be sure to refer to the manual for your device for proper installation procedures.

The Kernel Boot Process

After you restore the power, some program code executes to detect and configure devices.

The first code executed when a PC starts is the bootstrap code. This is a small program located in ROM (static memory) inside your computer. The code checks the internal system parts to see if any major failure is detected, such as memory corruption. Control then passes to the BIOS. When your system starts, you can see the memory test as the memory counts up to the amount of RAM you have in your system. The BIOS is the heart of your computer's input/output (I/O) subsystem. Its job is to detect the system components at start time and to work with the operating system to handle device calls. The code that appears on your monitor just after the video card name and before Linux starts is part of the BIOS. You may see a list of hard disks and then an information screen about your main system components. The BIOS is responsible for first detecting your hard disks, determining which one contains the kernel you want to boot, and optionally configuring any Plug and Play devices.

After BIOS completes various functions, it passes control to the first sector of your bootable hard disk (known as the MBR [Master Boot Record]). In older versions of MS-DOS or Windows, the MBR was used to contain DOS-MBR. In Red Hat Linux, it now contains LILO, the Linux boot loader, which simply tells the processor to load your Linux kernel.

NOTE LILO can, in fact, do much more, such as set a password, load many operating systems, and set geometry information for Linux. For the purpose of this morning's chapter, we'll assume that only the kernel is loaded. You can find more information on LILO on your Linux system by typing **man lilo**.

Once the BIOS and LILO have finished executing, the more complex part begins. The Linux kernel takes over to detect, configure, and manage all of the internal and external devices. It does so using complicated data structures, device drivers, and kernel processes. Without going into too many details, the following paragraphs describe the kernel start-up routine and how you can correct problems along the way.

All of the text that appears on the screen before you see the first Linux prompt explains what is being found by the kernel and various device drivers. It is important for you to understand that text so that you can later troubleshoot any hardware problems. A possible example appears in Figure 5-18.

The first line you see reports the kernel version and the version of the compiler that built it. It isn't really important to know this information unless you later want to recompile your kernel. Next, the speed of your CPU appears. The kernel detects that speed at boot time. It should be pretty close to the speed you know your CPU to be. For example, the CPU on the system could be a 333MHz Intel Pentium II. The kernel detected a speed of 334MHz, which is pretty close.

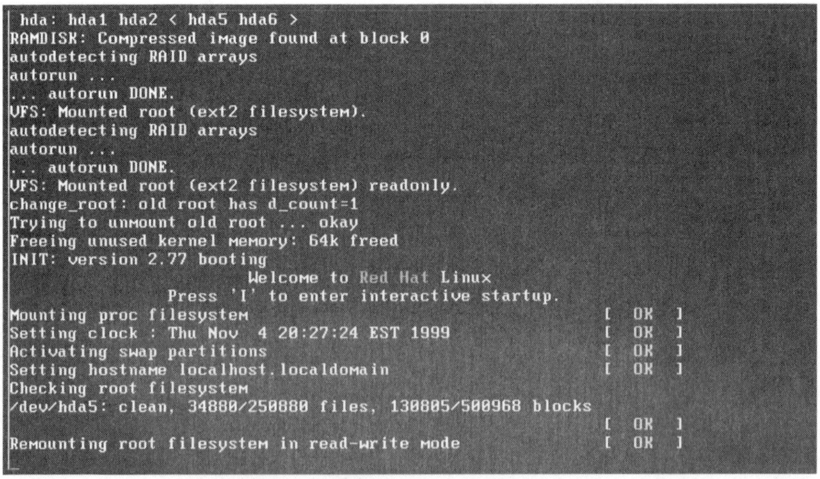

Figure 5-18

The boot process can inform you of any potential problems.

```
hda: hda1 hda2 < hda5 hda6 >
RAMDISK: Compressed image found at block 0
autodetecting RAID arrays
autorun ...
... autorun DONE.
VFS: Mounted root (ext2 filesystem).
autodetecting RAID arrays
autorun ...
... autorun DONE.
VFS: Mounted root (ext2 filesystem) readonly.
change_root: old root has d_count=1
Trying to unmount old root ... okay
Freeing unused kernel memory: 64k freed
INIT: version 2.77 booting
                    Welcome to Red Hat Linux
          Press 'I' to enter interactive startup.
Mounting proc filesystem                           [   OK  ]
Setting clock : Thu Nov  4 20:27:24 EST 1999       [   OK  ]
Activating swap partitions                         [   OK  ]
Setting hostname localhost.localdomain             [   OK  ]
Checking root filesystem
/dev/hda5: clean, 34880/250880 files, 130805/500968 blocks
                                                   [   OK  ]
Remounting root filesystem in read-write mode      [   OK  ]
```

The console line only tells you the currently used display font. You can set your Linux console to display any other font, but the default is standard fixed VGA 80 columns by 25 lines. You should ignore the line about BogoMIPS. It commonly is not the same as your CPU speed, and that is quite normal.

One very important line is the memory line. Here, the kernel is reporting how much RAM it detected in your system. This is a place where the kernel may be mistaken, especially if you have more than 128MB (megabytes) of memory, or if you have an old system. The details as to why this happens are unimportant, but it is easy to fix. For example, if you see a number near 16,000K and you really have 24MB of RAM, you will need to correct the lilo.conf file.

So, sticking with the example, if Red Hat Linux detects 16MB and you know you have 24MB, add the following line to the lilo.conf file:

```
append = "mem=24M"
```

The next lines display information gathered about your CPU. When the kernel has finished setting up the main hardware, it passes control to device drivers. Device drivers are small portions of code that can set up and control a particular device. For example, to handle a Sound Blaster card, you need a Sound Blaster-compatible sound driver. There are also less specific drivers that deal with things such as networking and your serial devices. All of these drivers are loaded at start time.

You should print the boot messages and read them all at least once. This will help you know your hardware a bit more and can help you diagnose problems. If you can't print messages while your system is booting, you can always review them by typing the **dmesg** command at your Linux console. If you have a printer attached, you can print the messages using the command **dmesg |lpr.**

What Is Auto-Detection?

The device drivers must configure your hardware to work with Linux. However, these drivers must first find the hardware. Linux has a very good auto-detection process. In this process, drivers will look for devices at likely places. For example, the NE2000 networking card driver knows that such a card will most likely be located at I/O address 0x300, 0x280, 0x320, 0x340, 0x360, or 0x380. It will probe these addresses to see if a card can be found. If found, a message will appear on the screen when your system starts. If your card is at another address, however, the driver may not find it and you must tell the driver where to look. You can find these settings using a variety of methods. If you have older hardware, you can alter settings using jumpers on the board itself. You can usually find the default settings in the board's manual, including the method used to change them.

Red Hat Linux 7 also has the utility Kudzu that attempts to detect new hardware on startup. Kudzu is an advanced form of device auto-detection. This little program keeps a database of installed hardware and, when the system starts, compares the installed hardware with the database. If new hardware is detected, Kudzu should allow you to configure it. Currently, this utility does not make your job much easier if the Linux kernel doesn't detect your device, but I believe that Red Hat will be moving in that direction in the future. You can review the database by looking at the file /etc/sysconfig/hwconf.

Configuring Your Devices

In the following sections, you will see how to configure any new hardware devices that you have added to your system. First, we'll run through the devices most likely to be detected at boot time, then focus on those that may need more attention from you.

The main devices in a system have device drivers already compiled in the kernel. These devices will be detected on system startup. These include

your CPU, memory, monitor, video card, floppy drive, IDE hard disks, and most CD-ROM drives, which means that most of the times you needn't worry about them. This section focuses on those devices that may not be so easily detected.

If a device is not detected at startup time, you first must determine whether the driver for that component was loaded. A driver can be loaded in two ways: by being compiled into the kernel itself, or by being loaded as a module. While this may seem complex, Red Hat has made it very simple for most devices. In your Red Hat Linux system, you have several graphical utilities that enable you to easily configure new devices. Since most drivers have been compiled into modules, you will seldom need to recompile your kernel.

To know if a device has been detected, you can use the command `cat /proc/devices`. This command lists all devices detected by your Linux system that use an IRQ detected.

Conclusion

This morning you examined two primary methods used to get new software on your PC: RPMs and setup applications. As Linux grows in popularity, you can expect that these processes will become even more automated.

Adding new devices can be a mystery, as you also learned this morning. You add a piece of hardware, and hope that the system will see it. Sometimes it works, sometimes it does not. Then begins the sometimes-complex task of troubleshooting. Thankfully, the Linux system becomes better every year, and with new kernel releases, more hardware is auto-detected. With more users, Linux also has more developers working on drivers for the latest and greatest devices sold at your local computer store.

The current kernel, and the one that comes with Red Hat Linux 7, is version 2.4. I hope that more companies will wake up and start making drivers for Linux and not only for Windows 98. Doing so would help users a great deal, thus solving many problems that exist with unsupported hardware.

This afternoon, you'll take a look at some of the applications that came with Linux; in particular, Netscape Communicator. You'll also explore the application you installed this morning: StarOffice 5.2 for Linux. Once finished, you'll start using Linux instead of configuring it.

Using Some Popular Linux Applications

✿ Using X Window Fonts

✿ Using Netscape Communicator

✿ Using StarOffices for Linux

By now its Sunday afternoon, and after all of this configuring and customizing, you're probably wondering: does Red Hat Linux actually *do* anything?

Indeed it does. For instance, when you hear people comparing Linux to Windows, one of the big gripes you will hear is the perceived lack of available Linux applications. At the moment, Windows has some 100,000-plus applications available. While there are not quite that many Linux applications, the number of available applications is nearer than many realize.

This afternoon, you will:

- ✪ Explore some of the essential tools packaged with Red Hat Linux 7
- ✪ Examine and configure Netscape Communicator to browse the Internet, read your e-mail, and read newsgroup messages
- ✪ Look at the StarOffice 5.2 for Linux application to see how it will give you office-suite power, all for free

Using X Window Tools

Because Linux applications typically are not commercially advertised, they aren't the household words that their Windows counterparts are. Word, WordPerfect, AmiPro—most people have heard of these applications. How many have heard of StarWriter? Not many. Those who have

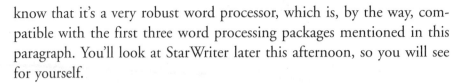

know that it's a very robust word processor, which is, by the way, compatible with the first three word processing packages mentioned in this paragraph. You'll look at StarWriter later this afternoon, so you will see for yourself.

GIMP is another prime example of an application that is just as feature-rich as its Windows counterpart, Adobe PhotoShop, is. Like most of its Linux brethren, GIMP is not on the public radar, so it's often treated as non-existent—for the time being.

The next four sections of this chapter briefly examine the tools and applications made available by Red Hat with its Linux 7 release.

Editors

Within X are three text editors that you can use to modify simple text files. Two work within the desktop environment, and the third, an old UNIX favorite, is a command-line application.

Known throughout the UNIX and Linux community as vi, VIM is an improved version of the old vi standby. You can't start vi from a menu (unless you create such a menu item for it); instead, you must run vi from the command line.

Within a terminal emulator or on the Linux command line, type **vi** to start the VIM editor. As you can see in Figure 6-1, the basic commands are displayed in its opening screen.

One very good use of VIM is to manually edit configuration files. To open a file in VIM, simply type **vi** *filename* on the command line.

◆ ◆

CAUTION   Before you edit any configuration file, be sure to save a backup copy to which you can revert if an error is made.

◆ ◆

To quit VIM, just type **:q**. VIM will close and return you to the command line.

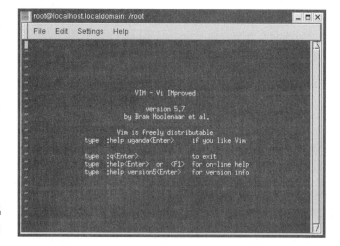

Figure 6-1

The VIM text editor.

The two X applications to use for text editing are gEdit and gnotepad+, both illustrated in Figure 6-2.

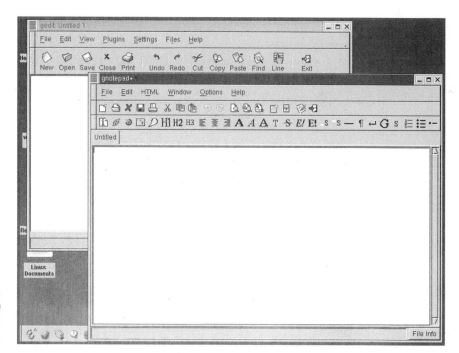

Figure 6-2

The gEdit and gnotepad+ editors.

As you can see from the illustration, the functionality of these applications is similar although gnotepad+ has extra tools that enable it to create HTML format commands. This makes sense because an HTML file is merely a text file containing textual codes that enable browsers to display enhancements such as font color and size changes.

Table 6-1 lists additional editors that are available in the Red Hat Linux 7 and whether they are installed as part of the default package set.

TABLE 6-1   ADDITIONAL AVAILABLE EDITORS

Application	Description	Installed?
abiword	A full-featured word processor	No
emacs	Another very popular Linux command line text editor	Yes

Graphics

With the influx of the Internet to the public, the need for applications that can handle graphics with ease has grown tremendously. Linux does not disappoint in this area, either, giving its users three tools for viewing and editing graphic files.

The first of these tools is Electric Eyes. Despite the odd name, Electric Eyes is an excellent, simple, graphics viewer. After you start the program, right-click anywhere in the application to open it's menu. Similar to most programs, the File, Open menu selection can be used to open a graphic, just like the example shown in Figure 6-3.

If you thought Electric Eyes had a weird name, then the GIMP application may set you back a bit. GIMP (short for GNU Image Manipulation Program) is a free-of-charge app often compared to Adobe PhotoShop because it has many of the same capabilities.

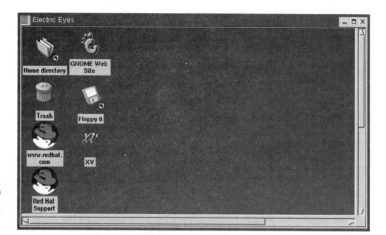

Figure 6-3

Viewing graphics in
Electric Eyes.

GIMP has some special features that make it necessary for you to perform
a secondary installation when you first start the application. When the
GIMP Installation dialog box appears, click Install. When the installation
is successfully completed, a message box will appear informing you of the
completed installation. Click Continue to open the GIMP interface,
shown in Figure 6-4.

The GIMP interface is sort of odd, in that there is no "canvas" screen
immediately visible—just a Toolbar and (if your options are set for it) a
Tip of the Day message box. But once you begin working with the program, you will find its capabilities amazing.

An entire book could be written just on GIMP alone, so we won't dwell
on it here. For further information, I highly suggest you peruse the
GIMP Manual, an electronic document that you can open from the
menu bar by choosing Xtns, Web Browser, GIMP Manual.

Finally, Xpaint is an application that will let you *create* sharp-looking
graphics, not just view them. Found within the AnotherLevel Menus
option, Xpaint lets you make your own pictures (such as the hypnotic display shown in Figure 6-5) and save them in a variety of formats.

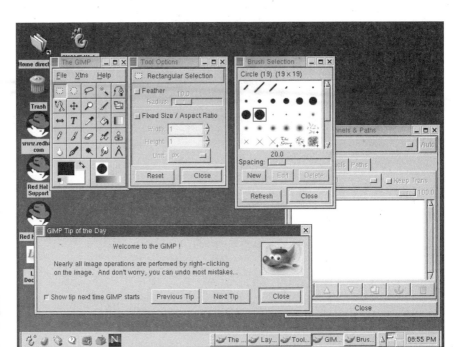

Figure 6-4

The unusual GIMP interface.

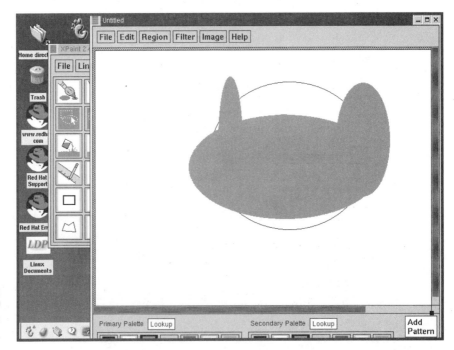

Figure 6-5

Making your own art in Xpaint.

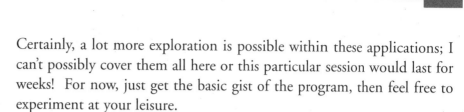

Certainly, a lot more exploration is possible within these applications; I can't possibly cover them all here or this particular session would last for weeks! For now, just get the basic gist of the program, then feel free to experiment at your leisure.

Personal Information Managers

I don't know about you, but my days are hectic. I often find myself going from meeting to meeting, appointment to appointment, until it seems that a 24-hour day is just not long enough. For me, it's just a matter of getting organized.

This is where having a personal information manager (PIM) comes in handy. The electronic equivalent of a day-planner, a PIM can track appointments and help avoid scheduling conflicts.

The primary PIM within Red Hat is the Calendar application. This application serves as a scheduler and task manager. Its interface may be very familiar to users of Microsoft Outlook or Symantec Act, as shown in Figure 6-6.

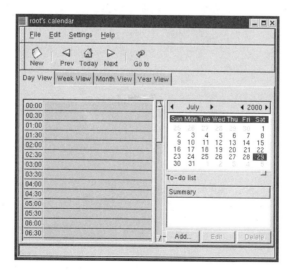

Figure 6-6

The Gnome Calendar application.

A more simplified PIM is lcal, another AnotherLevel application provided in Red Hat Linux 7. As you can see from Figure 6-7, it merely tracks your schedule, not tasks. If that's all you need, however, it's a nice little application to use.

There is only one other PIM application available in KDE: kOrganizer, KDE's answer to the Gnome Calendar.

Internet Tools

If the previous categories of applications seemed a bit sparse, that's about to change. Linux provides many Internet-based applications, not the least of which is the commercially available Netscape Communicator (see Figure 6-8).

Netscape Communicator is an all-in-one application that provides Web browser, e-mail, and newsgroup reader capabilities. This one program will fill most of your Internet needs. You'll learn about it in greater detail later this afternoon.

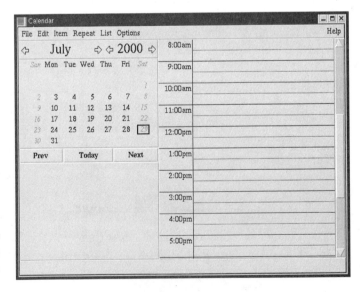

Figure 6-7

The lcal application.

Figure 6-8

Surfing the Internet
with Netscape
Communicator.

Even though Netscape provides most of the tools needed for Internet use, Linux provides many more Internet tools for advanced use. Because of the volume of utilities in the toolset, they are listed in Table 6-2.

The preceding table should give you the idea that Linux wants you to be connected to the Internet.

Many other types of applications are available too, of course. The number of games alone would fill another book. You should explore the remaining Linux applications available on the CD-ROM on your own. When you do, you will see the true power of the Linux operating system: its applications.

Using Netscape Communicator

As indicated in the previous section, there are several Internet tools for users included with Red Hat Linux 7. Of these, the most encompassing application is surely Netscape Communicator 4.74.

TABLE 6-2 INTERNET APPLICATIONS AVAILABLE IN RED HAT LINUX 7	
Application	**Description**
elm	A popular e-mail client
exmh	A mail client that can read mh mail folders
fetchmail	Remote mail retrieval and forwarding utility
finger	An Internet tool that obtains information about a specific Internet user
gftp	An FTP application for Gnome
lynx	A text-only Web browser
minicom	An Internet-based remote terminal emulation tool
mutt	A Linux e-mail client
ncftp	A more robust FTP tool
pine	Another popular e-mail client
slrn	A newsreader client
talk	An Internet chat tool
telnet	An Internet-based remote terminal emulation tool
tin	A newsreader client
trn	A newsreader client
whois	An Internet tool that obtains information about a specific Internet domain
xchat	An IRC client
xrn	A newsreader client

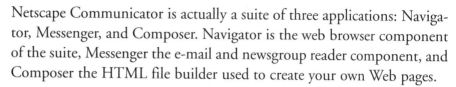
Netscape Communicator is actually a suite of three applications: Navigator, Messenger, and Composer. Navigator is the web browser component of the suite, Messenger the e-mail and newsgroup reader component, and Composer the HTML file builder used to create your own Web pages.

With all of these capabilities, you might think you would have a bit to set up—and you'd be right. The Navigator component alone has several settings that can make surfing the Web even faster.

Configuring Netscape Navigator

In the olden days of the Internet (all of seven years ago), life was uncomplicated. The simple concept of hyperlinks on a text page was just emerging. Some links went to other pages; others to files to be downloaded—perhaps a picture or two. Browsers such as Lynx only had to contend with text—life was good.

In 1993, everything changed forever. The National Center for Supercomputing Applications (NCSA) at the University of Illinois created Mosaic—a browser capable of displaying text and pictures. Suddenly, users could see illustrated Web pages, which facilitated the flow of information. A year later, one of the Mosaic developers left NCSA and launched his own browser—Netscape Navigator 1.1.

Since then, the capability of browsers has grown even more in response to more complex content. Need to hear a sound file? No need to download, save, and then play the file with another application. Browsers now begin to either play the sound themselves or automatically start that third-party application for you. Need to view a Shockwave file? Not only will a browser display it for you, the browser can automatically go get the required viewer if you don't already have it.

These sophisticated features are a long way from the early Internet days, that's for sure.

To make all of this work for you, there are a few settings you can adjust within Navigator such as the rudimentary home page and personalized start page settings. You can also alter the size of the cache and choose which helper applications Netscape will use when it encounters a file it can't display itself.

Home Page and Other Easy Stuff

Most of us have used browsers before, and we know that a user's home page is the first HTML file loaded when the browser starts. That home page can be a local file or one on the Internet. You can specify this setting with ease, as shown in the following steps.

1. Click the Netscape icon in the Panel to open Netscape.
2. Click Edit, Preferences. The Netscape Preferences dialog box will open (see Figure 6-9).

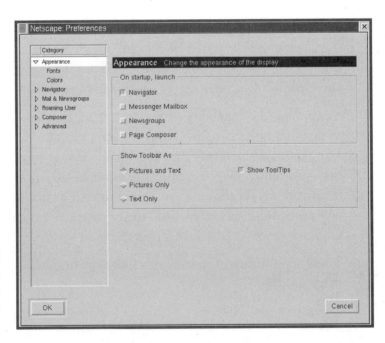

Figure 6-9

All of the Netscape configuration changes are made in this dialog box.

3. Click Navigator in the Category pane to open the Navigator settings window.

4. Type the URL of the Internet page you want to use as your home page (see Figure 6-10).

TIP If you want your home page to be a local file, click the Choose button to open the Netscape File Browser dialog box. There, navigate to the desired file and click OK. The full path to the file will appear in the Location field.

5. Click OK. Navigator will now use your new home page when the browser starts or when you click the Home button on the Navigator toolbar.

When you click the Netscape Communicator icon on the Gnome or KDE Panel, by default the Navigator component starts first. However, if

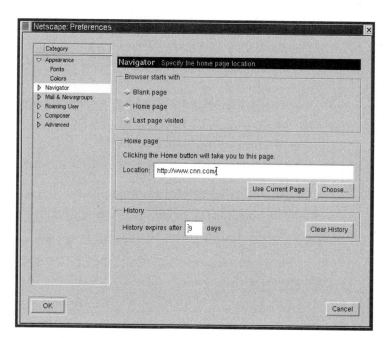

Figure 6-10

Any page on the Internet can be your home page.

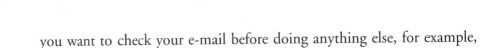

you want to check your e-mail before doing anything else, for example, you may prefer to have Messenger start before Navigator.

1. In Netscape, choose Edit, Preferences. The Netscape Preferences dialog box will open.

2. Click any of the four options in the On Startup, Launch group.

> **TIP**
>
> If you want more screen real estate in Netscape, change the Toolbar setting in this dialog box to Picture Only or Text Only.

3. Click OK. Communicator will now open the selected component each time the application starts.

Netscape also provides its registered users the ability to create their own personalized start page. This start page, which can also serve as a home page, can contain information from a variety of categories that you pick. What's nice about these pages is that you can access them from anywhere, not just your Linux PC and not just with Navigator as your browser.

1. In Netscape, click the My Netscape icon in the toolbar. The Netcenter Web page will appear (see Figure 6-11).

> **CAUTION**
>
> If you are already a registered Netscape user, click the Find it! link on the default Netcenter page to enter your username and password.

2. Click the Personalize icon on the left side of the page. The New Member Sign-Up page will open (see Figure 6-12).

> **TIP**
>
> If you are a returning Netcenter member, click the Sign In icon to customize your page.

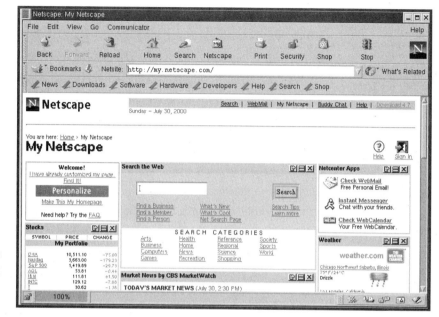

Figure 6-11

The default
Netcenter Web
page.

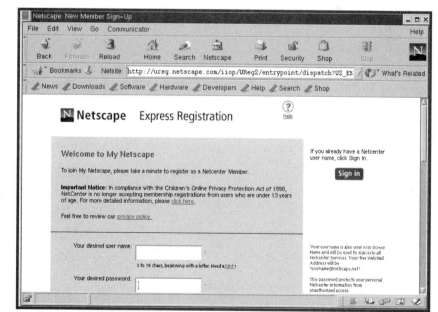

Figure 6-12

Express
Registration
enables you to
register with
Netcenter before
personalizing your
start page.

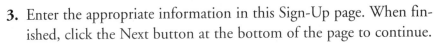

3. Enter the appropriate information in this Sign-Up page. When finished, click the Next button at the bottom of the page to continue.

4. The Email Confirmation Sent screen will appear. Read the screen to confirm the information, then click Next to continue.

5. Figure 6-13 displays the Welcome page that will appear. On this page, click an option's check box to include it on your start page, clicking the check box again to clear any that you want to remove.

TIP To see a preview of the information each option will display, click the option's link. When you're finished, click the toolbar's Back button to return to the Welcome page.

6. Next, select your time zone using the drop-down list near the bottom of the Welcome page.

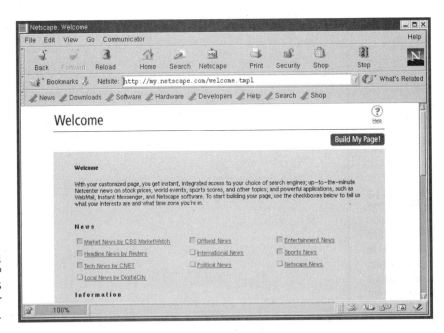

Figure 6-13

Choose the options you want to appear on your start page.

7. When finished, click one of the Build My Page buttons on the top or bottom of the page.

8. The new start page will appear, as shown in Figure 6-14.

9. Besides selecting the channels that will appear, you can also customize each channel. Customizing is especially handy if you chose a local channel and your city is not the default. To begin, click the Customize channel button for the channel you want to modify.

10. In this example, we chose to customize the local news channel. Find and select your desired city in the Select a News Category field. (See Figure 6-15.)

11. Click the Add icon to move the selected city to the Selected News Categories field. Repeat if you want to add additional cities.

12. To remove any cities you no longer want to see, click their names in the Selected field and then click the Remove button.

Customize channel icon

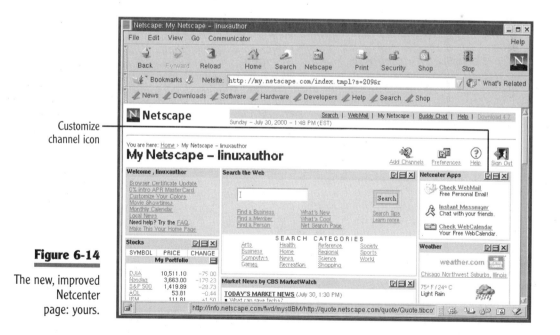

Figure 6-14

The new, improved Netcenter page: yours.

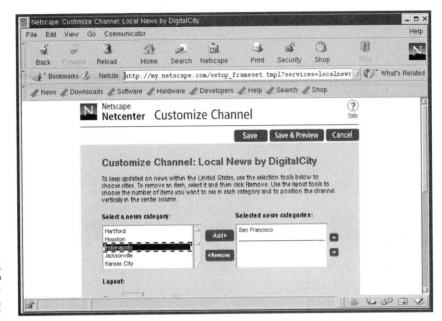

Figure 6-15

Local news at 11?
Get it anytime!

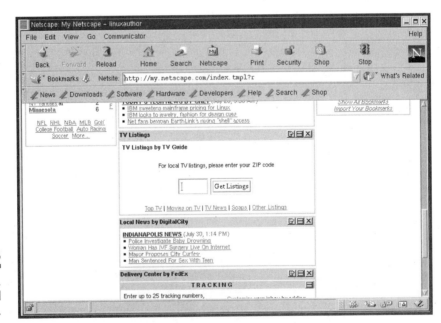

Figure 6-16

My city's news.
Maybe I should
move. . . .

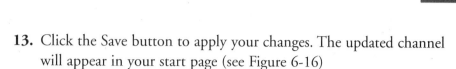

13. Click the Save button to apply your changes. The updated channel will appear in your start page (see Figure 6-16)

14. If you want to change the layout of the page itself, select the Preferences link that appears near the top of the page. The Preferences page will open (see Figure 6-17).

15. Make the changes you desire and click the Save button. Your updated page will be displayed with all of your changes, as shown in Figure 6-18.

CAUTION

◆◆

If you decide to customize both color and general preferences in a single trip to the Preferences page, be aware that only your color changes will be applied to the start page when you click Save. Therefore, you should set your general preferences first, and then set your color choices later.

◆◆

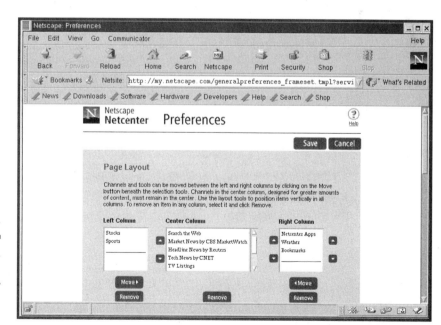

Figure 6-17

Page layout, color, and other personal preferences are handled from this page.

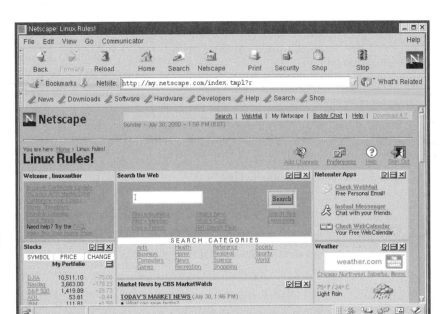

Figure 6-18

You may want to practice some restraint in designing your page.

Setting Cache Properties

A vast majority of Web pages to which you may surf are heavily laden with graphics and other little gimcracks that take up memory and therefore lengthen download times. Caching is a way to accelerate the downloading process.

◄◄

Cache: A specific amount of memory set aside to keep compressed versions of visited Web pages and their graphics. On a return visit to the Web site, any unchanged elements from the page are loaded from the cache first, thus rendering their download unnecessary.

◄◄

When it is first installed, Netscape has a fair amount of memory set aside for caching: a total of 8 megabytes (MB). If you often visit graphic-intense sites (or a lot of sites in general) you may want to change this figure.

1. In Netscape, choose Edit, Preferences. The Netscape Preferences dialog box will open.

2. Click the expansion icon next to Advanced.

3. Click Cache. The Cache window will open (see Figure 6-19).

TIP Unless your system has a lot of RAM, it is a good idea to leave the memory cache settings where they are. You do not want to devote a lot of system resources to caching.

4. Increase the disk cache value to a level you feel is appropriate for your system. I recommend at least 10MB, unless you are using a smaller or older PC.

5. Click OK to close the dialog box.

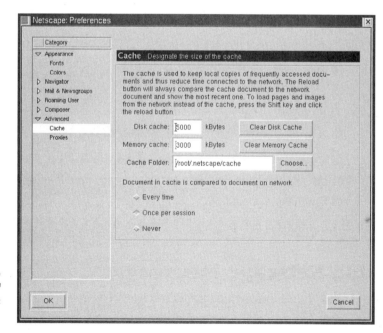

Figure 6-19

The cache preferences.

Defining Helper Applications

Helper applications are those used by Netscape to display or otherwise use certain file types you may find on the Internet. There are basically two types of helper applications: plug-ins, which are essentially mini-applications that work seamlessly with Netscape to open or display a file, and true third-party applications started by Netscape when a particular file type is encountered.

The next steps demonstrate how to add third-party applications to Netscape Navigator, in this case the StarOffice application for reading WordPerfect files.

1. In Netscape, choose Edit, Preferences to open the Preferences dialog box.

2. Click the expansion icon next to the Navigator listing.

3. Click the Applications listing. The Applications window will appear.

4. Scroll to the WordPerfect description and select it.

5. Click Edit. The Application dialog box will open.

6. Click the Application option and then click the Choose button. The File Browser dialog box will appear.

7. Navigate to the StarOffice application file and click OK.

8. Click OK to close the Preferences dialog box.

TIP You can also configure StarOffice to open any file from Microsoft Office's Word, Excel, and PowerPoint applications.

Configuring Netscape Messenger

One of the more useful features of Communicator is the all-in-one capability to receive e-mail and read newsgroups. Before you can begin,

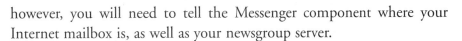

however, you will need to tell the Messenger component where your Internet mailbox is, as well as your newsgroup server.

The next two sections of this chapter will examine exactly how to provide Messenger with the information it needs.

Setting up E-Mail

E-mail messaging has changed the course of the business world considerably. It's gotten to the point where using the phone is considered a last resort for many companies.

So that you can receive e-mail on your PC, you first need to tell Messenger where to pick up your mail. E-mail rarely arrives directly at your computer. Instead, it resides on a mail server (usually at your ISP's location) until you query that server and download your messages into your computer.

The following steps demonstrate how to enter this information.

1. In Netscape, select Edit, Preferences to open the Preferences dialog box.

2. Click the expansion icon for the Mail & Newsgroups listing.

3. Click the Identity listing. The Identity window will appear (see Figure 6-20).

4. Enter all of the necessary information. Click Mail Servers in the Category pane to open the Mail Servers window (see Figure 6-21).

5. Select the default Incoming Mail Server and then click Edit. The POP dialog box will open (see Figure 6-22).

TIP Click on the Remember Password option to facilitate mail pickup.

6. Set any options you require in the General panel. Click the POP tab to view the POP panel.

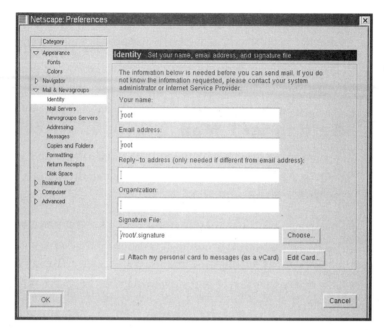

Figure 6-20

Telling Messenger
who you are.

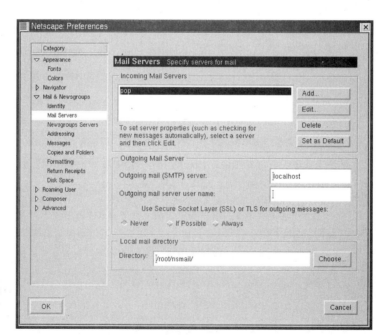

Figure 6-21

Finding your
Internet mailbox.

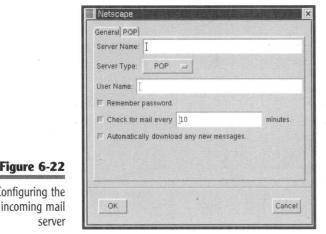

Figure 6-22

Configuring the
incoming mail
server

TIP If you use more than one computer to check your e-mail, I recommend choosing one
computer to be the central client repository and setting all other computers to leave
messages on the mail server. In this way, all incoming mail is seen in at least one place.

7. When finished, click OK.

8. Enter the pertinent information in the Outgoing Mail Server fields.

9. Click OK to complete the task.

Messenger can now pick up your messages.

Setting up Newsgroups

Reading newsgroups on the Internet works similarly to getting your
e-mail. The only differences here are that you are looking at servers to
which everyone has access and you can view a lot more messages!

1. In Netscape, select Edit, Preferences to open the Preferences
   dialog box.

2. Click the expansion icon next to the Mail & Newsgroups listing.

3. Click the Newsgroups Servers listing. The Newsgroups Servers
   window will appear (see Figure 6-23).

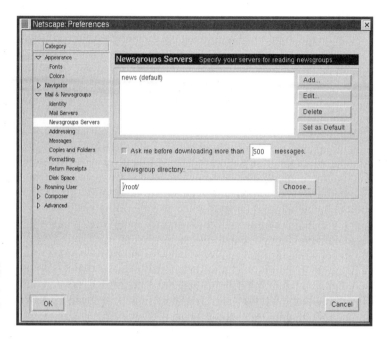

Figure 6-23

Identifying from
where newsgroups
will be read.

4. Click Add. The news server dialog box will open (see Figure 6-24).

5. Type the descriptive name of your news server and click OK to close the dialog box.

TIP

The port setting should be left alone, unless you know for sure that your news server uses a different port.

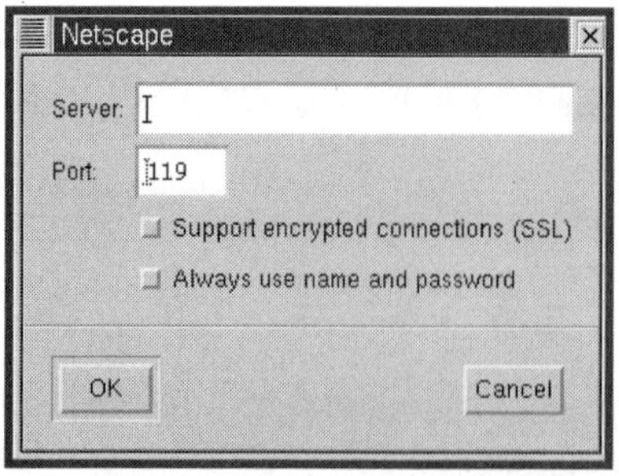

Figure 6-24

Configuring the
news server.

6. Select the new newsgroup and then click the Set as Default button.

7. Select the original newsgroup (which is a dummy setting) and click Delete.

8. Click OK to close the Preferences dialog box.

To begin using the news server, start the newsgroup reader, right-click the server listing, and then select Subscribe to Newsgroups.

Using StarOffice 5.2 for Linux

Advertising in the modern age has grown to outlandish heights. Day after day, images and sound exhort us to drink this, see that, and wear these blue jeans. Mostly the hype is just that—hype. A certain huge sci-fi movie released in the summer of 1999 demonstrated this point rather well.

Nevertheless, every once in a while, the hype has some substance to it, so we keep listening. StarOffice is a product where we should definitely pay attention. Is StarOffice the *Greatest Office Suite Ever Made*? No. Everything can be improved upon, and not everyone will like using StarOffice. But StarOffice does offer something other office suites do not: a unique, totally integrated interface that seamlessly blends its different components.

Since you successfully installed StarOffice on your Linux PC this morning, it's time to start it up and see for yourself how this powerful office suite is put together.

StarDesktop: A Better Interface

The best place to start any tour is at the beginning. With StarOffice, the beginning starts on the StarDesktop.

Getting to the StarDesktop is very simple: just start StarOffice. If you are running the KDE interface that comes with Red Hat Linux, do this by selecting the StarOffice 5.2 menu option on the Application Starter menu.

In Gnome, StarOffice does not have a Launcher on the Main Menu, so you will have to place one there yourself. Until you do, navigate to the ../office52/program directory and type ./soffice on the command line. This will start StarOffice in Gnome (and KDE, too, if you don't want to use the menu).

NOTE

When StarOffice starts for the first time after installation, it asks you to configure the Internet settings using the Internet AutoPilot. Follow the steps in the AutoPilot, which is a lot like a Wizard in Microsoft Windows, to tell StarOffice how you want to connect to the Internet.

TIP

StarOffice, like many other commercial applications, displays a logo during its startup. You can save some time by turning this feature off. Simply select the Tools, Options menu command. In the Options dialog box, select General, View from the options tree on the left. This shows the View options in the right section of the dialog box. Here you can select the Don't Show option in the Logo field. Click OK when complete. The next time StarOffice starts, the logo will not appear.

When the startup completes, you first see the StarDesktop (see Figure 6-25). A quick examination will be helpful because StarDesktop is key to the workings of the entire StarOffice application.

The center of the screen holds the Desktop section. This displays the contents of any directory you want to see. Items within the Desktop can be opened with just a double-click. In many ways, StarDesktop serves not just as a launch pad for the StarOffice applications, but also as a robust file navigator. But it is first and foremost the starting point for all documents within StarOffice.

On the left side of the screen is the Explorer window. This vertical bar can display a variety of items, from files in your computer to work folders containing all of a project's work. The structure of this window contains

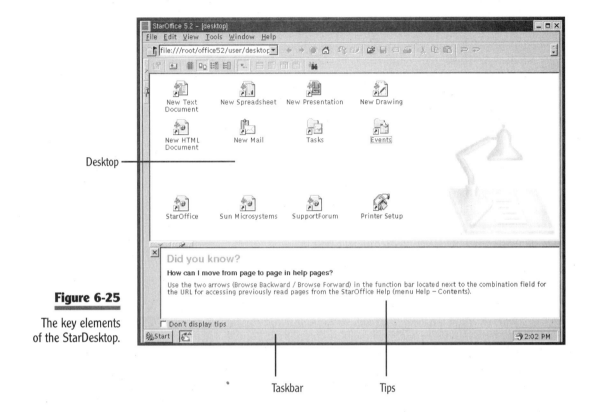

Desktop

Figure 6-25

The key elements
of the StarDesktop.

Taskbar   Tips

groups, such as E-mail & News, Work Folder, and Tasks. An Explorer
group uses a tree directory structure very similar to the Windows 98/NT
Explorer to navigate the files on your PC.

Along the top of the Desktop is the Beamer. The Beamer is similar in
functionality to the Explorer, as it displays folder contents. The Beamer
window (shown in Figure 6-26) displays the contents of any folder selected in the Explorer window. If you have been experimenting with the
interface (and who could blame you?) you may have noticed that you can
get the same effect by double-clicking any folder in the Explorer window
and seeing the folder contents in the Desktop window. But, by *single-
clicking* folders in Explorer, the Beamer can show the same contents without supplanting what is in your Desktop window.

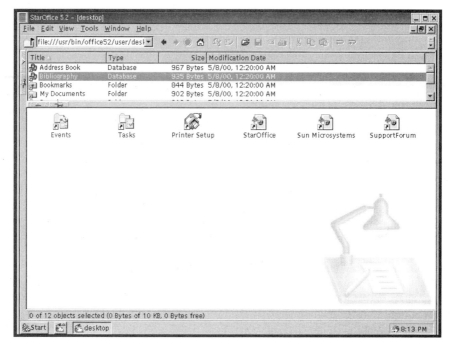

Figure 6-26

The Beamer in action.

As a document viewer, StarDesktop has the ability to configure itself to accommodate whatever type of file you have opened. Thus, when you open a StarCalc file, the toolbars, Navigator, and Stylist all change to StarCalc-specific tools. The same effect occurs when you open a Star-Writer document or a StarImpress presentation.

NOTE   In truth, there are no individual applications within StarOffice, as there are in Microsoft Office. You will not find an "on switch" for StarWriter or any of the other components. You activate them on an as-needed basis. For example, if you create a new StarImpress presentation or open an existing presentation file, then StarImpress automatically starts.

This dual functionality of file navigator and universal document viewer makes StarOffice unique. It is a powerful feature, but admittedly one that can trip up a user if they're not careful.

StarWriter: A New Way to Write

If StarDesktop is the center of StarOffice, then it can be safely said that StarWriter is the focal point.

The written word is still a major component of our daily lives. Newspapers, Web pages, and books—the written word comprises them all. Even our audio and visual media stems from written scripts and news copy.

StarWriter was the first product developed by the original Star Division and, as such, is the most developed component of Sun's new office suite. You can see this robust nature in Figure 6-27, which shows a typical StarWriter window. You can see that StarWriter offers a number of tools. Three tools unique to StarWriter—and the entire StarOffice suite— include the Navigator, Stylist, and Help Agent.

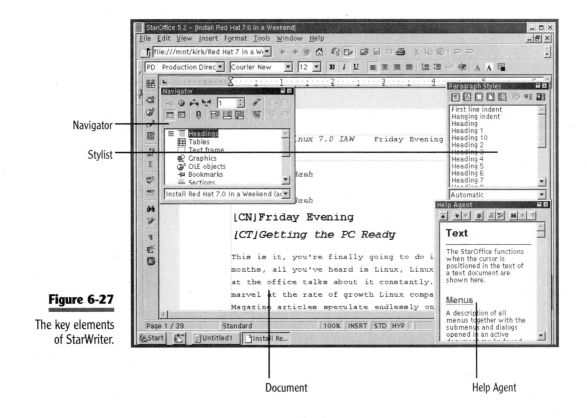

Figure 6-27

The key elements of StarWriter.

The Navigator enables you to navigate your cursor to any point in a document. For instance, the Navigator inventories and lists the total number of tables, figures, and other unique objects within a given document. If you wanted to jump to, say, Figure 6-20 of your document, then you would just click on that entry in the Navigator and your cursor appears at Figure 6-20.

The inventory feature of the Navigator also makes it easy to manage documents with large numbers of extra elements. If your document were supposed to have nine pictures, it would be embarrassing to discover after it comes back from the printer that only eight were actually inserted.

The Stylist brings forth the concept of styles. This may not be a new concept to you, as styles have been around for a few years.

◄ ◄

BUZZ WORD   *Styles*: A collection of various formatting attributes that you assign to whole sections of text, usually at the paragraph level.

◄ ◄

Styles typically have proper names that describe their features. The Stylist in Figure 6-27, for example, has paragraph styles of Heading 1, Heading 2, and so on. The naming makes it easy to ascertain where to use these styles.

● ●

NOTE   Styles in today's word processing programs stem from a concept found in Standard Generalized Markup Language (SGML). SGML is a text-only format that uses tags to highlight portions of a document. Any text in between the tags takes on the attributes assigned to the tags. A <Bold> tag makes text **bold**, for example. If this sounds familiar, it should. SGML is the parent language for another little language you may have heard of: HTML, the language of the World Wide Web.

● ●

The Help Agent proactively provides context-driven help on any part of StarOffice. If you are new to StarOffice, having the Help Agent on while you work can be useful. Click on a toolbar button and, as the action takes place, an explanation of what the button does appears in the Help Agent.

TIP

■■■

Don't use the Help Agent forever, just until you get comfortable with StarWriter and the rest of the StarOffice components. As nice as it is, Help Agent takes up some of your screen's real estate, which you could use for something else.

■■■

The uses for StarWriter are as boundless as your imagination. You can create any form of written document and use elements from any other part of StarOffice to suit your needs.

StarCalc: Figure It All Out

Spreadsheets get their name from the old-fashioned ledger sheets used by desk-bound accountants. In their work, they would lay out numbers on what were at times huge sheets of grid-lined paper. Sometimes these sheets would be yards long and if a mistake were made in just one cell . . . well, let's just say the mistake would be rather tedious to find and fix.

The concept of these paper sheets has been carried over to electronic form. It made sense to keep data in this familiar tabular format. Thus, the first spreadsheet program, VisiCalc, was born. Though no relation to StarCalc, a lot of the concepts introduced in VisiCalc provide the basis for StarCalc's design.

Figure 6-28 shows the basic elements common to all spreadsheets: cells, rows, and columns. You can't have a spreadsheet without these elements. Spreadsheet programs differ in the way they present and utilize these elements.

Cells are the heart of a spreadsheet. They contain the data. The data values can be numbers, letters, words—whatever you want to keep track of. Cells can also contain formulas. Formulas are mathematical equations that take the value of one cell and relate it to the value of another cell to come up with a unique answer. If needed, formulas can equate whole ranges of cells.

StarCalc helps you organize your data in other ways. In Figure 6-29, you can see the tools and navigational aids within StarCalc.

Column Heading   Column   Cell

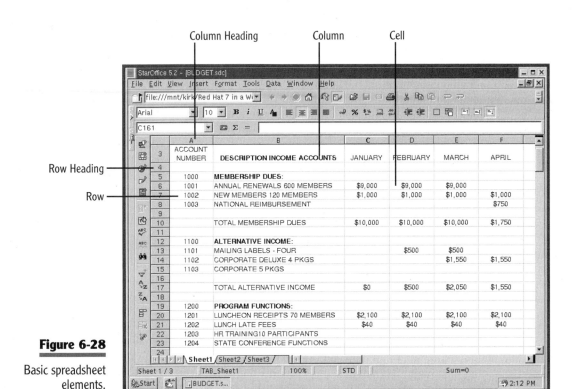

Row Heading

Row

Figure 6-28

Basic spreadsheet elements.

The Navigator and the Stylist function in much the same way as they do in other StarOffice components. The Formula bar is one of the more powerful StarCalc tools. In it, data or text values can be entered, as well as any formula you can create.

◆ ◆

CAUTION   Don't get carried away with your formulas. You can only use up to 256 characters to create a formula.

◆ ◆

The Function List window aids in the creation of formulas. This ingenious tool enables you to point and click to create a formula. Simply find the function you want to use and double-click it. The syntax of the

Formula bar

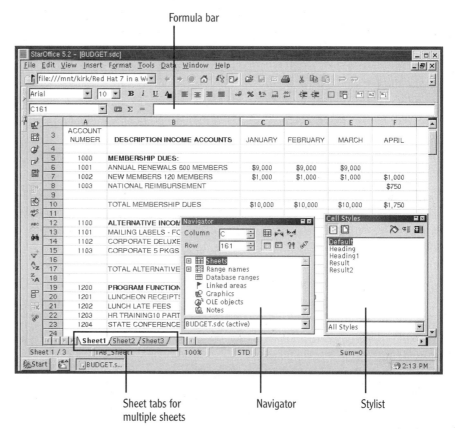

Figure 6-29

StarCalc tools.

Sheet tabs for multiple sheets

Navigator

Stylist

formula appears in the Formula Bar. All you have to do is fill in a number or cell value.

StarCalc does not just display data in neat little columns and rows. Nor does it just perform mathematic functions, though it does so rather well. With StarCalc's Scenario functions, you can create multiple scenarios with your data. What would happen to my overall revenues if the price of asparagus rockets to a new high this season? How much profit can I make if asparagus stays at its current level? StarCalc is a great way to plan for mortgages, loans, and other business concerns.

StarCalc is not the only math wizard in the StarOffice suite. Two smaller components can help you display your math talents: StarChart and StarMath.

StarChart: What Those Numbers Mean

While tables offer a nice way to look at your data, they can be counter-intuitive at times. In certain instances, seeing your work in a graphical format can be more productive.

StarChart works with StarCalc to help create detailed charts to display the data in your spreadsheet. These can be bar charts, pie charts, or line charts, to name a few. Many of these charts can be shown in three-dimensional format, as seen in Figure 6-30.

The charts you create in StarChart don't have to stay within StarCalc. These charts can be embedded or linked to any other StarOffice document.

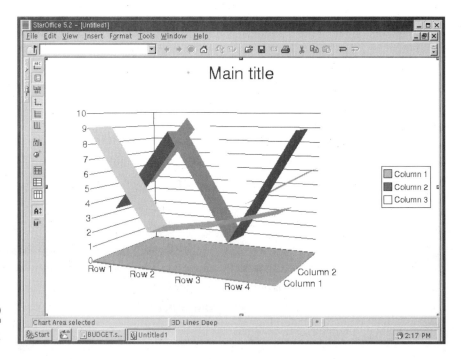

Figure 6-30

A 3-D line chart.

StarMath: Equation for Success

Let's face it: math is generally a misunderstood subject with low popularity. Sure, we use math on an every day level to balance the checkbook or count how many jellybeans are in the jar. But higher math? Who needs it?

Well, to tell the truth, you do. Algebra and calculus come up a lot more than you might think. As technology becomes more and more pervasive in our daily lives, the need to communicate mathematically grows.

A good example of how StarMath operates is seen in Figure 6-31, where the formula for gravitational force appears within StarMath.

To try this in Word or WordPerfect would be exceedingly difficult. In Word, the same formula would look like this:

$$F = Mm/r^2$$

Though accurate, this is not as clear. As an extra bonus, after you create a formula in StarMath, you can insert it within any other document. This

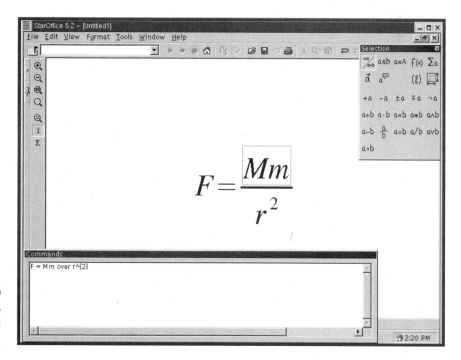

Figure 6-31

Here's what keeps your feet on the ground.

makes StarMath very useful for students and scientists creating reports. StarMath can also help children learn math, too.

StarBase: Track Your Data

Databases are scary. There, it's said, out in the open.

Many people often think of databases as dark, shadowy beasts that lurk in their PCs, chewing up and spitting out data and reports only if coaxed out with strange and cryptic queries.

Not necessarily. In recent years, personal databases have become more friendly and intuitive. StarBase is no exception.

Of all the StarOffice components, StarBase needs the most input from the user before creating a database. As simplified as databases have become, you still can't snap one together with a single command. You need to know what tables will hold what data, what the data entry form will look like, and what reports the database will need to generate.

Sounds scary again, doesn't it? It's really not, and to demonstrate this, StarOffice does have an example StarBase database for you to begin experimenting with: the Address Book (see Figure 6-32).

This Address Book contains a few sample addresses to show you the way. Basically, you can use it as a fully functional electronic Rolodex.

Figure 6-32

A brand new Address Book for you to use.

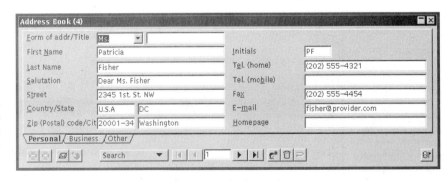

StarBase also includes a sample Bibliography for you to use. As you do so, you will begin to see how StarBase puts databases together. From there, you can easily start building your own database.

StarImpress: Show What You Know

There was a time in the business world when average workers were not expected to share their knowledge with the rest of the workplace all at once. In these days of open communication, however, more and more opportunities arise for people to do what they often hate the most: public speaking.

StarOffice has a component that helps relieve some of that anxiety. StarImpress is a robust presentation tool designed to show your ideas to the world. Figure 6-33 shows a sample StarImpress presentation.

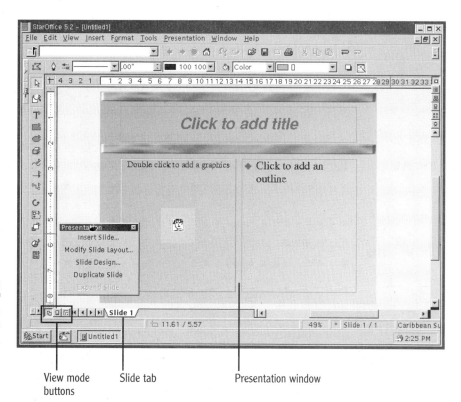

Figure 6-33

Beginning a StarImpress presentation.

View mode buttons   Slide tab   Presentation window

StarImpress can let you create a presentation from scratch, or build one from an existing outline. You can use the Presentation AutoPilot to add templates, backgrounds, and even additional slides all in one easy process.

Perhaps best of all is that any presentation created in StarImpress can not only be used in a standard slide show, but can also be converted for use on the World Wide Web, giving you a chance to create flashy Web pages in a snap.

StarDraw: Create Works of Art

The Mona Lisa. Whistler's Mother. Dogs Playing Poker. Brilliant pieces of art that have graced museums and walls the world over. If you have ever wanted to create art to join these masterpieces, StarDraw might be a good place to start.

Kidding aside, StarDraw is a wonderful tool (see Figure 6-34) for creating some good-looking art for your documents and presentations—even if you are not an artist by trade.

StarDraw is unique among drawing tools that come with other office suites as it uses vector-based technology. Other low-end art packages, such as Microsoft Paint, use raster-based technology.

◄ ◄

BUZZ WORD   *Vector-based graphics*: Graphic images based on computer-generated lines.

◄ ◄

◄ ◄

BUZZ WORD   *Raster-based graphics*: Graphic images based on computer-generated dots.

◄ ◄

For you, this means that StarDraw produces smoother, more even lines and curves, as opposed to the jagged effect that a raster-based drawing tool produces. You typically only find this kind of technology in high-end, expensive applications such as CorelDRAW.

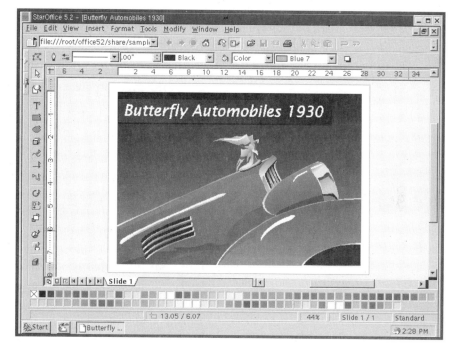

Figure 6-34

Draw like a
professional.

StarMail: Communicate with the World

Not only does StarOffice offer productivity tools, it offers communications tools as well. With StarMail, you can send and receive e-mails just as you can in Netscape or any other Linux e-mail client.

Sun Microsystems makes it a point throughout all of its marketing literature to "work in one place." By including e-mail capabilities within StarOffice, they have certainly taken a big step towards that goal.

You can create a new message from any point in StarOffice and you can send the message off at any time as well.

StarMail does more than let you send e-mails back and forth. Files can be attached to messages, creating an easy transfer method for sharing your work.

StarDiscussion: Join Online Communities

StarOffice also enables you to tap into an interesting, and at times controversial, portion of the Internet known as newsgroups.

If you have a question or a statement, you can use StarDiscussion to post a message to the appropriate newsgroup, just as you can in Netscape Messenger. Visitors to that newsgroup see your post and may answer it. Or they may not. It's very much like a town meeting.

StarSchedule: Keep Your Life in Order

With all of this document writing, presentation planning, and e-mailing, you'll be a very busy person. With time being a precious commodity these days, a way to keep track of your busy life is not a luxury, but a necessity.

That's where StarSchedule comes in. This Personal Information Manager allows you to create and update appointments, meetings, and tasks (see Figure 6-35).

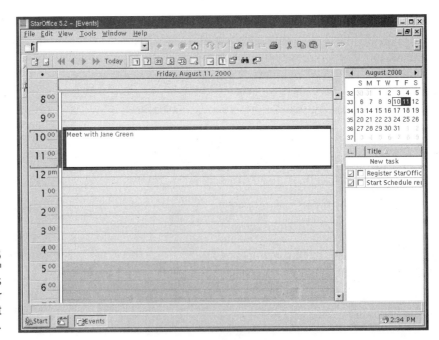

Figure 6-35

StarSchedule lets you find time for the important things, like eating.

◀ ◀

Personal Information Manager (PIM): An application designed to act as an electronic personal organizer. Such applications typically include calendar, address book, and to do list functions.

◀ ◀

Because of its integration with StarOffice, you can embed documents within your appointments and reminders, to help you find them when it comes time to work on them.

Conclusion

By now, you have seen just some of the many applications that are offered to the Linux platform. One thing to keep in mind is that this is just the tip of the iceberg. There are thousands of applications out there to be used, many of them free or low-cost. Moreover, the number keeps growing everyday.

Since its likely time for Sunday dinner, you may very well be all set to go with your Linux PC. If so, congratulations! This is not a perfect world, however, and sometimes there are pitfalls that pop up on our journeys. If things have not gone well for you this weekend, or if something hung you up, fear not. This evening's chapter may make all the difference!

Clean Up Any Messes

- ✿ Troubleshooting Installation
- ✿ Resolving Hardware Issues
- ✿ Resolving Software Isssues

This may sound odd at first, but I hope you are not reading this chapter.

That's because you should only read this chapter if something goes wrong during the installation and configuration of Red Hat Linux 7 this weekend. This chapter is unique, then, because you may not be reading it on the actual suggested day.

This evening, you will:

- ✿ Learn what to do when your installation does not work well
- ✿ Discover how to solve hardware problems
- ✿ Troubleshoot your Internet and networking configuration

Some of the material in this chapter may seem technically daunting. Don't let it shake you. Just look for what you need and take it from there.

Installation

This section will discuss issues surrounding Linux pre-installation, installation, and post-installation. We'll examine various problems that may arise, along with a few tips to make your experience more successful.

Decisions made during installation are a crucial part of your Linux success. Prior to installation, you decide how your system will be organized, such as the hard disk partition structure and the size of swap file you require. In this phase, you need to install those packages that will help you later do your work and troubleshoot problems.

Before even getting into troubleshooting the installation process, let's review a few tips about getting the software and preparing for installation.

Red Hat Software is the company that makes the Red Hat Linux distribution. With each new version, it sells a box containing a CD-ROM and printed manuals for around $40. The same files that appear on the CD-ROM are also available on its public FTP server. This means that anyone with a fast Internet connection (like a cable modem or DSL line) and a "writeable" CD-ROM drive can download the whole package and create their own CD-ROM. This is free, except for the cost of the blank disk.

For people like me who don't want to spend much money and don't have access to a fast Internet link, there's a third option. A few companies download each new version as it is released, create hundreds of CD-ROMs containing the complete Red Hat distribution, and then sell them for about $5. This is perfectly legal and will cost you less than the original packaged box from Red Hat Software. You must be aware, however, that two important items will be missing from that low-cost option. First, free limited support from Red Hat Software is missing. When you buy the distribution from Red Hat itself, a certain amount of free technical support is included. If you decide to purchase the low cost CD-ROM, you are on your own. Second, no printed manuals are included but are available in electronic form on the CD-ROM itself. You can, therefore, read them on your screen or print them out on your printer. Three known companies that sell low cost Linux CD-ROMs are LinuxMall, Cheap*Bytes, and Linux Central.

Of course, you should already have the Red Hat 7 CDs that accompanied this book, you lucky devil. While these publisher's versions are not the full version of Red Hat 7, they are more than adequate to get a great Red Hat PC up and running.

Once you have the Red Hat Linux 7 CD-ROMs, you should check the parameters for your hardware components as reported by your existing operating system (most often Microsoft Windows 95 or Windows 98). In Windows 95 or 98, these settings are found in the Device Manager. This is an important step; you should write everything down, including the type of device, name, IO port, and IRQ settings for all components. Knowing this information will help you troubleshoot many hardware problems in the future.

Another step you must consider before installing Linux, is what type of organization you want for your hard disk. If your hard disk contains another operating system, such as Microsoft DOS or Windows, you must decide if you want to keep it, or if you want to devote the entire hard disk to Linux. The easiest way to keep both operating systems is to have two hard disks, with the old operating system on the first disk and Linux on the second one. If you only have one hard disk, you can use a resizing program to maintain your existing operating system while making room for Linux. If you don't have one, such as Partition Magic from PowerQuest, you can use fips, the free partitioning program provided on the Linux CD-ROM. Be aware that the Linux fdisk or disk druid commands are not able to resize a partition. You must make your partitioning decisions before beginning the installation. Once you use fdisk or disk druid, any partition you delete will be gone for good, as well as access to the data it contained.

Boot Issues

When you modify scripts and configuration files in your Linux system, you may unwittingly make your system unbootable, either by setting incorrect parameters or by deleting important files. A good way to enable booting so that your mistakes can be corrected is by specifying the following command on the LILO text prompt:

```
boot: linux init=/bin/sh
```

TIP To get the text version of the LILO prompt, type Ctrl+x when the blue graphical LILO screen appears.

This command launches the Linux kernel and sets the init parameter to /bin/sh. This allows Linux to bypass the boot scripts, which may be faulty, and launch a console shell as root. You are then allowed to make modifications to your system in the console. This can be useful to repair problems, but it can be a big security hole. Anyone is able to use this (and many other tricks) to access your system and read your data. Physical access to your system is required, so the solution is to make sure your system is as off-limits as possible to undesirable people. You can set a BIOS password if you want a more secure system, but this still doesn't prevent someone from opening the system and removing the drive. Security is a huge subject—beyond the scope of this book—but you should be warned that anyone with physical access to a system can get data from it.

One of the most disconcerting problems is signaled when you boot your system and receive the error message:

```
VFS: Can't mount root filesystem
```

This means that the partition on which the Linux kernel is found could not be mounted. There are three common causes for this error.

If you recompiled your kernel and forgot to add basic features like IDE support and you use IDE disks, the kernel can't read the disk at all.

This message might also appear if you forgot to include support for ext2, the Linux file system. The disk will be read, but the kernel won't understand the file system.

Finally, you'll see this error message if the drive has failed. If the hard disk has died or if the controller has problems, then the kernel may not be able to read the entire disk. In these situations, you must use the rescue disk to boot your system. You can then begin to investigate the problem.

Note that these errors typically occur after a recompilation of the Linux kernel, which is a pretty advanced task that you should only undertake with a firm knowledge of the task.

X, Your Monitor, and Your Video Card

When the Linux installation is nearly over, it will launch a program called Xconfigurator, which will ask you questions about your video card and monitor with the purpose of configuring the X Window System. X is the common graphical environment in Linux, and is used by nearly all Linux users. It is important, therefore, that the configuration succeeds. X is able to detect your hardware and configure itself in most cases. There are a few instances, however, where it will fail.

For example, Xconfigurator may fail to configure X with your particular system. I recommend you install another configuration program, XF86Setup, which is included on your Red Hat Linux CD-ROM. XF86Setup requires that the XVGA16 package also be installed.

If Xconfigurator fails to install the graphical environment properly, run the XF86Setup command when the installation program is finished. XF86Setup will launch a graphical program that prompts you for information about your video and monitor hardware and may have more success configuring X. XF86Setup may be successful where Xconfigurator failed.

Another X problem that occurs occasionally, especially on laptops, is that graphic acceleration causes the screen to display black spots and lines. The X system uses acceleration for many cards in an attempt to make your graphical experience better. If you determine that this is causing a problem, it can be disabled. To disable acceleration, you need to edit the /etc/X/XF86Config file manually. Add the following line in the [monitor] section:

```
option "noaccel"
```

Fixing LILO

Dual boot using the LILO boot loader is straightforward. You simply have to install each operating system in a separate partition or disk, and LILO on your master boot record (MBR). LILO is then able to boot both Linux and other operating systems. Make sure that Linux is installed last so that nothing overwrites the MBR after LILO has been installed.

Things get more complicated if the other operating system is Microsoft Windows NT. Windows NT has a special loader called NTLDR, which must be placed in the MBR. This means that you cannot overwrite it with LILO or Windows NT will refuse to boot. There is a way around this limitation. Make sure you install Windows NT first, so it can write its loader to the MBR. Now when you install Linux, set the Linux partition as the active (bootable) one. When it is time to install LILO, specify that you want it installed on the Linux partition, rather than on the MBR. This way, when the system boots, the Linux partition gets loaded before NTLDR, and LILO can ask you which system you want to boot. If you select Windows NT, it will then load NTLDR, allowing both systems to coexist without problems.

A common problem with big disks was the early inability of the BIOS to recognize more than 1024 cylinders. Now, however, many large hard disks have more than 1024 cylinders. These are commonly hard disks greater than 8.6 GB. LILO will most likely not be able to load Linux, or any other system, if it is placed after the first 1024 cylinders. The way to handle this problem is to place your root partition, which is the one with your kernel, at the beginning of the disk. Do the same for your C: drive if you have DOS or Microsoft Windows installed. At the end of the drive, you can create some data or swap partitions. This will ensure that LILO has no problem loading any OS on your machine.

Hardware

Hardware-related problems are often the most difficult to resolve because there are so many hardware devices using so many different protocols. Fortunately, Linux tools exist to help you deal with these problems.

I Can't Hear You!

Sound cards can be a big problem. They are common, but they use all kinds of incompatible technologies, and many half-clones exist. Thankfully, with sndconfig most of these problems are no longer encountered. Before attempting to set up your sound card with the sndconfig utility, you should determine the type of chip on your card. If the card is an original Sound Blaster 16, configuration should be easy. However, if it is a clone, then it may not work with the Sound Blaster driver.

For example, you can have a card that is advertised as a Sound Blaster and Windows Sound System compatible card, but it really uses an ESS Maestro chip, which requires the ESS driver.

The lesson here is, make sure you know what kind of hardware you really have.

Making Printers Work

This same lesson applies to printers. If you have a printer that is not directly compatible with Linux, you need to determine the other printers with which it is 100 percent compatible and which printer it can emulate.

A Canon BJC-210 is not listed in the printtool utility, for example. However, it is compatible with the BJ-200, which is listed. If you are shopping for a new printer, make sure it is supported by Linux. Although expensive, the best type of printer to buy is one that supports PostScript, since Linux can support any PostScript-capable printer, regardless of the brand or model.

Some other problems can arise with printers. For example, the printer daemon lpd may be running, but if queried using lpq, it responds that the printer has not been found or is offline. There may be many reasons for this. First, perhaps the printer really is offline. Be sure to check. Or, perhaps the cable is bad. This message can also appear because the correct modules were not loaded. If you recompile your kernel or use some other custom kernel, make sure support for parallel port, PC-style port, and printer support are enabled.

The printer can also have another kind of problem. Printer/system communication occurs, but the output may have a staircase effect or look totally wrong. If this happens, it means you are using the wrong filter. You should go into the printtool program to correct it.

Those Touchy USB Devices

A few pages regarding universal serial bus (USB) devices is included here for two reasons. First, the USB bus is unlike any other port on your system. While you can't connect a monitor to a serial port, or a modem to your keyboard port, you can connect any type of supported device to a USB port. There are USB monitors, modems, network interfaces, mice, sound devices, scanners, printers, etc. Because of this, USB is the wave of the future—the second reason USB is discussed.

USB is a bus. It may look like a simple port on your system, but its inner workings are unlike the other ports. On a serial port, unless you use some special circuit workaround, only one device can be connected. You can connect hundreds of devices to a USB port. There are USB hubs available that can be connected to the USB port. These USB hubs offer 6 or 12 ports to connect various other devices. Another interesting thing about USB is that it also provides electrical power to the devices connected. Most serial devices must be plugged directly into an electrical outlet, but many USB devices don't have the same requirements. Devices that require a large amount of power include a power supply, but many won't.

When configuring USB in Linux, you must be aware that there are two parts of the USB bus to be supported—the USB controller and the device. USB controllers are made by various companies, but they follow a few standards. Linux currently supports those that comply to the UHCI and OHCI standards. Most USB controllers comply, so your controller should be supported.

TABLE 7-1 SUPPORTED USB DEVICES	
Type of Device	**Devices**
Mice and keyboards	Many Logitech USB mice are supported, including the N48, M-BA47 and Wingman Gaming Mouse. The Microsoft IntelliMouse Explorer also is supported. A few keyboards from Belkin, Cherry, Chicony and QTronix are supported.
Video and imaging products	The ZoomCam 1595, Kodak DC 240, 260, and Mustek MDC 800 are supported.
Hub devices	The USBH-600 hub from ADS Technologies is supported. Asante FriendlyNet also makes a supported hub. The Cherry MY3000 and Edimax hubs are also supported.
Mass storage	The Iomega USB 100M Zip drive is supported.
Printers	The Lexmark Optra S 2450 is supported.
Audio devices	The Philips Electronics USB Digital Speaker System is partially supported.
Scanners	HP Scanjet 4100C and 6300C scanners are supported.
Misc. devices	The Anchorchips EZUSB and Cypress Thermometer are supported.

While there are many USB devices now on the market, not all are supported. Table 7-1 lists a few of the supported, popular, USB devices. For a complete list and more information about the devices listed below, refer to the USB project Web site.

You should note that all of the supported devices are not in your current kernel. You *may* need to download a recent development kernel, and may also need third party software. Kernel 2.2.7 and later contain the basic USB code, and support for a few devices. Each new kernel supports new devices. You must also recompile the kernel to enable USB support in the configuration screen, where you also must enable support for a controller and device.

You can expect USB support to become more and more available in Linux and other operating systems. More information about the topics covered in this section and other supported USB devices can be found at the USB project Web site, **www.linux-usb.org**.

Software

Software is the primary reason computers are used. Many software packages come with your Red Hat Linux distribution. This section will cover a few problems that may occur when running some of them, along with a few tips that may help you use them productively.

Connecting to the Internet

As you learned this weekend, a popular application under Linux is Netscape Communicator, a well-known Web browser. One nice feature of Netscape that is used by few people is its Personal Toolbar. When downloaded, Netscape includes a Personal Toolbar with buttons that you may not find useful, such as taking you to the Yahoo and Netscape home pages. Most people, therefore, either turn off the Toolbar or ignore it. The Toolbar can be a more useful tool than Bookmarks.

What appears on the Personal Toolbar is simply what's listed in the Bookmarks, Personal Folder. Within the Personal Folder, you can create subfolders for news sites, Linux sites, and so on. To set up the Personal Toolbar, move your bookmarks into the Personal Folder using the Edit Bookmarks menu option. In this way, all of your frequently used bookmarks can be accessed directly from a Toolbar button.

Many Linux users use a program called Pine to get their e-mail messages. Pine is a console-based e-mail client that has many features and is very easy to use. It is, by default, configured to access only the e-mail messages on your local system, in a standard Unix mail format. Here's how you can use Pine both with local mail and with POP mail from your Internet provider, without first using fetchmail or some other tool to get POP mail. Start by using multiple config files:

```
pine -p localmail
pine -p popserver
```

The two configuration files specified in the last commands are identical, except for the mail fetching parameters. Now, configure Pine to use your POP server. Start Pine with the popserver argument. Next, choose Setup, Config. Set your inbox-path parameter similar to:

```
{pop.server.com/pop3/user=myid}INBOX
```

The server name and user ID you should use are provided by your Internet provider. Now restart Pine. You will be prompted for your password and then connected to the remote server from where you can now use Pine just as if you were accessing local mail while continuing to use the localmail configuration file for local mail handling.

You may also want to host Web pages with your Linux system. Your system may be on a static link, with a hostname, but you may want to support multiple hostnames such as www.domain1.com and www.domain2.com. The next paragraphs describe how to make virtual hosts in Apache, a popular Web server.

The common way to create a virtual host is to assign one IP for each hostname. But what if you want to host multiple hostnames on a single IP? Apache allows you to do so. The trick is a single command in the httpd.conf configuration file:

```
NameVirtualHost 1.2.3.4
```

Replace 1.2.3.4 with your real IP address to tell Apache the IP on which it should serve the virtual hostnames. You can add *virtual* commands for every hostname:

```
<VirtualHost www.domain2.com>
ServerAdmin webmaster@domain2.com
DocumentRoot /home/httpd/domain2
ServerName www.domain2.com
</VirtualHost>
```

These commands add a virtual host and specify the files that exist for that site. In the DNS database, the actual www.domain2.com hostname must point to your system. Next, update the record so that the host points to your server. You can do so yourself if you own the domain2.com domain name and control its name server. If not, ask the owner or technical representative to do it for you.

You may also want to create a secure Apache server, by adding an encryption library to the Apache sources. These sources and documentation are available from the Apache-SSL project site, **www.apache-ssl.org**. The encryption library can be a bit complex to install, so here are a few general-purpose hints. The goal is to compile the encryption module into the Apache binary file. You'll need to first uncompress them both in the same directory and then compile the library. With a provided patch, you can integrate both together. Once the compilation is done, continue installing the server as you would when installing a normal Apache Web server. Finally, you will need to create a certificate for your server. Using certificates is a complex topic, but you can create a temporary certificate in your Apache-ssl distribution until you purchase one from a company.

Networking Fixes

Networking is a very old concept. In fact, many people were having e-mail discussions and electronic chats in 1969. We still do the same thing, but on a much larger scale. While networking was reserved to scientists and the military in 1969, anyone with a computer can now be linked. Most networking problems have also been fixed. In the beginning, Unix systems talked on all kinds of networks, including the ARPAnet, fidonet, and, of course, on UUCP networks. While all of these protocols—and many more—are still included with your Linux distribution, you will most likely be connected on a IP network, or on an UUCP link. This section will show you how to resolve common problems related to networking issues.

Getting E-Mail Working

Many people use their Linux system as an e-mail server. There are two popular e-mail servers: Sendmail and Qmail. The one that comes with your Red Hat Linux distribution is Sendmail. If you read the documentation for Sendmail, it will suggest that you complete configuration of the entire system before building the sendmail.cf file, which contains the resulting configuration. This is a long and complex process, and needs to be done with the sources of the Sendmail package. Many people found it much easier to edit the sendmail.cf file itself. In most cases, it's only necessary to edit the first part of the file to set your domain name and various information about your server.

Another common problem occurs if you want to allow systems on your own LAN to send e-mail using the e-mail server for SMTP communications. You need to list every hostname that will use your e-mail server for outgoing mail in the file /etc/mail/relay-domains.

The Qmail mail server can bring problems too. If you want to allow other hosts to send e-mails with your server, you will need to add the following line to the file /etc/hosts.allow:

```
tcp-env: ip1, ip2, ip3: setenv = RELAYCLIENT
```

Replace ip1, ip2,.. with hostnames or IP addresses of the systems that will send e-mail via your server.

Security Alert

You can easily access files on remote Unix or Linux systems without the necessity of configuration steps or rebooting. First, make sure the remote system is running the NFS server and is allowing you to access its files. You need to specify the remote system in /etc/exports. (You can find a good example in the exports man page.) When the remote system has your system in its exports file, you can simply mount the remote directory the following way:

```
mount -tnfs 1.2.3.4:/remote-directory /mnt/remote
```

As you saw in the previous command, you specify the IP address of the remote system, and the mount command handles the rest. NFS is one of the oldest methods to share files, and it remains easy to use.

Because security is such an important topic, additional discussion is merited to help in your attempts to keep your system safe. If possible, install ssh, the Secure Shell. ssh can replace, in a secure, encrypted manner, the Telnet and FTP services. All of the communication through ssh is encrypted. Further, to connect to your system, a user must also have the ssh package.

Some people have reported speed problems on PPP dial-up connections. For example, they use a 56K bits per second (bps) modem, but actually connect at much lower speeds. The principal program used to make a PPP dial-up connection is PPPd, which will attempt to connect at a default speed of 33800 bps. If you want a higher rate, it must be specified. Many graphical dial-up clients allow you to specify a default speed. Alternatively, by calling PPPd manually, you can specify a default speed on the command line. Note that if you specify an invalid speed, the dial-out program will go back to its default speed of 33800 bps. See the PPPd man page to see the configuration settings.

Another reason for speed losses is the number of unwanted packets on the line. The Internet uses many protocols, and one of these is ICMP. This protocol is of no use to you unless you are running a server or router. You can use the ipchains command to disable it.

Internet hostnames are resolved to IP addresses using the Domain Name System (DNS). For this to work, you must have access to a DNS server. In your netcfg utility, you can specify one or more addresses for name servers. These are the servers that will resolve the hostnames. You should specify more than one, in case your primary name server goes down. You can also specify the name servers in the file /etc/resolv.conf.

Your system probably has many Internet ports opened: one for Telnet, another for DNS, and one for the FTP service. To see a list of all opened ports, type the command:

```
netstat -an
```

This command will list every open port and every host connected to your system. Ports are only numbers. You may see numbers you don't recognize and want to know which service is using a port. The fuser command will tell you that information. For example, if you want to know which service is using the UDP port number 1024, type:

```
fuser -v -n udp 1024
```

fuser reports the process using that port and the user who owns the process.

Conclusion

There was a lot of information jammed into this chapter, and ideally you found the solution to your needs. If you still need additional help, be sure to check out Appendix B, "Online Resources," to find more sources of information.

The weekend is almost over now, and you have completed a pretty significant task: the installation of Red Hat Linux. Now it's time to sit back, put your feet up and play one more game of Reversi before going to bed.

Good night!

The Linux Primer

N ow that you've successfully installed Linux on your computer, it's time to log on to your system and get familiar with working in Linux. You're probably already familiar with using a GUI, and you can find your way around unfamiliar GUIs such as KDE or GNOME pretty easily. After all, you just experiment with pointing and clicking on icons or menus until you find one that does what you want. With a command-line interface (CLI), however, you might have a little more trouble getting around if you don't know what's going on.

Getting Started: The Login Prompt

When you start your computer, and Linux has finished booting, you get a prompt to log in that looks something like this:

```
Welcome to Linux 2.4.0.
Odin Login:
```

The name in front of Login is the name you've given your computer when you set up networking. If you haven't given your computer a name (shame on you), the default is localhost.

If you've set up a regular account for yourself, type in your username at the prompt. If you haven't set up a normal user account for yourself, however, type in root.

CAUTION ◆◆

It is a bad idea to do all of your work on your system as root if you aren't very familiar with Linux. Actually, it's a bad idea to do all of your work as root even if you are very familiar with Linux. Linux is an obedient operating system—it does whatever you tell it to do as long as you have the proper permissions. This means it is possible to delete your entire directory tree without any fuss from the system. Consider yourself warned.

◆◆

Using Passwords

After typing in your username, you will be prompted for your password. For security reasons, your password does not display as you type. Furthermore, if your computer is exposed to other users — even if just through a dial-up Internet connection — you probably should change your password from time to time and use a password that includes numbers as well as letters. Passwords made up of regular words are weak because you can find them in a dictionary, making them vulnerable to what is known as a dictionary attack. Don't be so clever with your password that you forget it, though — especially if you don't use Linux every day. On a dual-boot system it's very easy to install Linux, forget about it for a while, and then go back to find you've forgotten your password! There are ways to fix this, but it's easier not to worry about it in the first place.

TIP If you are having trouble with your password, but you're certain you're typing it correctly, make sure that the Caps Lock key is not toggled. Linux passwords are case-sensitive. You'd be surprised how often this happens.

Now that you're logged in to the system, it's time to start getting familiar with how to navigate the Linux OS from the command line.

Getting Familiar with Multi-User Operating Systems

Linux is a multi-user operating system. That means you can have several people logged in to one Linux machine who are all working simultaneously. Typical desktop operating systems are designed to handle only one user at a time. A typical Linux machine can have one user logged in locally and several other users logged in remotely over a network connection.

Using Virtual Terminals

Another way to make use of Linux's multi-user functionality is to log in to multiple virtual terminals. While you're logged in to the system, press Alt+F2. Another login screen appears. This enables you to work on several things at the command line simultaneously, just by alternating between virtual terminals.

You can be logged in to several virtual terminals at a time, which is very useful. If you find you need to do something as root, for example, you can log in to a virtual terminal and execute the commands you need to as root. Once you finish with the system administrator stuff, you can log out again so you aren't tempted to work as root on everyday tasks.

Using the whoami Command

If you're logged in to five virtual terminals, some as yourself and some as root, what if you forget which is which? Easy. At the shell prompt, type in **whoami.** The system will display the name of the user currently logged into that terminal. Figure A-1 shows an example of the output of the whoami command.

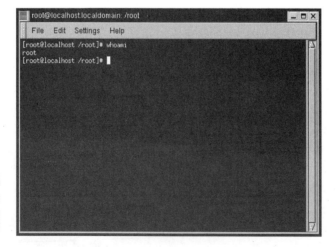

Figure A-1

An example of the output from the whoami command

Another sign to look for is the shell prompt. Under bash, the shell prompt is a dollar sign ($) when you are logged in as a regular user. When logged in as root, the shell prompt is a pound sign (#) instead.

Understanding and Using File Permissions

The key difference between the root user and the typical user on a Linux system is the permissions each has on the system. As the name implies, permissions indicate what a particular user is allowed to do. If you have permission to manipulate a file, Linux lets you do so. If you do not, however, the system returns a permission denied error message.

Permissions are very important for a multi-user operating system. They prevent unauthorized users from accessing files vital to the system, and they prevent users from accessing or accidentally overwriting each other's files.

NOTE This also makes Linux a great OS for home use. When a family shares a computer, Mom, Dad, and the kids each have separate home directories in which they can save their own files without worry. With legacy operating systems, such as Windows, files belonging to one family member often are misplaced or deleted by another family member who doesn't realize the files are important. This often has the effect of contributing to Dad's ulcer when his report due Monday morning was deleted to make more room for a game Junior downloaded.

There are three types of permissions: read, write, and execute. These permissions can apply to the owner of the file (the user), the group to which the file belongs (the group), and all other users (the others). By making a file owned by a particular user and group, and then setting permissions for the user, the group, and the others, you can control precisely who can access the file (see Table A-1). Typically, the user who created it owns a new file. The file has read and write permissions for that user and read access for anyone else. If you don't want anyone else to be able to read the

TABLE A-1   MEANINGS OF PERMISSIONS

Permission	File	Directory
Read	File can be read.	Directory contents can be listed.
Write	File can be modified.	Files can be created and deleted in the directory.
Execute	File can be executed.	Directory can be opened.

file, be sure to remove the read option from the file for the group and for all other users. To do this, execute the following command:

```
chmod 600 file
```

Running the chmod (change mode) command on a file changes the mode of access to the file, depending on the arguments you pass to the file when you run it. In the preceding example, you pass the octal notation for the level of permissions allowed for that file. The first digit describes the permissions for the user, the second digit is for the group, and the last is for all other users. Also, note that no matter what permissions are set on a file, the root user can always access a file.

NOTE   The octal notation, 0-7, represents the file permissions numerically. 0 indicates no permissions, 1 indicates execute permission, 2 indicates write permission and 4 indicates read permission. When you add the numbers together, you have between 0 and 7. Thus, if you have read and write permission, the number would be 6, for example. For some people it is easier to remember number schemes than the other way round.

It's also possible to tell chmod only what permissions to change, rather than give it an entirely new set of permissions. For example, if you wanted to allow everyone in the file's group to write to it, you could use this command:

```
chmod g+w file
```

You refer to the user, group, and others with the letters u, g, and o. A plus sign sets the permissions; a minus sign clears them. The permissions themselves are indicated by r for read, w for write, and x for execute. You can specify multiple letters at once.

To find out what permissions are currently set on a file, run the ls command with the -1 argument, as follows. I use my own screen name as a placeholder for these examples.

```
$ ls -1 testfile
-r--------  1 BKP    users              0 Sep 26 15:28 testfile
```

The first – is not related to permissions; the next three relate to my (BKP) permissions; the next three relate to my group's permissions; and the final three are the permissions for all users. As you can see, I only have read access to the file, and no one else can read the file. If I had read, write, and execute access, the output would look like this:

```
-rwx------  1 BKP    users              0 Sep 26 15:28 testfile
```

Files stored under MS-DOS or Microsoft Windows can also have permissions, but you'll have fewer options since those are not multi-user operating systems.

Finding Hidden Files

Unlike MS-DOS files, which can have a flag set to make them hidden, Linux files are hidden when they begin with a dot (period).

◄ ◄

Linux files that begin with a dot are hidden. These are commonly called *dotfiles*.

◄ ◄

Many common configuration files are stored in dotfiles in each user's home directory. You normally don't see these files unless you ask to see them, as in this example:

```
$ ls -a
./       .Xdefaults    .bash_profile   .emacs    .mailcap   .zshrc     tmp/
../      .bash_logout  .bashrc         .kderc    .vimrc     Desktop/
```

Working at the Shell

The default command shell under Red Hat Linux is the GNU Bourne Again Shell, or bash. The shell is the command interpreter for Linux, much like command.com is for MS-DOS or its GUI equivalent, the Windows Explorer, under MS Windows. The bash shell executes commands from standard input or from a script. Shell scripts under Linux are the functional equivalent of batch files under MS-DOS, except that they are much more powerful than the average batch file.

The bash shell is not the only command shell available for Linux. Three other popular shells are csh, which is similar to the Berkley UNIX C Shell, and the enhanced version of csh, tcsh, as well as the Z shell, zsh.

As is often the case in Linux, there is a dizzying variety of options, far too many to cover in a book concerned with brevity and simplicity. Generally, the Bourne Again Shell is probably the only shell you ever need to know. However, there are plenty of other shells available if you find you want to experiment.

You do not need to do anything to initialize the bash shell; it is available after you install Red Hat and runs whenever you log in to the computer. However, there are options for the bash shell you can use to configure the way bash behaves. When you log in to Linux, bash looks for a file called /.bashrc in your home directory. If this exists, bash reads the file and executes the commands that you put in the file.

Under Red Hat Linux, ~/.bashrc is not created by default. However, if you wish to customize bash, you can easily create your own /.bashrc.

Keep in mind that /.bashrc is not the same to Linux as bashrc. The /.bashrc file is a dot file, which means it is normally a hidden file. Most configuration files under Linux are dotfiles found in the user's home directory.

Understanding the Linux Philosophy

You probably notice that I mention piping and redirecting output and input several times in explaining commands in this primer. The reason is that the UNIX philosophy is that every command should be a filter and operate on input and output. You can pipe or redirect almost any command's output into a file, a device, or another command. Linux follows the basic idea of UNIX in this fashion. I explain a few simple ways to utilize this in this appendix, but I barely can touch the surface of the capabilities of Linux. You should experiment with redirection and pipes a little on your own. You might be surprised what kind of timesaving shortcuts you discover.

Piping Input and Output

Piping is taking the output of one command and making it input for another command. For example, to pipe the output of the ps command to the grep command to search for a process ID, issue this command:

```
ps -ax | grep netscape
```

The | is the pipe symbol. If there is a Netscape process running, grep outputs the lines with netscape in them to standard out (the monitor).

Using Direction and Redirection

You can redirect input or output with the symbols > and <. The > symbol redirects output to a file or device. The < symbol changes a command's input to come from a file or device rather than from the keyboard.

You can use the > symbol to create a file by redirecting output from a command to a filename. Be careful not to overwrite an existing file with this redirection. If you would rather append the output to an existing file, use >>, which tells the shell not to clobber the file, but instead append to it. If you want to overwrite a file, use >|, which tells the shell to go ahead and overwrite the file without asking. Some shells treat > and >| the same, never asking you if it is okay to overwrite the file.

 **CAUTION** As always, be careful with redirection symbols. You can easily overwrite an important file.

Common Commands

To get around better in Linux, you should familiarize yourself with some common commands. Even if you plan to spend most of your time in KDE, GNOME, or one of Linux's other GUIs, you find using these commands in a term or at the console very useful. You will also find you are able to combine commands with each other to simplify everyday tasks.

Some commands have a large number of options, and they might not all be covered in this text if they aren't likely to be used in normal situations. For a complete list of options, you can consult the command's man page.

Copying Files: The cp Command

Name: cp

Function: To copy files and directories.

Syntax: cp [options] file(s) destination

Description: The cp command is similar to the MS-DOS command copy; it's used to copy files or directories from one place to another. You can copy one file to a new file, one file to another place, or a large number of files all at once to a new place. When you copy a file, you do not delete the original file by default. If you wish to move a file rather than make a copy of it, use the mv command instead.

Usage: To use the cp command, type **cp**, followed by any options, and then type the directory or filename(s) you want to copy, followed by the destination. If you want to copy multiple files, you can use wildcards, or you can list multiple files separated by spaces.

Options:

-f Force. Remove any existing files of the same name.

-i Interactive. Prompt the user if there is an existing file of the same name in the destination directory.

-p Preserve. This option tells the cp command to preserve the original file's permissions, if possible.

-R Recursive. Copy directories located under the starting directory. The default is not to copy subdirectories.

Example 1: Copying a File into Another Directory

Let's say you download a /.tgz file called ~/program.tgz — which contains source code — into your home directory, and you want to unzip and untar it, but you don't want to do it in your home directory. You can cp the file into the /tmp directory and work with it there. To do this, type in the following:

```
cp program.tgz /tmp
```

Note that you do not get an error message if the file already exists unless you use the interactive option. If the file exists, you are asked whether you want to overwrite the file or not, like this:

```
cp -i program.tgz /tmp
cp: overwrite  /tmp/program.tgz'?
```

If you answer **y**, the file is overwritten; if n, the file is not overwritten.

Example 2: Copying Multiple Files into Another Directory

If you have a group of files you want to move into another directory without having to type each filename individually, you can use wildcards. If you want to copy all files in the current directory to another directory, type

```
cp * /tmp
```

This copies all files in the directory to the /tmp directory; however, it does not copy directories unless specifically told to. To copy files and directories, use the recursive option.

```
cp -R * /tmp
```

NOTE Note that -r and -R are not equivalent. Unlike MS-DOS and Windows, Linux is case-sensitive. Be careful when typing commands under Linux, as interchanging uppercase and lowercase letters might cause unwanted and possibly disastrous results!

If you'd like to copy all files with a specific extension to another directory, you can use wildcards to selectively copy groups of files like this:

```
cp *.jpg *.gif images
```

This copies all JPEG and GIF files to the image directory, without copying any other files with them. You can also use the question mark character (?) to match a single character rather than a group of characters.

Moving Files: The mv Command

Name: mv

Function: To move or rename files and directories.

Syntax: mv [options] file(s) destination

Description: The `mv` command can be used to move a file or files to another directory, or to rename a file or files. The `mv` command is similar to the `move` command under MS-DOS, but the `mv` command is much more powerful than its MS-DOS equivalent. The `mv` command does delete the original file that is being moved, so be sure to use the command carefully. The `mv` command is also used to rename files under Linux, so it also takes the place of the `REN` command under MS-DOS.

Usage: To move a file, type `mv`, followed by any options, then the name of the file(s) or directories to be moved, and then the destination to which you want the file(s) moved. As with the `cp` command, you can use wildcards to move multiple files rather than typing individual filenames.

Options:

-b Backup. The backup option creates a backup file of any files that would be overwritten by moving a file. By default, backup files have a tilde character (~) extension.

-f Force. Removes any files of the same name when trying to move a file without prompting the user.

-i Interactive. The interactive mode of mv prompts the user if moving the current file will overwrite another file. If there are no conflicting files, mv simply moves the file with no complaint.

-S Suffix. Appends a suffix to any backup files. By default, the tilde suffix is applied, but you can specify any type of suffix, such as .bak or .tmp.

Example 1: Moving a File to Another Directory

To move the file `index.html` to another directory without making a backup or being prompted in the event of an overwrite, use the `mv` command, followed by the name of the file and its destination:

```
mv index.html /home/BKP/backup/
```

If you're not certain whether a file of the same name already exists, use the interactive mode of mv. If the file already exists, your output looks like this:

```
mv -i index.html /home/BKP/backup/
mv: replace /home/BKP/backup/index.html'?
```

Example 2: Moving Multiple Files to Another Directory

You can use wildcards to move more than one file to another directory. Be careful! The mv command can move directories as well as regular files. Be sure you actually want to move everything under a directory before using the wildcard (*).

If you want to move all of the .html files in the current directory to the /home/httpd/ directory, you use this command:

```
mv *.html /home/httpd/
```

The *.html specifies that you want to move all files that end in .html to another directory. If you want to move all files in the current directory to the /home/httpd/ directory, you type

```
mv * /home/httpd/
```

This moves all files in the current directory, except any dotfiles. To move dotfiles, you have to be more explicit:

```
mv .* /home/httpd/
```

Example 3: Renaming Files with mv

Linux does not have a separate rename command, so the mv command is used to rename files. If you want to rename index.html to index.html.old, for instance, you use the mv command like this:

```
mv index.html index.html.old
```

As far as Linux is concerned, moving a file and renaming it is the same thing.

Creating Directories: The mkdir Command

Name: mkdir

Function: To create new directories.

Syntax: mkdir [options] directory

Description: The mkdir command is pretty straightforward. It behaves the same way that the MS-DOS command MKDIR works. The Linux command does have some additional functionality — you can set the permissions of the directory when it is created.

Usage: To create a new directory simply type mkdir and any options and then the name of the directory you wish to create.

Options:

-*m Mode.* To create a directory with specified permissions.

Example 1: Creating a New Directory

To create a new directory called /html under the current directory, use the mkdir command followed by the name of the new directory:

```
mkdir html
```

If you want to create a new directory called download under the /tmp directory that has read-only permissions for other users and members of your group, and read and write permissions for you, use the mkdir command plus the proper octal mode:

```
mkdir -m 644 /tmp/download
```

This creates a directory named download under the /tmp directory. You do not need to be in the /tmp directory to create a subdirectory for it. If a file or directory named /download already exists in the /tmp directory, you receive the following error message:

```
mkdir /tmp/download
mkdir: cannot make directory  download': File exists
```

Listing and Finding Files with ls

Name: `ls`

Function: To list the contents of a directory.

Syntax: `ls [options] [directory or file(s)]`

Description: The ls command lists the contents of a directory. This command is similar to the MS-DOS command DIR. In fact, typing `dir` under Linux is the same as typing `ls -c`. The `ls` command is one of the commands you use the most under Linux. You can also use the `ls` command to get information about a specific file in a directory.

Usage: To use the `ls` command, you simply type the command, followed by any options you want to invoke and any filenames (including wildcards) that you want to specify.

Options:

-a All. Using the -a option lists all files in a directory, including hidden files.

-A Almost all. Lists all files in a directory, except for . and . . .

-i Inode. Prints inode number of each file.

-l Long. In addition to the filenames, lists the file type, permissions, owner name, size of the file and the last time the file was modified. Also known as the verbose mode.

-r Reverse. Lists the directory contents in reverse order.

-sk Kilobytes. Lists file sizes in kilobytes. The s specifies that, yes, you want to see the sizes.

-X Extension. Sorts files by their extension; files with no extension will be sorted first.

Example 1: Listing Files in Your Home Directory

You probably want to know what files are in your home directory from time to time, so it's a good idea to know how to check. To list the files in your home directory, type the following command:

```
ls ~
```

That's all you need to type. The ~ character is a shortcut that refers to your home directory. The output for the command looks something like Figure A-2.

NOTE Did you notice on your screen that not only are the files in the current directory listed, but that they're in color? That's one of the ways Linux makes your life a little bit easier.

Figure A-2

Output of the ls command

Example 2: Listing Hidden Files in a Directory

If you decide you want to edit resource files, you probably have to find some hidden files. To list all files in a directory, type in the following:

```
ls -a
```

When listing all of the files in your home directory, you find there are quite a few more files than you might have thought.

Example 3: Listing All Files and Their Attributes

If you want to see all of the files in a directory and their attributes, combine the -a and -l options, as follows:

```
ls -al
```

You see a listing of all files in the directory, as well as their permissions, modification dates, to whom they belong, and the size of the files. The first letter indicates whether it is a file, directory, link, or other. A file is a dash (-), a directory is d, a symbolic link is an l, and a hard link is represented as a regular file. Other characters indicate it is a special type of file. After that letter comes the permissions. There are three groups of three letters. The first set is the permissions given to the owner of the file. The next set of three is for the group of the file, and then finally the permissions for everyone else. Then you see the owner of the file, followed by the group to which the file belongs. By default, the size of each file is displayed in bytes. Next in the listing is the last time the file was modified (edited), then the name of the file itself.

NOTE   The expression touch is not one I coined. On UNIX-style operating systems, a file is said to be touched when it is modified by a user in some way. A file is not touched when you just list the contents of a directory the file is in, or view the contents of the file.

Making Links

Name: ln

Function: To create a hard link or symbolic link to a file.

Syntax: ln [options] source [linkname]

Description: The ln command creates a link to a file or directory. By using the ln command, you can create either a symbolic link or a hard link. A symbolic, or soft, link is a special file that contains a pathname. Hard links are actually another name for a file, rather than a pointer to that file like symbolic links. As long as a name (that is, a hard link) for a file exists, it remains on disk. Even if you create a file, create a hard link to it, and then delete the original file, the data remains safely on disk. If you create a symbolic link pointing to a file and delete the original file, the file ceases to exist and the soft link is left pointing to nothing.

The other major difference between symbolic links and hard links is that symbolic links can cross filesystems. Hard links can only point to files on the same filesystem. For instance, if you have your /home directory on one hard drive partition, and the /opt directory on another, you could not create a hard link from something in the /home directory to something in the /opt directory. However, you could create a symbolic link between the two with no problem.

Usage: Use the ln command to create symbolic or hard links to files or directories. If you do not specify the name of the link, ln attempts to create a link with the same name as to what you're linking.

Options:

-f Force. Removes files if they already exist with the link's name.

-i Interactive. Prompts the user if files exist.

-s Symbolic. Makes a symbolic link rather than a hard link.

Example 1: Creating a Symbolic Link to a Directory

Let's say you do a lot of work in the `/home/httpd/Webpages/uri/` directory, but don't feel like typing the entire directory name each time you want to change to that directory. You can create a symbolic link to that directory in your home directory called `/Web` and then you only have to type `cd /Web` to change to the `/home/httpd/Webpages/uri/` directory. To create that link, use the following command:

```
ln -s /home/httpd/Webpages/uri/ ~/Web
```

As long as there are no files in your home directory called `/Web`, you have created a symbolic link to the proper directory. This can be very useful and save quite a bit of typing!

Moving around the Command Line Interface: cd

Name: `cd`

Function: change the working directory.

Syntax: `cd [directory]`

Description: The `cd` command changes your working directory to another directory that you specify. This command is used to navigate the directory structure in Linux. Typing only `cd` returns you to your home directory. The `cd` command works similarly to the `CD` command under DOS. However, the `cd` command is a little more flexible in that it allows you shortcuts to change between your home directory and the previous working directory.

Usage: Use the `cd` command to change directories. Specifying no directory returns you to your home directory.

Options: none

Example 1: Changing to the Parent Directory of the Current Working Directory

As in DOS, the parent directory is always .. . To go up one level in the directory structure, simply type the following:

```
cd ..
```

NOTE You must have a space between the .. and cd. If you type **cd..** with no space (as you might be used to doing under DOS), you get an error message telling you that the command cd.. is not found.

If you want to go up several levels in the directory structure, you can do so by typing this:

```
cd ../../
```

This moves you up two levels from your current directory.

Example 2: Changing to a Specific Directory

To change to a specific directory, issue the cd command, then type the name of the desired directory. If you're working in your home directory and decide to switch to the /tmp directory, you use this command:

```
cd /tmp
```

NOTE It is important to note that /tmp and tmp are not the same in this instance. The /tmp tells the shell you want to go to the tmp under the / (root) directory and not a tmp directory under the present working directory.

Example 3: Going Home Quickly

To get to your home directory quickly, simply use the cd command with no arguments, like this:

```
cd
```

If you do not specify a directory, the bash shell assumes you wish to go back to your home directory. You can also use the tilde (~) symbol to specify your home directory, as in the following example:

```
cd ~
```

Example 4: Going Back to the Previous Working Directory

If you want to quickly jump back to the directory you were last in, without typing the full pathname of that directory, type this shortcut:

```
cd -
```

Once you get the hang of the cd command, and Linux's directory structure, you find that using the command-line interface is not as unfriendly as you might have thought when you first started using Linux. If you try using DOS after using Linux for a while, you really find yourself missing Linux.

Where the Heck Am I? Using pwd

Name: pwd

Function: To print the name of the present working directory.

Syntax: pwd

Description: The command pwd is about as straightforward as you can get. It's a one-trick pony. If you have lost track of where you're at in the directory structure, you simply use pwd to get the shell to print the present working directory to standard out.

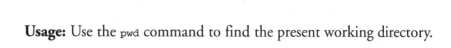

Usage: Use the pwd command to find the present working directory.

Options: None.

Example 1: Using pwd to Find the Present Working Directory

At the command shell, type in

pwd

The output is the current working directory. The pwd command does not take any options or arguments.

Mounting Filesystems

There are two commands under Linux that are pertinent to accessing filesystems: mount and umount. The mount command is used to mount a filesystem, and not surprisingly, the umount command is used to unmount a mounted filesystem.

Name: mount

Function: To make available, or mount, a filesystem.

Syntax: mount [options] device [directory]

Description: Unlike other operating systems you might be used to, Linux requires that you mount a filesystem before you can use it. Generally, most of this happens during the boot-up procedure, and you don't do it manually. CD-ROMs and floppies have to be mounted as you wish to use them, and unmounted when you are finished. Normally you have to be the superuser (root) to issue the mount command. You do not normally need to specify the filesystem type or the directory to mount in if the device is already listed in the /etc/fstab file. If you want to make a device mountable by a user, or all users, include that information on the device line in `/etc/fstab`. Open your favorite text editor and put an entry in the `/etc/fstab` file like this:

```
/dev/hdd /cdrom iso9660 ro,user
```

From left to right, that line includes the name of the device, the directory it should be mounted under, the filesystem type, an option specifying read-only, and an option specifying that non-root users can mount the device. Be sure to separate the options only with commas but no spaces, otherwise Linux doesn't understand what you're saying.

Currently mounted filesystems can be found in the `/etc/mtab` file. Do not edit the `/etc/mtab` file by hand, because it is updated dynamically by your system. It is useful to be able to read the `/etc/mtab` file, however, to see what devices are currently available and what filesystems they are mounted as.

Usage: To use the `mount` command, type **mount** followed by any options, and then the device name you wish to mount and optionally the directory under which you want the device mounted. In Red Hat Linux, the default directory for the CD-ROM is /mnt/cdrom. If you have additional devices you need to access, you can create directories for them under the `/mnt` directory (or wherever else you like, but the `/mnt` directory is the standard location).

NOTE Another nifty thing about Linux (and there are plenty!) is that it can handle quite a few filesystem types. Linux can read disks in its own native format (ext2), the FAT16 and FAT32 formats used by MS-DOS and Windows 9x, the Macintosh filesystem HFS, the Joliet filesystem used by Windows 9x for CD-ROMs and the standard ISO9660 CD-ROM format, as well as many others. I found this very handy when I was sent a Zip disk with art files in Macintosh format. Using Windows I would have had to buy an expensive program to read files from a Mac disk; using Linux I just had to recompile the kernel to support HFS and mount the disk like any other Zip.

Options:

-a Auto. Determines file system type automatically, if possible.

-n No write. Mounts the device without writing in `/etc/mtab`. Useful if `/etc/mtab` is a read-only file.

-t Type. Specifies the filesystem type. The following filesystem types are common:

- **ext2**. The native Linux filesystem
- **msdos**. FAT16 file system
- **umsdos**. UMSDOS file system
- **vfat**. The FAT32 file system
- **minix**. The Minux file system
- **nfs**. Network file system
- **smbfs**. SMB shares from Windows or Samba
- **iso9660**. Standard CD-ROM file system
- **hfs**. Standard Macintosh file system

-v Verbose. Prints any messages to standard out.

-o Options. Filesystem-specific options are specified by `-o` followed by a comma-separated list of options. Note that I am only listing the most common options. Most of these apply to all filesystem types, but some filesystems may support additional options.

- `auto`. Can also be specified by -a
- `defaults`. Uses the default options (rw, suid, dev, exec, auto, nouser, async)
- `exec`. Permits the execution of binaries on the filesystem
- `noexec`. Does not permit the execution of binaries on the filesystem

- ⚙ **ro**. Mounts the file system read-only, does not allow writing to the filesystem

- ⚙ **rw**. Mounts the file system read-write, allows writing to the filesystem if the user has the privileges

Example 1: Mounting a CD-ROM

To use a CD-ROM you need to mount it. By default, Red Hat Linux comes with a /mnt/cdrom directory. To mount a typical CD-ROM, type this command:

```
mount -t iso9660 /dev/hdd /mnt/cdrom
```

This tells the system that the filesystem type (-t) is iso9660, the CD-ROM standard, and that your CD-ROM is located on the fourth IDE channel (hdd). Typically, your hard drive is hda; if you have a second it usually is hdb, and so on. On most PCs, you'll find two IDE controllers that each support two devices, allowing for hda through hdd. The master device on the first controller is hda; the slave device is hdb. The master device on the second controller is hdc, and the slave device is hdd. The final argument to the mount command is the directory under which you want the CD-ROM mounted. Now, unless there are errors, you can access the CD-ROM from that directory.

Example 2: Mounting a Floppy

To mount a MS-DOS floppy in what would be drive A under MS-DOS, use the mount command like this:

```
mount -t msdos /dev/fd0 /floppy
```

This mounts an MS-DOS (FAT16) floppy under the /floppy directory. By default, it allows read and write access. If you do not want to allow write access to the floppy, you can specify that with the -o ro option, like this:

```
mount -t msdos -o ro /dev/fd0 /floppy
```

If your `/etc/fstab` file is set up correctly, you can save typing. You only have to tell the `mount` command what device to mount; it tries to assume the rest by reading `/etc/fstab`. So to mount your floppy, usually all you really need to type is this:

```
mount /dev/fd0
```

Unlike Windows, Linux does not assign drive letters to devices. Devices become part of the filesystem when mounted. Although this probably seems foreign to you at first, it actually tends to make more sense. For one thing, you're not limited to 26 devices on your system! Okay, you probably won't hit this limit at home, but it is a real concern in a networked environment.

Unmounting Filesystems

NOTE •

When I first started using Red Hat, I kept trying to unmount CD-ROMs and floppies using `unmount` instead of `umount`. It's a common mistake. I eventually started remembering that it was umount instead of unmount, but you don't have to. If you want to type a more logical command, go to the `/bin` directory and make a symbolic link to `umount` called `unmount`, like this: `ln  -s  umount  unmount`. Then the system finds a command called `unmount` after all. The `-s` provides a symbolic link to the command `umount`, thus providing for those who think `unmount` is more logical.

• •

Name: `umount`

Function: To unmount a device attached to the filesystem.

Syntax: `umount [options] directory`

Description: The `umount` command unmounts a mounted device. You probably only need to use `umount` on devices such as your CD-ROM drive or floppy drive, though it can also be used to unmount any device on the system that is not currently being used. It is the opposite of the `mount` command.

Usage: To use the umount command, type **umount** followed by any options and then the directory name the device is mounted under. You can also use the device name instead of the directory, but it's usually easier to type the directory name.

NOTE   Note that if the filesystem is in use, Linux does not allow you to unmount it. If you are in the /cdrom directory, for instance, it does not let you unmount a CD-ROM mounted under that directory.

Options:

-n No write. Unmounts without writing in the /etc/mtab file.

-r Read only. If unmounting fails, this will try to remount read-only instead.

Example 1: Unmounting the CD-ROM

To unmount a CD-ROM mounted under the /cdrom directory, type

```
umount /cdrom
```

As long as no one is currently accessing /cdrom or is in that directory, the device is unmounted with no error messages or other output.

Example 2: Unmounting the Floppy

The syntax for unmounting a floppy is the same. Type:

```
umount /floppy
```

Deleting Files

Name: rm

Function: To remove files and directories.

Syntax: rm [options] file(s)

Description: The rm command is similar to the DEL command under MS-DOS, but it is much more powerful.

◆ ◆

Unlike MS-DOS, Windows, or the Mac OS, Linux assumes you know what you're doing. This means if you have the permissions to remove files, Linux lets you and it doesn't complain that it might damage the system. Be very careful when removing files under Linux; once they're gone, they're gone. There is no command to undelete in Linux, so be sure to exercise this command with caution. You can wipe out your entire directory tree and Linux happily lets you. This is a good reason not to do your work when you are logged in as root. Normal users don't have the permissions to really mess up the entire system. The root user, on the other hand, can delete the entire filesystem with one command.

◆ ◆

Usage: To remove a file, type **rm**, then any options, and then the name of the file to be removed.

Options:

-f Force. Do not prompt the user for confirmation, and give no error messages for non-existing files.

-i Interactive. Ask before removing each file.

-r,-R Recursive. Remove directories and their contents recursively.

-v Verbose. Print the names of files being removed.

Example 1: Removing a File

To simply remove a file use the rm command with no options, and only one argument—the name of the file you wish to remove, like this:

```
rm file
```

This removes the file with no error message or output of any kind as long as the file does exist and you have permissions to remove it. If the file doesn't exist or you don't have permissions, rm produces an error message.

Example 2: Removing a Directory and All Files under It

To remove an entire directory and any contents in the directory, use the rm command along with the recursive (-r or -R) option and the name of the directory, like this:

```
rm -r tmp/
```

As long as you have the proper permissions, and the directory exists, there is no prompting or messages; Linux simply removes the directory and all of its contents. This is a good argument for using the interactive option as well, like this:

```
rm -ri tmp/
```

As you can see from the Figure A-3, you have several chances to change your mind about removing the file under the tmp directory, and removing the directory itself. Unless you are very sure of yourself, and even if you are, I recommend using the interactive option of the rm command. It takes a little longer, but there's less chance of deleting an important file. Granted, deleting a vital part of your system helps you build valuable troubleshooting skills, but that's probably not the way you want to build them.

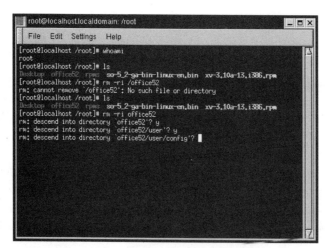

Figure A-3

Using `rm` interactively.

Example 3: Deleting Multiple Files with Wildcards

You can use wildcards to delete multiple files at once without having to type individual filenames.

CAUTION ◆◆◆
Be very careful with wildcards. You can very easily destroy files you do not want to delete.
◆◆◆

If you have multiple files that only differ by one character, you can use the ? wildcard to represent only one character, like this:

```
rm -i temp?
```

That command deletes any file named temp1, temp2, and so on. It does not delete a file named temp22, stuff, or just plain temp.

The * wildcard in the next example deletes any file that begins with temp in the current directory. You can use the * wildcard to match a few files, like this:

```
rm -i temp*
```

Or you can use the * wildcard to match all files in a directory, like this:

```
rm -i *
```

NOTE ●●
The interactive option is not necessary, but I'm putting it in the examples to encourage you to use it, at least until you're very familiar with Linux.
●●

Example 4: Utter Insanity

If you're just fed up with your system, you can delete the entire directory tree with the following command executed as root under the / directory. Be sure you've got installation disks ready to go.

```
rm -rf *
```

Do not try this at home, and no, I haven't tried it to make sure it works.

Viewing and Manipulating Files with cat

Name: `cat`

Function: Concatenate files and print on standard out.

Syntax: `cat [options] [file(s)]`

Description: The `cat` command basically takes a file (or standard input, if you don't specify a file) and prints it to standard output, which is another name for the display. This is somewhat useful for quickly viewing files such as `/etc/fstab` or one of the other configuration files. The `cat` command really becomes useful in conjunction with other commands, either by piping the output of `cat` to other commands, or creating files with the output.

Usage: To concatenate a file to standard output, type **cat** followed by any options, and the name of the file. Generally `cat` is used with some sort of redirection.

Options:

-b Number. Number all lines that are not blank.

-s Squeeze. Replace multiple blank lines with one blank line.

-n Number all. Number all lines.

-v Show nonprinting. Show nonprinting characters as well as regular characters.

-T Tabs. Show tabs in a file.

Example 1: Concatenating a File to the Display

The simplest use of `cat` is to display the contents of a file to the screen, with no options. This can be useful to quickly view the contents of a file, without opening the file in vi or Emacs. To see what filesystems are currently mounted you can cat the contents of /etc/mtab to the display (standard out), like this (see Figure A-4):

```
cat /etc/mtab
```

This is somewhat useful, but cat becomes very useful when you redirect the output of the command to a file or another command.

Example 2: Redirecting the Output of a Concatenation

To redirect the output of cat, you should either pipe the output of cat to another command, or redirect the output into a file. Here's how you redirect output from cat into another file.

```
cat file > file2
```

The preceding command overwrites the contents of the file if it already exists, and creates the file if it doesn't exist. Basically, this is a poor man's copy.

If you want to append the contents of one file onto another, without overwriting the original contents, you can use the following command:

```
cat file >> file2
```

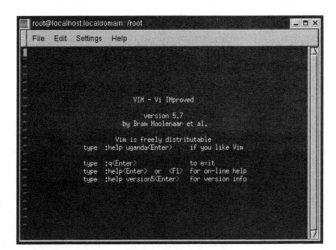

Figure A-4

The output of cat /etc/mtab.

This tells the shell to append the output of `cat` to the file rather than overwriting it.

`cat` is also used frequently in conjunction with the `less` command and the `grep` command. Say you have a text file where you save all of your friends' names and addresses, phone numbers, and email addresses, and you want to find one quickly. You can `cat` the file and pipe the output to `grep` and use `grep` to search for your friend's name. For instance

```
cat phonenumbers.txt | grep Bob
```

The preceding command outputs every line with Bob in it, saving you the hassle of searching through all of your friends' information in that file. You can even create a file just for Bob by redirecting the output to `/Bob.txt`, like this.

```
cat phonenumbers.txt | grep Bob > Bob.txt
```

Viewing Files with less

The `less` command is also useful to view files, especially longer files. It also enables you to navigate files in a way that `cat` does not.

Name: `less`

Function: The `less` command reads a file (or standard input, if no file is given) to standard output. It is similar to the `more` command, but allows forward and backward movement.

Syntax: `less [options] [file]`

Options:

-E End. Tells less to exit when it reaches the end of a file.

-f Force. Forces non-regular files to be opened. No error message is given when opening a binary file.

-i Ignore. Causes searches to ignore case.

-p Pattern. Starts less on the first instance of a given pattern.

-s Squeeze. Display multiple blank lines as one blank line.

-S Chop lines. The -s option causes long lines to be truncated rather than wrapped. In other words, lines too long for the display are chopped to fit and the remainder is discarded.

-u Printable. Carriage feeds and backspaces to be treated as printable characters.

Example 1: Displaying a File with less

```
less /etc/rc.d/rc.modules
```

The preceding displays the file /etc/rc.d/rc.modules and enables you to navigate the file without having to open a text editor.

To move around in less, use the following keys:

- **Enter**. Move one line forward.
- **d or Ctrl+d**. Move forward one-half screen at a time.
- **b or Ctrl+b**. Move backward one-half screen at a time.
- **Left arrow**. Move horizontally to the left.
- **Right arrow**. Move horizontally to the right.
- **F**. Scroll forward.
- **g**. Go to the beginning of the file, or if preceded by a number, go to that line.
- **G**. Go to the end of the file, or if preceded by a number, go to that line.
- **h**. Display a summary of less commands.
- **Space**. Scroll forward an entire screen.

Viewing Running Processes with ps

Name: ps

Function: Display running processes.

Syntax: `ps [options] [pid(s)]`

Description: The `ps` command displays process status to standard out. You get a static report of what processes are currently running. The `top` command is similar but provides a continually updating report of processes and their status. The `ps` command is useful to see what processes are running, who has created the process, and what the process statuses are.

Usage: To use `ps`, type **ps** followed by any options, and a process ID if you want to check a specific process and know its ID. If you don't know the ID of the process, you can run `ps` to find out!

Options:

-l Long. Give lots of information.

-u User. Give username and start time of processes.

-m Memory. Give memory usage.

-a All. Show processes created by other users as well.

-x Detached. Show processes that are not associated with a terminal.

-C Command. Show processes with the given command name.

-w Wide. Don't truncate output to fit on one line; display full information.

-r Running. Only show running processes.

pid(s) Process IDs. Show only the process IDs given. If you specify several process IDs, separate them with spaces.

Example 1: Show User's Current Processes

To show your processes, use the simple `ps` command:

```
ps
```

This only displays processes owned by the user who runs the ps command. The ps command also appears on the list of running processes.

Example 2: Show All Processes

To display all currently running processes, use the ps command with the -a and -x options (see Figure A-5):

```
ps -ax
```

The first number in the output is the process ID (pid). The next column in the output is the terminal from which the command is being run, and the third column displays the status of the command. Processes can have a status of running (R), sleeping (S), stopped (SW), or zombie (Z). The fourth column displays the amount of time the process has been running, and the final column displays the command name.

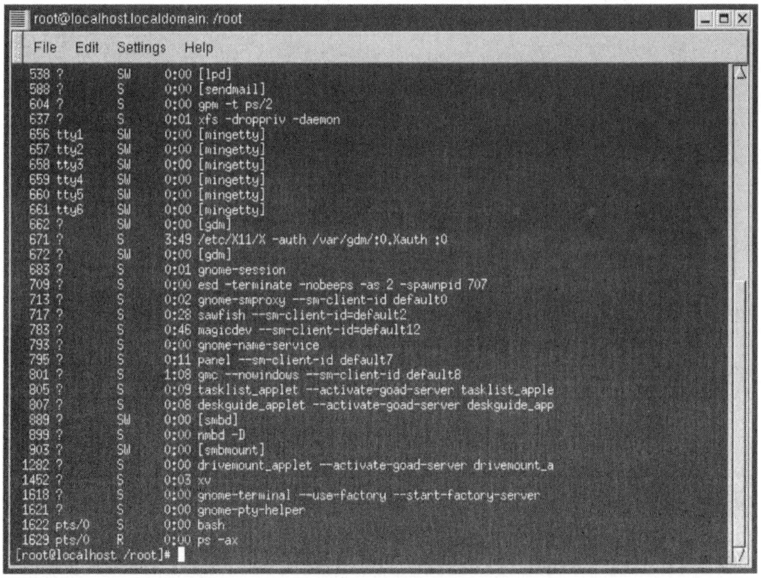

Figure A-5

Output of ps -ax.

Stopping Processes with kill

Name: `kill`

Function: The `kill` command sends a signal to a process. By default, `kill` sends the SIGTERM (terminate) signal.

Syntax: `kill [option] pid(s)`

Description: Generally, the `kill` command is used to terminate a process that does not terminate in another fashion. `kill` can send other signals to a process as well. The `kill` command can also list the signal names.

Options:

-s Signal. Specify which signal to send, which can be given as a name or number.

-p Print. Tells `kill` not to send a signal to the process, but only to print the pid of the process.

-l List. List the signal names and numbers.

pid(s) Process IDs. Specifies the processes to which the signal should be sent. If you want to send the signal to several processes, separate the IDs with spaces.

Example 1: Killing an Errant Process

If a process has stopped responding, you can use the `kill` command to stop the process. If the process ID you want to kill is 212, the following should stop the process. Note that you can only `kill` a process you did not create if you are the superuser on the system.

```
kill 212
```

This tells the process to exit, but it first gives it a chance to clean up — perhaps it will save any data it has before exiting.

If the default signal sent by `kill` does not terminate the process, signal 9 (SIGKILL) should always terminate the process.

```
kill -9 212
```

You should use `kill -9` only when a normal `kill` won't do it, because this method forcefully terminates the process without giving it a chance to clean up.

◆◆◆

CAUTION   Be very careful using `kill`. If you terminate the wrong process ID while you are root, you could very easily cause problems for yourself or other users on the system.

◆◆◆

Getting Help with the man Command

Name: man

Function: Displays the man (manual) page for a command.

Syntax: man [options] command

Description: The man command is your friend. Really. If you commit no other command to memory, learn this one. If you know the name of a command, the man page tells you how to use it, providing the man page is installed on your system. (Hint: Don't save disk space by not installing documentation; you'll need it later!)

There are nine sections of man pages. They are:

○ **Commands**. Commands a user can execute from a shell.

○ **System calls**. System calls available from the Linux kernel. These are usually only useful to programmers.

○ **Library calls**. Functions available in libraries. These are usually only useful to programmers.

- **Special files.** Pages for files found in /dev.
- **File formats.** The format of files such as /etc/fstab and other useful files.
- **Games and demonstrations.** 'Nuff said.
- **Other.** Things like the man man page.
- **System commands.** Commands only root can execute.
- **Kernel information.** A manual section that contains information about kernel code.

Usage: Using man is simple. Just type **man** followed by the desired command or the name.

Options:

-f Output. Equivalent to the whatis command.

-h Help. Displays a brief help message.

1–9 Manual section. Specifically names the man page section to search. Useful if the same command appears in multiple sections.

Example 1: Displaying the man Page for cp

To display cp's man page (see Figure A-6), simply type **man**, followed by the command you want displayed–cp, in this case.

```
man cp
```

The man pages are a bit cryptic — they're not necessarily written for non-Linux or non-geek types. However, the man pages display and explain, sometimes tersely, the options and syntax for each command. They're extremely helpful in a pinch.

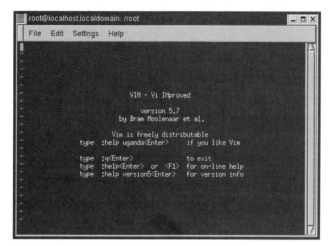

Figure A-6

The cp man page.

Directory Structure

The directory structure under Linux is much different from that of the directory structure of typical desktop operating systems. Linux's directory structure is patterned after UNIX — everything is in a single directory tree. This tree includes all your files, your hardware devices, any devices you have mounted, and even dynamically generated information about your system.

The / Directory

The / directory is typically called the root directory, not to be confused with /root, which is actually the home directory of the root user. All other directories fall under the root directory. Under Red Hat, this includes the following top-level directories:

- /bin
- /boot
- /cdrom

- ✿ /dev
- ✿ /etc
- ✿ /home
- ✿ /lib
- ✿ /lost+found
- ✿ /mnt
- ✿ /opt
- ✿ /proc
- ✿ /root
- ✿ /sbin
- ✿ /tmp
- ✿ /usr
- ✿ /var

NOTE You also can create other directories under the root directory if you want, although you should exercise some restraint. On systems that have Microsoft Windows or MS-DOS, I usually mount the DOS filesystem under /c or /Fat-c so I can use files between Linux and Windows when needed. Remember, Linux can read FAT and FAT32 filesystems, but you won't be able to see your ext2 filesystems under Windows or MS-DOS. It's probably a good idea to store all of your personal files under your home directory rather than just piling them under the root directory. This helps you keep your system well-organized and keeps clutter to a minimum.

The /bin Directory

The /bin directory is where the most basic binary executable files that are used system-wide are stored. As you may have guessed, /bin is short for binary. Executable files are often referred to as binaries on UNIX-style systems, which is probably a bit misleading. If you use WordPerfect under Linux, for example, the files are stored in a binary format, but they're not executable. Also, shell scripts are ASCII files that are flagged as an executable file, but they aren't stored in binary format.

Under the /bin directory you find most of the common commands like ls, touch, mount, cd, and other commands used by all users on the system. These fundamental commands are kept in this directory, separate from other programs (such as Emacs or games,) to make it easier to recover a sick system.

The /boot Directory

Not surprisingly, the /boot directory contains files related to booting your Linux system. There is nothing very interesting in this directory, and it is probably best to leave it alone. You only modify files in this directory if you compile your own kernel.

The /dev Directory

The /dev directory is not a typical directory. It contains special files that represent devices attached to your system. Some of these are block devices, meaning they deal only in big chunks of data. Your hard drive is a block device. Others, such as your mouse, are character devices that only give and take a single character at a time. By reading and writing to and from these files, programs can communicate with your hardware. For example, the input from your mouse usually comes in to Linux from the file /dev/mouse. For a little fun, go to the /dev directory, type in **cat mouse**, and move your mouse around a bit.

```
cd /dev
cat mouse
```

NOTE If you follow the previous steps, you start seeing a bunch of gibberish on the screen, because instead of directing your mouse input to the normal destination, you're directing it to standard output — namely your screen. Don't worry, you haven't broken your computer. Type in Ctrl+c to quit sending the mouse signal to standard out. See what your computer has to put up with?

If what you type is now gibberish too, blindly type **reset** and hit Enter to restore sanity.

Your hard drive is represented in this directory. It probably is /dev/hda. You used this device when you configured partitions during installation. Advanced users might even read and write directly to these devices to make byte-for-byte copies of the hard drive.

Another popular destination under the /dev directory is /dev/null. This is basically the same as "File 13" — anything sent to /dev/null basically is being thrown away. This is sometimes useful for programmers to send output to /dev/null rather than write it to disk when there is output that has to go somewhere.

A final interesting device in this directory is /dev/zero. Like /dev/null, this isn't an actual physical piece of hardware, but Linux treats it as if it were one. This device continually spits out zeroes. What good is that? For any politicians out there looking for a modern paper shredder, here's a quick way to totally blank a floppy:

```
cat /dev/zero > /dev/fd0
```

You probably don't have to worry about /dev too much, but there might be occasions when you can find use for directing input from a device to a file rather than to its normal destination — mostly for troubleshooting purposes. You also should be familiar with this directory when you are configuring new hardware.

The /etc Directory

The /etc directory, usually pronounced "etsee," contains configuration files and several other directories that contain more configuration files. Some of the more important files contained in /etc are the /XF86Config file, the /fstab and /mtab config files and the /rc.d directory. The /XF86Config file contains the configuration information for XFree86, including which X server it should use, the refresh rate of your monitor, and information about your mouse and keyboard. You probably never need to edit this file directly, but it is there if you do need to edit it.

The other two files, /fstab and /mtab, are short for Filesystem Table and Mount Table, respectively. The /fstab is created when you install Red Hat. If you add a hard drive or other storage device, you have to manually add a line for it to the /fstab. The /mtab is updated dynamically, depending on which devices currently are mounted on the system. For instance, if you mount a MS-DOS floppy (mount -t msdos /dev/fd0 /floppy), the /mtab gains a new line:

```
/dev/hda3 / ext2 rw 0 0
/dev/hdb1 /usr ext2 rw 0 0
/dev/hdb2 /opt ext2 rw 0 0
none /proc proc rw 0 0
/dev/fd0 /floppy msdos rw 0 0
```

The first entry /dev/hda3 / ext2 rw 0 0 is my root partition, which is located on the third partition on my first IDE hard drive. It is an ext2 filesystem that is mounted with read and write enabled.

The /usr and /opt directories are actually mounted on separate physical partitions on my second IDE hard drive. They are also ext2 filesystems, mounted with read and write enabled. The floppy is device /dev/fd0 mounted under /floppy and is an MS-DOS (FAT16) filesystem. If I had a second floppy drive, it would be /dev/fd1, and so on. If I unmount the floppy drive, the /mtab drops that entry. The /mtab exists for programs to read to see what devices are mounted.

The `/etc/rc.d` directory contains configuration scripts for the different runlevels under Linux, as well as the files that control the console font, Samba, the serial port, and other fun things. You also find the ppp directory, which is where the config files for ppp are found. You might need to edit these to use ppp on your system.

The /home Directory

The `/home` directory contains the home directories of all users on the system (with the exception of the root user, whose home directory resides in `/root`.) If your username is bsmith, for example, your home directory would be `/home/bsmith`.

Because Linux is a multi-user system, having separate home directories for each user is a necessity. Other desktop operating systems allow users' files to be intermingled. Linux forces them to stay separate, giving you a bit of privacy and security.

The `/ftp` and `/httpd` directories are under the `/home` directory as well. If you are running an FTP or Web server, these directories contain the files visible to the outside world.

The /lib Directory

Under the `/lib` directory you find library files. Library files are files that are required when compiling or running many programs under Linux. Library files are similar to DLL files under Windows. `/lib` is another directory that it's best not to muck about in unless you need to and know what you're doing.

The /lost and found Directory

The `/lost+found` directory generally is empty. If your computer shuts down without properly unmounting the drives, Linux does a filesystem

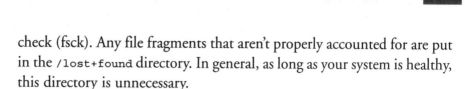

check (fsck). Any file fragments that aren't properly accounted for are put in the `/lost+found` directory. In general, as long as your system is healthy, this directory is unnecessary.

The /mnt Directory

Red Hat put devices like the CD-ROM or floppy drive directories under `/mnt`.

The /opt Directory

The `/opt` directory contains optional programs — generally large programs. If you download a new version of Netscape, it might install here. The K Desktop Environment installs in the `/opt` directory by default as well.

The /proc Directory

The `/proc` directory does not contain actual files; it is generated on the fly by Linux. It contains information about running processes and the status of the hardware. You can get information about hardware devices or running processes by using the cat command on these files. For instance, you can find out what filesystems your kernel supports by running the following command:

```
cat /proc/filesystems
```

Alternatively, you can find out what interrupts your hardware devices are using by running this command:

```
cat /proc/interrupts
```

Generally, the `/proc` directory is an area for power users only, but on occasion you might be instructed to get information from the `/proc` directory in order to troubleshoot or configure devices.

The /root Directory

The /root directory is the home directory for the root user. When logged on as root, the cd command brings you to this directory. It is kept separate from the home directories in /home so that the root user can maintain the system, even if the /home directory is destroyed.

The /sbin Directory

The /sbin directory contains more binary files. This directory is similar in purpose to /bin, except /sbin contains system binaries. Most are related to system upkeep. Typically, you must be root to use these binaries.

The /tmp Directory

The /tmp directory contains temporary files. This is a good place to stick a file you plan to delete. Many programs automatically create temporary files in the /tmp directory. KDE creates files in /tmp for the K File Manager and a few other programs while it is running, so it's a good idea not to delete anything in the /tmp directory while you're in KDE or X Windows.

The /tmp directory is a handy place to decompress and compile programs that you've downloaded. Once you've compiled and installed a program you should be able to delete all of the remaining unnecessary files from the /tmp directory. Be sure to keep an archived copy of the .tgz files you download in another area, though.

The /usr Directory

The /usr directory and its subdirectory /usr/local are often kept on separate partitions because of their size. The /usr directory is one of the larger directories, because it contains the majority of software on your system: the X11 directories, development tools, library files, and games.

The directory layout within /usr/local mimics what you see in /usr. Usually, Red Hat packages install in /usr. If you compile your own software, it goes in /usr/local.

The /var Directory

The /var directory contains variable files, mostly system logs. Generally, files under /var aren't of much interest unless you want to monitor the health of Linux or a Web server.

Directory structure under Linux is a bit more complex than under MS-DOS/Windows, but in the end, it also makes more sense. Under DOS and Windows, directory structure tends to be a bit haphazard, and many third-party programs put program directories wherever they feel like it, with little rhyme or reason. There is actually a method to the madness under UNIX-style OSes, which should comfort you when you're getting used to the system.

Conclusion

This Linux Primer should give you a good idea of how to get around in the Linux CLI. Most users who are new to Linux and just want to use Linux as a workstation or desktop operating system probably don't need to be gurus at the shell prompt, but it never hurts to have an idea of how to get around the shell if needed. You might even find that using the CLI is better in many cases. The nice thing about Linux is that you don't need to make a choice between GUI and CLI; you can fire up KDE (or whatever your favorite window manager/desktop environment is) and open several console windows and go to town!

APPENDIX B

Online Resources

Throughout this book, you have read about a lot of Linux configuration tips and tricks. Linux knowledge grows on a daily basis, as more and more Internet sites are devoted to the care and feeding of this now-tame beast.

This appendix will list, by category, a few of the many Internet addresses you can visit for more Linux information and knowledge.

This list is just the tip of the iceberg, and if you want to find more information, just use your favorite Internet search engine to help you on your way.

ONLINE RESOURCES	
General Linux Information	
Red Hat Linux	http://www.redhat.com
Linux	http://www.linux.org
Linux Kernels	ftp://ftp.kernel.org
X Window	http://www.x.org
Prima Linux	http://www.primalinux.com
Linux Planet	http://www.linuxplanet.com
Freshmeat	http://freshmeat.net
Window Managers and Desktop Environments	
GNOME	http://www.gnome.org
KDE	http://www.kde.org
Sawfish	http://sawmill.sourceforge.net
Desktop Themes	http://www.themes.org

Editors

emacs	http://www.gnu.org/software/emacs
gedit	http://melt.home.ml.org/gedit
gnotepad+	http://ack.netpedia.net/gnp
jed	http://space.mit.edu/~davis/jed.html
joe	ftp://ftp.std.com/src/editors/
Vim	http://www.vim.org

Graphics

ElectricEyes	http://www.labs.redhat.com/ee.shtml
GIMP	http://www.gimp.org
xfig	http://epb1.lbl.gov/homepages/Brian_Smith/xfig/

Internet

elm	http://www.instinct.org/elm
fwhois	http://www.oxygene.500mhz.net/software.html
gftp	http://gftp.seul.org
ircii	http://www.eternal.com.au/ircii
Lynx	http://lynx.browser.org
mutt	http://www.mutt.org
ncftp	http://www.ncftp.com
Netscape	http://www.netscape.com

pine	http://www.Washington.edu/pine/
slrn	http://space.mit.edu/~davis/slrn.html
tin	http://www.tin.org
trn	http://www.clari.net/~wayne
ytalk	http://www.eleves.ens.fr:8080/home/espel/ytalk/ytalk.html
Games	
Linux Game Tome	http://www.happypenguin.com
Linux Games	http://www.linuxgames.com

Hardware Compatibility Journal

As you gather hardware information about your PC, feel free to fill out this form as a journal of the data you find.

s you gather hardware information about your PC, feel free to fill out this form as a journal of the data you find.

CPU

Manufacturer

Model

Speed

Motherboard

Manufacturer

Model

Buses

Manufacturer

Model

Memory (RAM)

Size

Video Card

Manufacturer

Model

Video RAM size

Monitor

Manufacturer

Model

Horizontal Synchronization Rate

Vertical Synchronization Rate

Hard Drive

Manufacturer

Model

Size

Type

SCSI

_____

IDE

_____

Network Card

_____

Manufacturer

_____

Model

_____

CD-ROM Drive

_____

Manufacturer

_____

Model

_____

Size

_____

Floppy Drive

Manufacturer

Model

Size

Modem

Manufacturer

Model

Transmission Speed

Printer

Manufacturer

Model

Mouse

Manufacturer

Model

Type

PS/2

Serial

Keyboard

Manufacturer

Model

Number of Keys

Language

SCSI Card and Devices

Manufacturer

Model

Type of Device Controlled

IDE Adapters

Manufacturer

_____

Model

_____

Type of Device Controlled

_____

ZIP/JAZ Drive

Manufacturer

_____

Model

_____

Size

_____

Tape Drive

Manufacturer

Model

Size

Sound Card

Manufacturer

Model

Scanner

Manufacturer

Model

Infrared Device

Manufacturer

Model

Type of Device Controlled

Joystick

Manufacturer

Model

Serial Device

Manufacturer

Model

Type of Device Controlled

Parallel Device

Manufacturer

Model

Type of Device Controlled

PCMCIA

Manufacturer

Model

Card Type

BIOS Settings

Network Settings

INDEX

A

accounts, configuration, 67–68
adapters, SCSI, 30
Add a Printer Entry dialog box, 170
alias, 152
Anaconda, 51–53
applets, 85
Application Starter button, 92
    starting programs, 93
AT&T Global Network Services, 14
ATAPI CD-ROMs, 26
auto-detection, 212

B

Backup (Microsoft) application, 31–36
Backup Progress window, 35
Backup Wizard, 32–35
Backups, preparing for Red Hat Linux installation, 30–36
Ball, Bill (author of *Linux for Your Laptop*), 29
Basic Input Output System. *See* BIOS
/bin directory, 320–321
BIOS (Basic Input Output System), 10–14

/boot directory, 321
boot disks, creating, 49–50
booting
    dual, 78–80
        Windows 95/98, 78–79
        Windows NT, 79–80
    Kernel, 209–211
    troubleshooting, 265–267
branding (hardware), 17
browsers, Netscape Navigator. *See* Netscape Navigator
buttons, 88–90
    Application Starter, 92-93
    Desktop, 93
    Kill, 90
    Main Menu, 85–88

C

cache properties (Netscape Navigator), configuration, 236–238
Calendar (Gnome), starting, 86–88
case sensitivity, passwords, 68
cat command, 309
cd command, 136

CD-ROMs, 7–8
mounting, 304
supported by Red Hat Linux, 26
unmounting, 306
class A addresses, 158
class C addresses, 158
Clockchip Configuration screen, 103
color depth, 104
commands, 288–318
-r, 138
cat, 309
cd, 136
cp, 137, 288–290
kill, 316–317
less, 312
ln, 139, 297–298
ls, 135, 294–296
man, 317–318
mkdir, 138, 293
mount, 301–305
mv, 137, 290–292
piping, 286–288
ps, 313–315
pwd, 137, 300–301
rm, 138
rmdir, 138
unmount, 306
whoami, 282–283
compatibility
Hardware Compatibility List. *See* Hardware
Compatibility List
resources for checking hardware compatibility
Linux Hardware Database, 18-21
Red Hat support, 17–18
configurations
accounts, 67–68
desktops, 122–132
icons, 124–125
menu customization, 122–123

Panel icons, 125–126
themes, 126–132
devices, 212–213
filesystem, 133–139
functions, 135–139
permissions, 135–139
graphics card, xf86config tool, 112–114
keyboards
Control Panel, 115
xf86config tool, 108–109
LILO, 78–80
monitors, xf86config tool, 109–112
mouse
Control Panel, 116
xf86config tool, 107–108
Netscape Navigator, 227–238
cache properties, 236–238
helper applications, 238
home page, 228–235
Netscape Messenger, 238–243
network settings, 64–66
PPP Dialer configuration, 146–155
sound, sndconfig, 177–181
X Windows, 70–72
XFree86
Xconfigurator, 97–105
xf86config tool, 106–114
Configure Filter dialog box, 171
connections
dial-up, 14–16
troubleshooting, 272–274
Control Panel, 114
keyboard configuration, 115
mouse configuration, 116
copying files, 288–290
cp command, 137, 288–290
custom installation, 50, 57–58
Custom Monitor Setup screen, 101–102
customization, menus, 122–123

D

databases, Linux Hardware Database, 18–21
dead keys, 54
deleting
    files, 306–310
    partitions, 41–44
Desk Guide, 86
Desktop Switching tool, 119–120
desktops, 83–84
    buttons, 93
    configuration, 122–132
        icons, 124–125
        menu customization, 122–123
        Panel icons, 125–126
        themes, 126–132
    desktop environments, 119–120
    Gnome, 84–90, 95–96
        buttons, 88–90
        dialog boxes, 88–90
        menus, 88–90
    icons, 124–125
    installation, 192–194
    KDE, 90–93
    selecting, 117–118
        login options, 118–122
Destroy option, 90
/dev directory, 321–322
Device Manager (Windows), 6–8
devices
    adding, 206–209
        external, 207
        internal, 208–209
    configuration, 212–213
    gathering information on, 6–10
    USB, troubleshooting, 270–272
dial-up connections, 14–16
Dial-up Networking window, 14
dialog boxes, 88–90
    Add a Printer Entry, 170

    Configure Filter, 171
    Edit Internet Connection, 154
    Edit Local Printer Entry, 171
    Internet Connections, 155
    Microsoft Backup, 31–32
    Netscape File Browser, 229
    Netscape Preferences, 228
    Print, 9–10
    Select Sound File, 182
    System Properties, 7–10
    TCP/IP Settings, 15–16
Dialup Connection tool, 147
direction, 286–288
directories, 319–327
    /, 319–320
    /bin, 320–321
    /boot, 321
    changing, 298–300
    creating, 293
    /dev, 321–322
    /etc, 323–324
    /home, 324
    /lib, 324
    /lost and found, 324
    /mnt, 325
    /opt, 325
    /proc, 325
    removing, 308
    /root, 319–320, 326
    /sbin, 326
    /tmp, 326
    /usr, 326
    /var, 327
Disk Druid option, 60–63
disk partitions, 36–39
    partitioning software, 13
    PartitionMagic 5.0, 39–40
    removing, 41–44
    swap partitions, 37
DNS (Domain Name Service), 151

documentation, 48

Domain Name Service (DNS), 151

downloading Red Hat Linux 7, 48

dual booting, 78–80
Windows 95/98, 78–79
Windows NT, 79–80

DVD-ROMs supported by Red Hat Linux, 26

dynamic IP addresses, 64

E

e-mail
Netscape Messenger, configuration, 239–241
troubleshooting, 275–276

Edit Internet Connection dialog box, 154

Edit Local Printer Entry dialog box, 171

editing isapnp.conf, 185

editors, 218–220

emulators, 94

encryption, 276–277

/etc directory, 323–324

Ethernet Cards supported by Red Hat Linux, 24–25

exiting X Windows, 116–117

external devices, adding, 207

F

Failsafe login option, 121–122

FAT partitions, 40

fdisk, 40–44
removing partitions, 41–44

file permissions, 283–285

files
copying, 288–290
deleting, 306–310
finding, 285–286, 294–296
isapnp.conf, 185
listing, 295–296
moving, 290–292

names, 290–292
SETUP.EXE (Windows), 4
viewing, 309, 312–313

filesystems
configuration, 133–139
functions, 135–139
permissions, 135–139
Intel PCs, 38
mounting, 301–305
unmounting, 305–306

finding files, 285–286, 294–296

fips utility, 40

floppies
mounting, 304
unmounting, 306

functions, 135–139

G

gEdit editor, 219

GIMP, 220–223

Gnome, 84–90, 95–96
buttons, 88–90
Calendar, starting, 86–88
dialog boxes, 88–90
menus, 88–90
Panel, 85
RPM window, 192

gnotepad+ editor, 219

GNU Image Manipulation Program. *See* GIMP

graphical user interfaces. *See* GUIs

graphics
StarDraw, 256
tools, 220–223

graphics cards, configuration, 112–114

GUIs (graphical user interfaces), 83–84
Gnome, 84–90, 95–96
buttons, 88–90
dialog boxes, 88–90

menus, 88–90

KDE, 90–93

H

hard drives

logical, 13

physical, 13

supported by Red Hat Linux, 24

hardware

branding, 17

Hardware Compatibility List. *See* Hardware
Compatibility List

installation, 204–213

adding devices, 206–209

auto-detection, 212

device configuration, 212–213

Kernel boot process, 209–211

Red Hat Linux installation, 11–12

PCs, 6–10

BIOS, 10–14

supported by Red Hat Linux, 21–30

CD-ROMs, 26

DVD-ROMs, 26

Ethernet cards, 24–25

hard drives, 24

Jaz drives, 27

keyboards, 28

memory, 23

modems, 27–28

monitors, 23–24

mouse, 28

notebook computers, 28

printers, 28

SCSI adapters, 28

sound cards, 25–26

tape drives, 27

video card, 22

Zip drives, 27

troubleshooting, 268–272

Hardware Compatibility Lists, 9–10

resources for checking compatibility

Linux Hardware Database, 18-21

Red Hat support, 17–18

help

applications (Netscape Navigator), configuration,
238

man command, 317–318

Online Help, turning off, 53

/home directory, 324

home pages (Netscape Navigator), configuration,
228–235

hosts, 158

I

icons

desktop, 124–125

icon bar, 92

Launchers, 84

input, 286–288

installation, 11-12

desktops, 192–194

hardware, 204–213

adding devices, 206–209

auto-detection, 212

device configuration, 212–213

Kernel boot process, 209–211

Red Hat Linux 7, 48–52

account configuration, 67–68

Anaconda, 51–53

backing up data on PC, 30–36

boot disks, 49–50

completing install process, 72–77

custom installation, 50, 57–58

install options, 56–59

keyboard selection, 53–56

language determination, 53–56

installation *(continued)*
    LILO configuration, 78–80
    mouse settings, 53–56
    network settings, 64–66
    partition selections, 59–63
    selecting package groups, 68–70
    Server System option, 57–58
    text installation, 77–78
    time zone settings, 66–67
    troubleshooting, 263–272
    Upgrade option, 57–58
    Workstation option, 57–58
    X Windows configuration, 70–72
  software packages, 190–192
    desktop installations, 192–194
    StarOffice, 199–204
    Update Agent, 194–199
  troubleshooting, 268–272
Intel PCs, file systems, 38
internal devices, adding, 208–209
Internet
  account setup, 144–158
    connections, 155–158
    PPP Dialer configuration, 146–155
  connections, 14–16
    troubleshooting, 272–274
  tools, 224–243
Internet Connections dialog box, 155
IP addresses, 158–166
  dynamic, 64
isapnp.conf file, 185
ISPs, 146, 150
  AT&T Global Network Services, 14

J

Jaz drives, supported by Red Hat Linux, 27

K

K Desktop Environment. *See* KDE
KDE, 90–93
Kernel
  boot process, 209–211
  definition, 5
keyboards
  configuration
    Control Panel, 115
    xf86config tool, 108–109
  supported by Red Hat Linux, 29
keymap, 108
Kill button, 90
kill command, 316–317
killing processes, 316–317
KPanel control, 93

L

launchers, 84
  configuration, 125–126
less command, 312
/lib directory, 324
LILO (Linux Loader), 12–13
  configuration, 78–80
  troubleshooting, 268
links, creating, 297–298
Linux. *See also* Red Hat Linux 7
  compared to windows, 4
  shutting down, 116–117
Linux Hardware Database, 18–21
Linux Loader. *See* LILO
list command, 135
listing files, 295–296
ln command, 139, 297–298
local printers, adding, 168–173
logical hard drives, 13
login options, 118–122
login prompt, 280

/lost and found directory, 324
ls command, 135, 294–296
LucentVenus PCI modems, 27

M

Main Menu button, 85
    starting programs, 86–88
man command, 317–318
memory supported by Red Hat Linux, 23
menus, 88–90
    customization, 122–123
Microsoft Backup application, 31–36
Microsoft Backup dialog box, 31–32
Microsoft Office StarOffice, 31
mkdir command, 138, 293
/mnt directory, 325
modems
    LucentVenus PCI, 27
    supported by Red Hat Linux, 27–28
monitors
    configuration, xf86config tool, 109–112
    overclocking, 70–72
    supported by Red Hat Linux, 23–24
    troubleshooting, 267
mount command, 301–305
mounting, 134, 301–305
mouse
    configuration
        Control Panel, 116
        xf86config tool, 107–108
    supported by Red Hat Linux, 28
Mouse Configuration screen, 55
mouse settings, 53–56
moving files, 290–292
multi-user operating systems, 281–286
    file permissions, 283–285
    virtual terminals, 282
    whoami command, 282–283
mv command, 137, 290–292

N

names, files, 290–292
Netcenter, 229–235
netmask, 65
Netscape Communicator, 224–243
    configuring Netscape Navigator, 227–238
Netscape File Browser dialog box, 229
Netscape Messenger, configuration, 238–243
    e-mail, 239–241
    newsgroups, 241–243
Netscape Navigator, configuration, 227–238
    cache properties, 236–238
    helper applications, 238
    home page, 228–235
    Netscape Messenger, 238–243
Netscape Preferences dialog box, 228
Network Configurator, 160–163
networking, 158–166
    network cards, 164
    Network Configurator. *See* Network Configurator
    printers, adding, 173–176
    settings, 14–16, 64–66
    troubleshooting, 275–276
newsgroups, Netscape Messenger, 241–243
nicknames, 91
non-Linux partitions, 139–140
Norton System Utilities, 31
notebooks supported by Red Hat Linux, 29

O

Online Help, turning off, 53
online resources, 330–332
operating systems
    multi-user, 281–286
        file permissions, 283–285
        virtual terminals, 282
        whoami command, 282–283
    multiple, 36–44
/opt directory, 325

output, 286–288
overclocking monitors, 70–72

P

package groups, selecting, 68–70
Pager, 85
Panel icons, configuration, 125–126
panels, Gnome Panel, 85
PartitionMagic 5.0, 39–40
partitions, 36–37, 39
    FAT, 40
    installation selections, 59–63
    non-Linux, 139–140
    partitioning software, 13
    PartitionMagic 5.0, 39–40
    removing, 41–44
    swap partitions, 37
passwords, 281
    case sensitivity, 68
PCs
    backing up data, 30–36
    BIOS, 10–14
    Device Manager, 6–8
    hardware, 6–10
        BIOS, 10–14
    Intel file systems, 38
    network settings, 14–16
permissions, 135–139, 283–285
physical hard drives, 13
PIMs (Personal Information Managers), 223–224,
    259
piping, 286–288
pixmap arrows, 86
PnP (Plug and Play), 183–185
    dumps, 184–185
PPP (Point-to-Point Protocol), 145
    Dialer configuration, 146–155
Print dialog box, 9–10

printers, 167–176
    adding local printers, 168–173
    adding network printers, 173–176
    supported by Red Hat Linux, 28
    troubleshooting, 269–270
problems. *See* troubleshooting
/proc directory, 325
processes
    killing, 316–317
    viewing, 313–315
programs, starting
    Application Starter button, 93
    Main Menu button, 86–88
proprietary connections, 14
protocols
    PPP, 145
        Dialer configuration, 146–155
    TCP/IP, 145
ps command, 313–315
pwd command, 137, 300–301

R

RAM supported by Red Hat Linux, 23
raster-based graphics, 256
Red Hat Linux 7, 3. *See also* Linux
    downloading, 48
    Hardware Compatibility List, 9–10
    hardware supported by, 21–30
        CD-ROMs, 26
        DVD-ROMs, 26
        Ethernet card, 24–25
        hard drives, 23–24
        Jaz drives, 27
        keyboards, 29
        memory, 23
        modems, 27–28
        monitors, 23–24
        mouse, 28

notebook computers, 29
printers, 28
SCSI adapters, 30
sound cards, 25–26
video card, 22
ZIP drives, 27
installation, 48–52
account configuration, 67–68
Anaconda, 51–53
backing up data on PC, 30–36
boot disks, 49–50
completing install process, 72–77
custom installation, 50, 57–58
hardware information needed, 11–12
install options, 56–59
keyboard selection, 53–56
language determination, 53–56
LILO configuration, 78–80
mouse settings, 53–56
network settings, 64–66
partition selections, 59–63
selecting package groups, 68–70
Server System option, 57–58
text installation, 77–78
time zone settings, 66–67
troubleshooting, 263–272
Upgrade option, 57–58
Workstation option, 57–58
X Windows configuration, 70–72
starting, 280
support, hardware compatibility, 17–18
Web site, 17
Red Hat Package Manager. *See* RPM
redirection, 286–288
removing
files, 306–310
partitions, 41–44

renaming files, 290–292
resolution, video, 98
rm command, 138
rmdir command, 138
root account, creating, 67
/root directory, 319–320, 326
RPM (Red Hat Package Manager), 190–194
desktop installations, 192–194
running processes, viewing, 313–315

S

/sbin directory, 326
screen resolution, 98
SCSI adapters supported by Red Hat Linux, 30
security, 276–277
encryption, 276–277
passwords, 281
case sensitivity, 68
Select Sound File dialog box, 182
selecting desktops, 117–118
login options, 118–122
Server System option (installation), 57–58
servers, X, 22, 24, 95
setup application, StarOffice installation, 199–204
SETUP.EXE file (Windows), 4
shell, 286–288
shutting down Linux, 116–117
Skip X Configuration option, 72
sndconfig utility, 177–181
software
installation, 190–192
StarOffice, 199–204
Update Agent, 194–199
partitioning, 13
troubleshooting, 272–277
Internet connections, 272–274
networking, 275–276

sound, 176–183
cards supported by Red Hat Linux, 25–26
configuration, sndconfig, 177–181
events, 182–183
StarBase (StarOffice), 254
StarCalc (StarOffice), 249–252
StarChart (StarOffice), 252
StarDesktop (StarOffice), 243–246
StarDiscussion (StarOffice), 258
StarDraw (StarOffice), 256
StarImpress (StarOffice), 255
StarMail (StarOffice), 257
StarMath (StarOffice), 253
StarOffice, 31, 243–259
installation, 199–204
StarBase, 254
StarCalc, 249–252
StarChart, 252
StarDesktop, 243–246
StarDiscussion, 258
StarDraw, 256
StarImpress, 255
StarMail, 257
StarMath, 253
StarSchedule, 258
StarWriter, 247–249
Web site, 49, 200
StarSchedule (StarOffice), 258
starting
programs
Application Starter button, 93
Main Menu button, 86–88
Red Hat Linux 7, 280
StarWriter (StarOffice), 247–249
styles (StarWriter), 248
Subnet Mask, 65
swap partitions, 37
switches, 135

switching desktop environments, 119–120
System Properties dialog box, 7–10

T

Taskbar, 93
TCP/IP, 145
TCP/IP Settings dialog box, 15–16
text installation, 77–78
themes, 126–132
changing, 126–129
themes.org Web site, 130–132
time zone settings, 66–67
Token Ring cards, 25
Torvalds, Linus (Linux creator), 5
Transmission Control Protocol/Internet Protocols.
See TCP/IP
troubleshooting
e-mail, 275–276
hardware, 268–272
installation, 263–272
boot issues, 265–267
hardware, 268–272
LILO, 268
monitors, 267
video cards, 267
X Window, 267
software, 272–277
Internet connections, 272–274
networking, 275–276
USB devices, 270–272

U

unmount command, 306
unmounting filesystems, 305–306
Update Agent, 194–199
Upgrade option, 57–58
USB devices, troubleshooting, 270–272
Use Graphical Login option, 72

user accounts, creating, 67–68
/usr directory, 326

V

/var directory, 327
vector-based graphics, 256
video cards
    supported by Red Hat Linux, 22
    troubleshooting, 267
video resolution, 98
viewing files, 309, 312–313
VIM text editor, 219
virtual terminals, 282
VisiCalc, 249

W

Web browsers, Netscape Navigator. *See* Netscape
    Navigator
Web sites, 330–332
    Red Hat Linux, 17
    StarOffice, 49, 200
    themes.org, 130–132
whoami command, 282–283
wilcards, deleting files, 309
Window Manager, 95
Windows
    compared to Linux, 4–5
    Device Manager, 6–8
windows, 84, 91
    Backup Progress, 35
    Dial-up Networking, 14
    Gnome RPM, 192

Windows 95, dual booting, 78–79
Windows 98, dual booting, 78–79
Windows NT, dual booting, 79–80
wizards, Backup, 32–35
Workstation option (installation), 57–58

X

X server, 22, 24, 95
X Window System, 22
X Windows
    exiting, 116–117
    configuration, 70–72
    tools, 217–225
        editors, 218–220
        graphics, 220–223
        Internet, 224–243
        PIMs, 223–224
    troubleshooting, 267
Xconfigurator, 97–105
xf86config tool, 106–114
    graphics card configuration, 112–114
    keyboard configuration, 108–109
    monitor configuration, 109–112
    mouse configuration, 107–108
XFree86, 22–24, 95
    Xconfigurator, 97–105
    xf86config tool, 106–114
Xircom cards, 25

Z

ZIP drives supported by Red Hat Linux, 27